ANGLO-SAXON
GLOUCESTERSHIRE

ANGLO-SAXON
GLOUCESTERSHIRE

Carolyn Heighway

ALAN SUTTON &
GLOUCESTERSHIRE COUNTY LIBRARY
1987

The County Library Series is published jointly by Alan Sutton Publishing Limited and Gloucestershire County Library. All correspondence relating to the series should be addressed to:

Alan Sutton Publishing Limited
30 Brunswick Road
Gloucester GL1 1JJ

First published 1987

British Library Cataloguing in Publication Data
Heighway, Carolyn M.
    Anglo-Saxon Gloucestershire.
    1. Gloucestershire—History
    i. Title
    942.4'1'01   DA670.G5

ISBN 0-86299-364-4

Printed in Great Britain.

Contents

TO MY
PARENTS

Acknowledgements

Many people have helped me with this book. I am very grateful to all those who allowed me to use their drawings and photographs: Ashmolean Museum; Steve Bassett, Richard Bryant, Philip Cracknell, Cirencester Excavation Committee, the Crickley Hill Trust, Tania Dickinson, Gloucester City Museum and Excavation Unit, Alan Hannan, Della Hooke and Manchester University Press, David Miles and the Oxfordshire Excavation Unit, Philip Moss, Edward Price, the Society of Antiquaries, the Dean and Chapter of Bristol Cathedral, Harold Taylor, Jean Williamson and Mike Webber. Mick Sharp devoted much care to some excellent photographs, Linda Viner, Malcolm Watkins, and Jan Wills all helped me find other illustrations. An MSC team of the Crickley Hill Trust, working on an exhibition of the origin of Gloucestershire churches, have allowed me to use their plans and drawings; I am grateful to the team leaders, Sarah Butler, and Heather Brown, and to the other illustrators whose names are acknowledged in the captions. I was much helped by Rob Isles and Mick Aston who sent me proofs of *Archaelogy in Avon* (since published); and by Michael Ponsford who sent me the Bristol sections from the same volume. Eric Boore provided me with information on his excavations at Bristol. David Brown, at the Ashmolean Museum, gave me much help on the pagan Saxons and allowed me to use copies of his notes, and provided me with a number of drawings and photographs. Mick Aston, Mike Hare, and Richard Bryant all commented in detail on drafts of the text and rescued me from some of my greater errors; Mike Hare provided me with several chunks of unpublished material, and allowed me to draw on his survey of Anglo–Saxon sculpture in Gloucestershire Churches. Richard Bryant allowed me to use a number of his drawings from the same survey. I am particularly grateful to David Hill, of Manchester University, who not only read the text but gave up several hours of a family reunion weekend to hold an impromptu seminar, and who gave me the courage to rewrite the whole thing at the eleventh hour. The text was corrected (at final print-out stage, so she is not responsible for the mistakes that crept in later) by Cherry Lavell, of the Council for British Archaeology, who is the best proofreader and bibliographer in archaeology. I would also like to thank all the people who have in the past attended my evening classes, and who have so often prompted me into further research with their acute questions (some of which I am still trying to answer).

I owe a special debt to Richard Bryant, my husband, for fulfilling the quadruple role of illustrator, book designer, critic, and moral supporter. This is his book too.

Carolyn Heighway
Kings Stanley, Gloucestershire, July 1987.

Preface:
Discovering the Anglo Saxons

. . . Britain was attacked by waves of . . ..Angles, Saxons and Jutes who, landing at Thanet, soon overran the country with fire (and, of course, the sword) . . . The brutal Saxon invaders drove the Britons westward into Wales and compelled them to become Welsh; it is now considered doubtful whether this was a Good Thing.

W. C. Sellar and R. J. Yeatman, 1066 and All That.

But if England seemed for the moment a waste from which all the civilization of the world had fled away, it contained within itself the germs of a nobler life than that which had been destroyed. . . . War was no sooner over than the warrior settled down into a farmer, and the home of the peasant churl rose beside the heap of goblin-haunted stones that marked the site of the villa he had burnt. Little knots of kinsfolk drew together in 'tun' and 'ham' beside the Thames and the Trent. . .not as kinsfolk only, but as dwellers in the same plot, knit together by their common holding within the same bounds.

J.R. Green, A Short History of the English People, 1892.

John Richard Green published his book, *The Making of England*, in 1881, and his 'Short History of the English People' (in three volumes!) in 1892. He gave a dramatised version of the events depicted in the Anglo-Saxon Chronicle. Against a background of dense forests and hostile swamps, the Anglo-Saxon settlers fought to settle the new country in clearings hacked out of the primeval forest. The remnants of the Romano-British settlers, powerless and effete, retreated to woodland fastnesses or fled to the remote west. The Saxon settlers, shunning the ruins of towns and villas, built villages and laid out communal strip-fields, and so created England.

This account fired the imagination of generations, and vestiges of it were memorable enough to find their way into that summary of memorable history, *1066 and All That*. Even now, it often finds place in school history books, and the 'primeval forest' has outlasted the other components of the myth, appearing even in quite recent and learned works.

For a myth it most certainly is. Green's account was based on no evidence that would now be accepted. Even the battles of the Anglo-Saxon Chronicle, which formed the framework of his story, are no longer regarded as reliable history.

Scientific pollen analysis has shown that the Wildwood had mostly been destroyed long before the arrival of the Saxons; place-name studies and modern archaeology tell us that the British were very numerous, and many must have survived. Excavations have shown how Roman villas, though destroyed, died slowly rather than by fire and sword, and were replaced by other settlements. The humble huts both of British and Saxons turn out to be only part of the architectural repertoire, which included great timber halls with sophisticated carpentry. The Saxon peasant is no longer seen as forming a free commune, and his strip-fields, farmed in common, seem to be laid out only centuries later. As to the Saxon himself, as environmental archaeologists laboriously measure bones and peer through microscopes at human faeces, the whole life of the Anglo-Saxon, lice, worms and all, begins to emerge.

Historical studies have changed too, though perhaps less dramatically, and it would be hard to surpass in quality and quantity the sheer volume of work produced by the Rev C S Taylor at the turn of the last century. Yet more study of the documents, as in Della Hooke's recent work on the Hwicce, continues to give a better view of the past.

A few words are needed here about terminology. The term 'Dark Ages' was once used to describe the period from the end of Roman power (i.e. *c*. 400) to 1066. Occasionally it is still used to mean this, with everything after 1066 being 'medieval'. As research has gone on, the 'Dark Ages' have become shorter (and less dark) and nowadays the term, if used at all, usually means the centuries after Roman rule, but before the Anglo-Saxon invasions (a variable period, depending on when the Anglo-Saxons arrived). A better term for this is 'sub Roman'. A further confusion follows with the term 'medieval'; a relatively recent academic fashion terms the period from 400 to 600 'early medieval' – much more fair to the Celts and Saxons but terribly confusing to those who still label the period immediately after 1066 as 'early medieval'!

For the 'Dark Age' period in Gloucestershire I usually use the term 'sub-Roman'. It is a particularly vital time for Gloucestershire, which consisted of several small British kingdoms which survived for years after the end of direct Roman rule. Soon this period too will be better understood, and just as well, for in those two centuries lies the key to the society which followed, which we call 'Anglo Saxon Gloucestershire'.

★★★★★★

The first 'Gloucestershire' was created in the reign of Edward the Elder or of Athelstan, in the 900s; it was a smaller unit than the later one, having to the north the smaller shire of Winchcombe. In the reign of Cnut, in 1016, the two shires were combined. Before the shires were created, Gloucestershire formed the southern part of an Anglo-Saxon kingdom, known as the Kingdom of the Hwicce (pronounced Hwitchay). The kingdom did not include the Forest of Dean, but it did include Bath. When Gloucestershire was created, the area west of the Severn was part of Hereford; by Domesday the boundary had been pushed to the Wye. Later boundary alterations took place, but on the whole Domesday Gloucestershire remained until 1973, when its southern part became Avon. 'Gloucestershire' as described in this book is therefore a flexible area; it covers the pre-1973 County (more or less the Domesday one) but also, for the early centuries, includes Bath.

****

Gloucestershire includes three widely differing types of landscape. First, the Cotswolds to the east, an upland area with shallow soil over limestone rocks which for many centuries have provided excellent building stone for the district. West of the wolds, below the steep scarp slope with its hidden wooded valleys, is the broad plain of the River Severn and its tributaries, with its pasture and fertile arable on heavy clay soils. Thirdly, further west still, between the Severn and the River Wye, are the highlands of the Forest of Dean, often wooded, and with deposits of coal and iron ore and good quality sandstone available beneath the surface. The whole area, valley and upland, was exploited by man well before the Iron Age, the valley began to be cleared of trees for agriculture in the late Neolithic or early Bronze Age, c. 2000 AD. The Cotswolds may have been cleared of their woodland much earlier, about 3,000 BC, although there was plenty of remaining woodland in some areas and some of it, particularly along the scarp slope, is still there today. By the middle Iron Age (about 700–500 BC) the Cotswold scarp was occupied by a chain of fortified villages, of which Crickley Hill is a prime example, which profited from the wealth of agriculture in the valley below. The local tribe, the Dobunni, just before the Roman conquest, occupied an area which included the whole of the Severn Valley and the Cotswolds, as far south as Bath and including the Lower Avon Valley in the Worcester area. The principal centre of the tribe might have been Bagendon or Minchinhampton, where defensive dykes are still visible. The wealth and status of the upper levels of society are represented by the beautiful objects placed with a Celtic princess in the Birdlip Burial, now in Gloucester Museum. This Celtic world, with its formalised warfare and stratified social levels, must still have been a factor in the society which emerged after

Roman rule ended, when the veneer of imperial civilisation wore off. Indeed, it is noticeable that the area of the Dobunni coincides roughly with the much later Anglo-Saxon-dominated Kingdom of the Hwicce. It is beyond proof that they are connected, but tribal affiliations die hard. The coincidence will serve to represent the truism that the roots of post-Roman society should be sought in the pre-Roman Iron Age.

The Roman conquest brought about many changes: an intensification of agricultural exploitation, the promotion of towns as administrative and market centres. By the end of the first century Roman power was well established in Gloucestershire – an area which was one of the wealthiest and most fertile in Britain.

1
A Sub-Roman Kingdom

Roman Gloucestershire was full of people. A plot of the Roman villas alone would show intensive exploitation of the uplands, but there were many more sites than just these mansions of the rich. The traces of numerous Romano-British farms have been found, showing that there were many settlements in the Vale as well as on the Cotswolds. Recent work – keeping a wary eye on building sites for signs of Roman occupation – has greatly increased the number of Romano-British sites even in the Forest of Dean, previously thought to have a very low population at that time. One projection of population density, based on the distribution of sites seen during the construction of the M5 motorway, suggests that 'there should be 4,500 Romano-British sites in the Vale of Berkeley alone, of which around 4,400 remain to be discovered'. Indeed, for Britain as a whole it is becoming apparent that the Romano-British population was much higher than used to be envisaged. Estimates range between 3 and 4 million and one estimate suggests a total of 4–5 million. This compares with a population of perhaps 2 million estimated, for example, from Domesday Book in 1086. Figures of this order for Roman Britain have important bearing on subsequent history. If the population was so large, can it indeed have been wiped out by a few thousand Saxons?

What is more, in Gloucestershire there is the fact that there were precious few Saxons to do any wiping-out; until about 550 the Vale of Gloucester and Berkeley and much of the Cotswolds were still British. Indeed there is no archaeological evidence that more than a handful of Saxons ever arrived in the Vale of Gloucestershire.

So where did all those Romano-British farmers go? Today's historians and archaeologists tend to the view that, whatever disasters befell the economy around 400–500, the Romano-British or Romano-Celtic population remained, ultimately to intermarry with the politically dominant Saxons.

For Gloucestershire in about 400, however, the Anglo-Saxon conquest was in the future. For some it was a time of particular prosperity. The owners of the great villas, the 'country houses' of Roman Britain, enjoyed and even improved their premises, with their mosaics and baths, painted walls, and formal gardens. It is less certain what the towns were like: they may not have been as prosperous as they had been, and by the 300s they were sheltering behind heavily increased fortifications, designed to withstand siege warfare. Towns had been Roman civilisation personified; centres of administration and of wealth, they were also vulnerable to raiders. Barbarian raids were becoming commonplace – the Severn valley was particularly attractive to pirates and a Roman fleet may have been based here.

Roman Britain ended officially in 410, when it became independent of Rome. To us, looking back, it seems a sudden break, a catastrophe, an impression heightened by the fact that from this point on, texts are absent and coinage ceased to circulate, and the archaeologist or historian must thus flounder without dates. But to people at the time, 410 was just part of a slow decline. After all, Britain had been independent before, most recently under Magnus Maximus in 383, Gratian in 407, and then Constantine III. Roman power had always been re-asserted; many must have expected the same to happen again. But it did not, and there followed what can only be interpreted as a worsening economic crisis. The signs of this are provided by the archaeology. The great pottery factories, the archaeologists' index of trade and prosperity, ceased operating. The towns and villas could no longer be maintained, and they fell into ruin by the mid 400s. Without coinage (the coin supply had come via the Roman army) and without the military markets, the economy operated on a very much lower level, presumably relying on barter. Administration would have become increasingly local, and therefore more prone to intimidation and corruption.

There are several reasons why there is so little evidence for the 'sub-Roman' centuries; some have already been mentioned. The cessation of

The remains of the Roman city wall at Cirencester. Drawn by Richard Bryant.

factory-made pottery and coinage create grave difficulties for modern historians. It is these items, attached to levels in archaeological sites, that give the Romano-British period its confidently dated framework. Sites may have been found belonging to 450, or 500, but we would not know it. There are of course other dating methods, but these usually depend on organic substances suriviving – an event rare in our climate. The excavation of burials often provides information about the past, but for the 5th and 6th centuries there are almost no burials known. No-one knows why. It is possible that some burial rite, which left no trace of the body, was re-introduced after the Roman period. Another possibility is that burials are not found because they were scattered about the countryside. At Frocester, for instance, both the Roman villas are the sites of 5th century burials, showing that people, instead of being buried in ordered official cemeteries, were being interred in local plots attached to the farm where they had worked. A group of burials at Frampton on Severn, quite undated, could belong to this period, but there is no evidence from Gloucestershire as yet of the great Dark Age cemeteries that have been found, for instance, at Cannington in Somerset. It is possible, of course, that the burials of this date underlie present-day burial grounds, as was the case at St Peter's, Frocester.

If we turn to written history, we get little help. There are no contemporary historical texts for the 5th century; only a few scraps of comment from Continental writers. The only source relevant to Gloucestershire is the priest Gildas, and his sermon, 'The Ruin of Britain'. This is a difficult work in convoluted Latin whose purpose was to moralise, not to write history. It was written in about 540. By then Britain had been independent for more than a century. Gildas, as shown by his hopeless attempts to produce a history of Roman Britain, found it impossible to reach back a century to write about the fall of Roman Britain. It was already too far in the past.

The fate of the Roman villas seems to emphasise more than anything else the decline of Roman Britain. These great houses, with their luxurious fittings apparently representing aspirations so like our own: how did they suddenly come to an end? There is a good example of how it came about at Frocester Court, which differs from nearly all other villas in that it has been excavated archaeologically with its surroundings.

At Frocester Captain Gracie and Mr. Eddy Price have shown that the area was used for agriculture from the Bronze Age into the Roman period, and through that time the boundaries of the farmstead remained much the same. A major change was the creation, in the late 3rd century, of a stone 'villa'; at the same time there was a substantial alteration of property boundaries. The villa was used until the very end of the 4th century, with 'a gradual decline in the status of the occupants from that of gentlemen farmers to that of peasants'. Towards the end, one room of the villa was used as a stable.

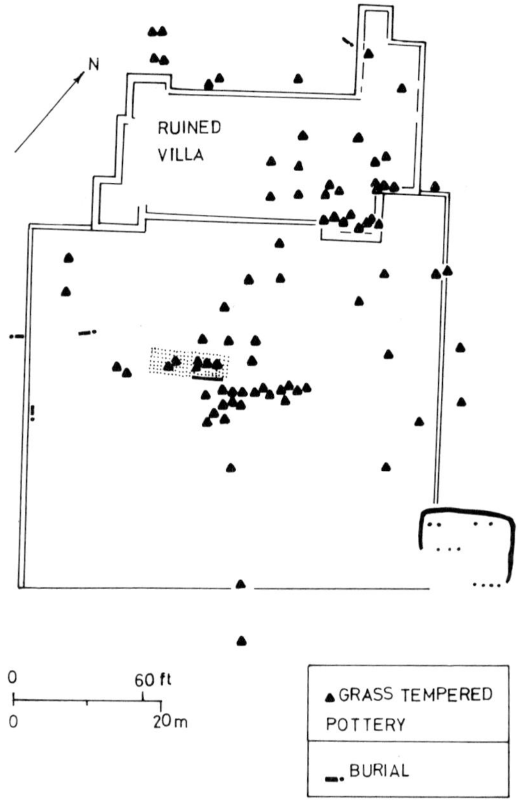

Frocester Roman villa: a plan of the villa area in the 5th century. Based on Price 1979, fig 6, with permission. The villa site went on being occupied after the Roman period, but by people using timber buildings, not stone.

Other rooms were badly repaired by 'DIY' methods, and part of the villa was burnt down. By the early 5th century the farmers had abandoned the villa-house altogether. A building 14m × 3m was put up in the courtyard; this had a stone and gravel floor and no post-holes, though the south-east side was defined by a shallow gully or drip line. Under the building was a 4th century pit into which the floor had sagged and been renewed three times. Though the excavators considered this building to be 'of very slight construction' it is probable that it was a rectangular hall built on sill beams laid flat on the ground. (There is evidence that this building technique was becoming popular at this time; and it was not unknown centuries earlier; very similar Roman buildings were excavated at Barnsley Park). Around this building, and in and under its floor, were dozens of sherds of 5th-century pottery, of a type known as 'grass-tempered' because the clay was mixed with straw or grass before firing. There were four graves also belonging to this period. At the same time, a timber building was erected across part of the courtyard wall: an area 12m x 9m was defined by a timber beam–slot, and there were internal postholes. This structure is far too wide to have been spanned by a roof, and maybe this is an enclosure with a building inside.

Whatever the exact status of these buildings, the general picture is clear. The stone villa was too difficult and expensive to maintain, so the farmer used it for a barn and outhouse and and built a new timber house in the villa courtyard nearby. Life and work went on, although without the former luxuries. For a long time the ruins of the villa were ploughed around and used for stone; only in the 1200s was it taken down altogether and ploughed over.

It is likely that many other Roman villas would tell a similar story, if they were as extensively excavated as Frocester has been. And not only the villas, but the many thousands of smaller settlements too, must have continued farming through the 500s and 600s.

The towns must have been very mournful places. In the 540s Gildas wrote,

> . . .The cities of our land are not populated even now as they once
> were; right to the present they are deserted, in ruins and unkempt.

Archaeologists have a struggle to show much activity in the towns beyond about 430; and probably the roots of the decline lay well in the past. Much of the walled area of Cirencester was not urban; by the 4th century there was at least one farmhouse inside the walls. At Gloucester, too, there was much space inside the walls in the 4th century, and a number of larger well-appointed houses. The suburbs of the city were contracting in the 3rd and 4th centuries. In the 4th century, public buildings were being divided up for use as industrial units. Events in the early 400s were dramatic: the forum forecourt was enlarged, the main street eliminated, and public buildings demolished. On their levelled ruins were constructed buildings set on timber sills laid on the ground – just as at Frocester. Buildings of this type leave no trace when they are demolished. In Gloucester such buildings occur from the late Roman period onwards. At 1 Westgate Street, the chance survival of a single timber betrayed their presence; at St Mary De Lode church, also in Gloucester, was a 5th century timber building of similar type. At Wroxeter, 80 miles north, a whole street was constructed in this way in the 5th century; its buildings were only detected in the 20th century by the most meticulous use of brush and trowel.

Many towns thus continued their life into the 500s, but it is difficult to show that they survived the end of the century. At Gloucester, for instance,

The ruins of Roman Gloucester, in the 600s. Detail from a painting by Richard Bryant. Copyright, Dean and Chapter, Gloucester Cathedral.

there are a few sherds of coarse pottery of the 6th century, associated with a collection of smith's tools; and one sherd of imported ware of the same century. All this is only enough to show that there were people in the town. At Cirencester, the defences were maintained into the early 5th century; the forum was kept clean to about 430, though there seems to have been no money for repairs. The main street ceased to be used in the early 400s, and in the roadside ditch two skeletons were found, apparently never properly

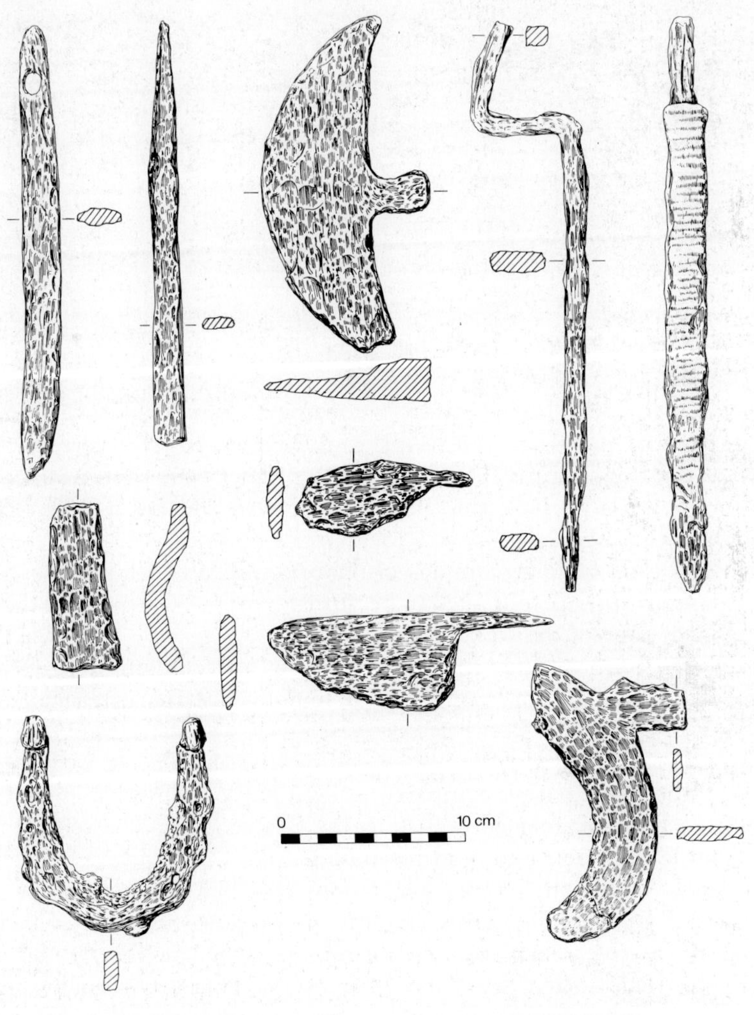

Iron tools from 6th century levels in Gloucester. These show that industrial activity was still continuing in Gloucester after Roman rule ceased. Drawn by Damyon Rey.

The Roman amphitheatre at Cirencester. After the decay of the town, the amphitheatre was occupied by 5th and 6th century buildings, and may have been a defended centre.

buried. Civic order had completely collapsed; there may have been an outbreak of plague. The latest people to inhabit the town were apparently living in the amphitheatre. Here in the 400s or later were timber buildings, including one large hall; this might have been the last refuge of the population of Cirencester.

At Bath, too, the huge complex of temples and baths fell into disrepair, yet its famous springs continued to be visited – even 400 years later the hot springs were one of the wonders of Britain.

In all the Roman cities the ruins of walls and columns remained to dominate the towns for centuries and to influence the pattern of later restoration.

Temples and shrines outlasted the end of Roman rule. At Lydney, for instance, the whole temple complex was built in the late Roman period and may have been maintained well into the 5th century. The temple was dedicated to the water god Nodens and hundreds of offerings of jewellery were made. In the 5th century adaptations involved the building of new ramparts in front of the temple, indicating continued use. At Uley, too, there was a temple which had religious origins in the late Iron Age but was rebuilt as a Roman temple in the 4th century. This was partially pulled down in the 5th century and replaced by a number of other structures. Other temples in the West have a similar history which may mean that the Romano-British were returning to their own native gods. At Uley there

A sixth-century warrior. His armour and weapons are modelled on late Roman prototypes. Chieftains such as these would have dominated the politics of Western Britain and Gloucestershire in the 5th and 6th centuries. Detail of a model by Richard Bryant.

was an additional puzzle, for one of the post-temple structures has in plan the appearance of a Christian church, as if the temple had been considered a suitable site for a conversion to Christianity. A possible Roman temple at Blaise Castle, near Bristol, became a burial-ground in the post-Roman period.

In fact, an unknown number of men and women in the 5th and 6th century would have been Christians. When the Gaulish bishop Germanus visited Britain in 429, sent to deal with heresy in the British church, he found well-dressed prelates and a Christian church still in operation. Gildas, writing in the sub-Roman west or north in the 6th century, described a country which was at least nominally Christian, and though he enumerated in lurid detail the rulers' sins, he did not include pagan practices among them.

The economic world of the fifth to sixth centuries must have been very different from what went before. The end of the towns meant that market centres and power centres shifted their location, probably to rural sites, – a reversion, in fact, to the pre-Roman Iron Age systems. In nearby south-east Wales, whose Roman history and fertile land was not so very different from that of Gloucestershire, Wendy Davies has shown how, after the decline of towns, economic life focussed upon the estate system. The profits went to aristocrats and 'kings', who continued to grant land using Roman formulae. In Wales and in the North, there survived into the medieval period a system whereby the king owned the head manor of a group of estates, and to the head manor (or 'royal vill') were paid dues and rents in kind and in the form of labour service. Possibly something like this system was operating in Gloucestershire in the 5th and 6th centuries.

We may be sure that the new rulers of 5th and 6th century society were unlikely to be benevolent to their subjects. Gildas described the rulers in unflattering terms . No doubt they collected tribute from their peasants and if need be backed up their claims with military force. As Gildas put it,

> Britain has kings, but they are tyrants; she has judges, but they are wicked. They often plunder and terrorize – the innocent, they defend and protect – the guilty and thieving. . .

And in her work on the Llandaff charters, Wendy Davies concluded of these early rulers:

> The evidence..suggests overwhelmingly that kingship was sought for power and property and not for office. . .and that the majority of kings used their powers for the benefits of self, family and companions rather than for those who had the misfortune to be subject to them.

Of these 'kings' we know little, having only a few traces. One of their earliest ancestors might have been the man buried at Kingsholm, Gloucester, his body placed in a special timber mausoleum, clothed in his best, including silver belt–fittings. Gildas names Aurelius Caninus, or Conan, to give him his probable British name, who ruled in the Severn Valley area in the early 500s. The genealogy of Vortigern, the British prince who is reputed to have first employed Saxon mercenaries, places one of his ancestors, Vitalinus, in the Gloucester area. Some of these men reinforced their right to rule by claiming descent from Roman public office of some kind.

Until recently, we did not even know where these rulers of Gloucestershire lived. In the Celtic West as a whole, their strongholds are well-known: they tend to be on fortified sites, often sites re-used from the pre-Roman Iron Age. At Dinas Powys, for instance, within the defended area of a promontory was a great hall, and excavation uncovered some of the valuable objects once made, traded, and given as gifts by the lord and his men. In Somerset a number of these defended Dark Age sites are known, notably Cadbury-Congresbury and South Cadbury. We might expect some of the Gloucestershire Iron Age hill forts to have been re-used in the Dark

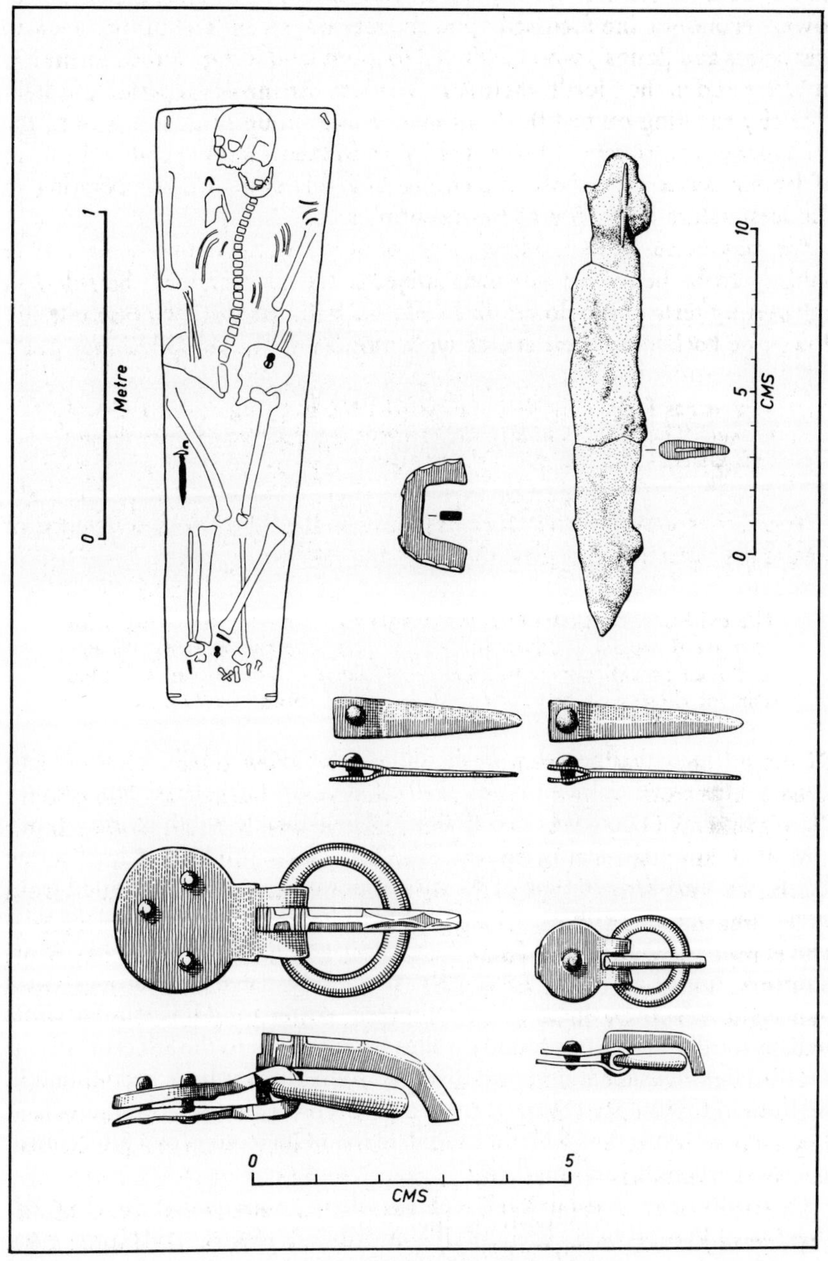

The early 5th century burial of a high-ranking man at Kingsholm, Gloucester. The site of this burial ground was later occupied by a Saxon palace. Drawing by Phil Moss.

A view of the Iron Age hill-fort on Crickley Hill. The remains of 5th century buildings have been found on the hill, showing it was re-used in the Dark Ages.

Ages, and recently there has been found, at Crickley Hill, traces of 5th century sub-rectangular huts, as well as remains of a large 5th century rectangular hall. There was also an unusual belt-buckle of 5th century type.

Most of the high status sites of the Celtic west produce at least a few sherds of a well-known type of glossy red pottery, which is imported from the Mediterranean. Gloucestershire has produced only one sherd of this, which is surprising if its contacts were similar to those of the Celtic West. Another sort of pottery, not nearly so closely dated, sometimes dates Gloucestershire sites: this is 'grass-tempered' pottery and it is humble stuff, perhaps locally made. It is found on sites from the 5th to the 8th centuries. It must be significant that no more than a few sherds of it have been found in the Roman towns. By contrast, there are dozens of sherds from the villa at Frocester, which is thus a better candidate than Gloucester for a 5th century centre – perhaps a rural market.

There must have been markets; centres where goods could be exchanged. These would not have been in the moribund towns, and large rural assemblies are most likely. What medium of exchange was used can only be guessed; iron bars, perhaps, as in the pre-Roman world, small jewellery items. Since the Welsh world reckoned its wealth in cattle and slaves, among other things, it is likely that these were used for the larger transactions.

So far we have said nothing of the peasants – those who did all the hard work. That is because we know very little about them, or even about how

A belt buckle from Crickley Hill dating to about 420. These military buckles represent some sort of continuation of the Romano-Celtic military organisation. Photo: Phil Dixon. Copyright: Crickley Hill Trust.

the land was organised. The Romano–Celtic system of agriculture was probably based on a number of small fields, held by individuals, and the landscape would have looked more like today's Devon and Cornwall, with many scattered farms, and few villages. The system of roads, lanes and tracks, inherited from the Roman and pre-Roman period, was still in being; and the Roman roads would have been in good repair. The saltways, in particular, can never have ceased to be used, for without salt the economy can hardly have functioned at all.

We can probably assume that the peasants were tied to the land and did their work in greater or lesser degrees of servitude. It was H. P. R. Finberg who first put forward for Gloucestershire the thesis of the essential continuity of estates and their workers; that estates were handed over from British to Saxon hands, complete with tenants, and that it was over-complex to assume that between the Roman tenants (who were tied to the land) and the Saxon serf of Domesday Book, there was somehow a period

Salters Hill, near Winchcombe. A section of the old salt route from Droitwich to the south-west. Photograph: Mick Sharp.

when the peasants won freedom and independence. Then a radical proposition, this view is much more accepted today: to quote Eric John, 'servitude is more stable than leadership, and more readily inherited.' The Romano-Celtic peasants no doubt inherited the condition of their parents and grandparents, and when the Anglo-Saxons took over – nothing changed. It would be a tied peasantry, for instance, which built, as part of their labour services, the great dyke of Wansdyke, east of Bath. It may be 6th or 7th century, and have been built either under Celtic or Saxon orders.

The daily life of people in the 5th and 6th centuries has to be reconstructed from very little evidence. Houses were of wood; Roman stone buildings were being replaced by buildings on timber sill-beams laid on the ground. But it should be remembered that even in the full Roman period, buildings all of stone were rare and were seen only in towns and temples. The great villas, though having stone sleeper walls, were mostly half-timbered. And ordinary people had continued to build in wood, as they had for thousands of years. Most domestic items, too; spades, hoes, wheelbarrows, butter churns, bowls, trenchers, and spoons – everything would have been wooden and so has not survived.

One very important domestic item would have been the cauldron; there would have been one in every home from the greatest to the least. The many Celtic legends featuring cauldrons, whether magic or not, show how important this item was. Unfortunately, because it was so precious, it was handed from generation to generation until beyond repair, when it would be melted down for scrap. The Celtic-inspired ornament on hanging bowls found in Anglo-Saxon graves is a reminder both of Celtic influence on the Anglo-Saxons, and of how important the cauldron was both to Celt and Saxon.

Clothes in the 5th and 6th century, as throughout history, depended on who you were. In the 5th century, and undoubtedly in the 6th, there was a wealthy richly dressed aristocracy, some of whom Germanus met in 429. They probably wore silk or furs, or at the least brightly dyed wool. Their dress would certainly have included jewellery, especially brooches and pins. There are a number of objects which it can be suggested were worn in the 5th century and perhaps beyond; these include penannular brooches, cross-bow brooches, certain plate brooches with animal ornament. Many of these are found at Lydney temple, which survived into the 5th century. One particularly unusual brooch (no 7 in the illustration) has no parallel, has both Saxon and Roman prototypes, and may be late 5th century in date. The type G penannular brooches (no 3 in the illustration) began manufacture in south Wales in the late Roman period and continued in use there and in the Severn Valley in the 5th and later centuries. Some were traded or exchanged with the Anglo-Saxons in the east. The bronze pins, known as 'proto-hand-pins', later developed into a much larger version well-known in Ireland. The two examples illustrated here from St Oswald's, Gloucester, were possibly late Roman, but may have gone on being used into the 5th century.

Men of post-Roman Britain wore a short tunic over woollen breeches, perhaps cross-gartered, suitable for the British climate. In cold weather, extra tunics were worn. Women would have worn a longer tunic, and cloaks were the usual outdoor wear, as they were to be for many centuries to come.

It is hard to imagine what it must have been like in the sub-Roman world of the 5th and 6th centuries. No doubt the Roman period seemed a golden age, when many were prosperous and the legions had kept the peace. Though the status of ordinary people remained the same in the sub-Roman world, life must have been very different. For one thing, the population must have fallen. A population as dense as that of Roman Britain does not occur again until the time of Domesday or later, and some time in the 5th and 6th centuries a severe loss of population must have occurred. Plagues, mentioned by Gildas and by Continental writers at this time, may have been one factor. Climatic change could have been another. An alteration in annual average temperature as small as 1°C. would be enough to reduce the

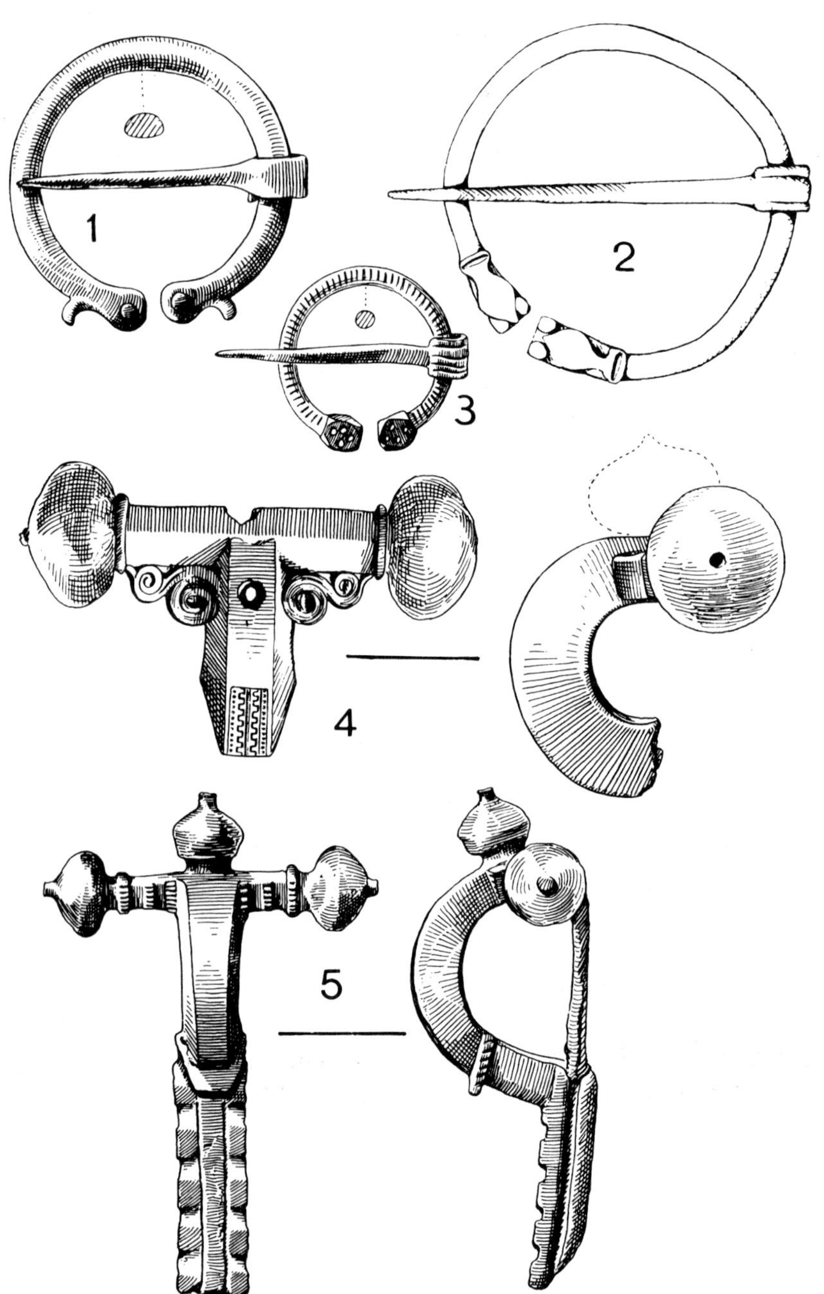

Some pieces of ornamental metalwork which may, in the Severn Valley, date to the 5th century. (1) Penannular brooch, type B3, from Wheeler 1932, fig 14, no 40. (2) Penannular brooch, Type F; from Gracie 1970, Fig 13, no 39. (3) Penannular brooch, type G, from Wheeler 1932, fig 14, no 39. (4) Cross-bow brooch from Lydney, from Wheeler 1932, Fig 13, nos 25 and 27.

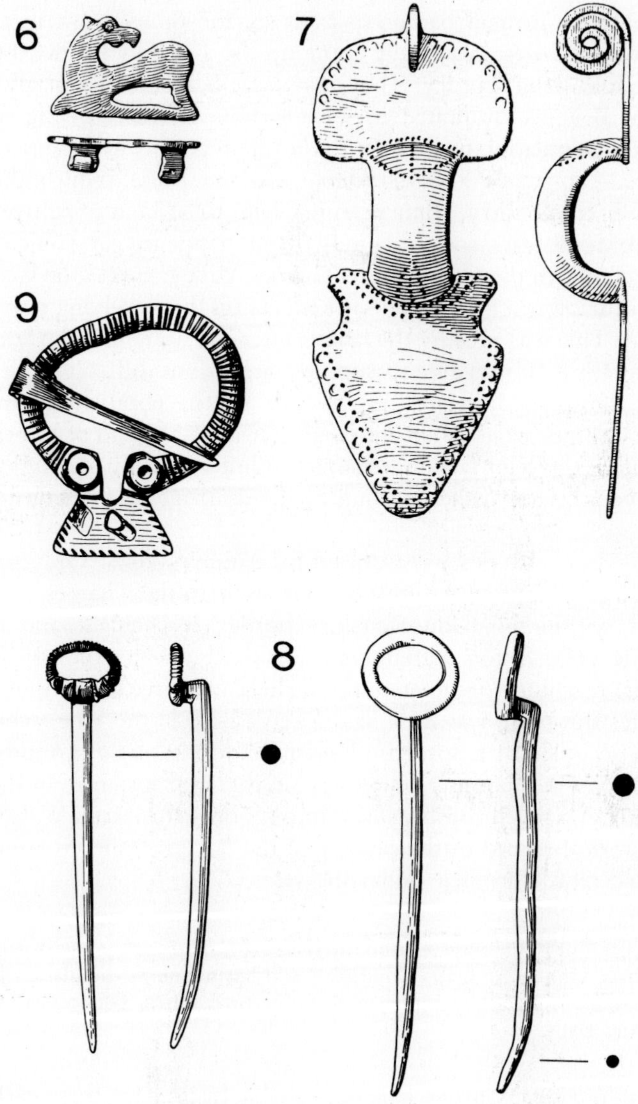

Possible 5th century metalwork (6) Animal-style plate brooch , which has some affinities with Anglo-Saxon metalwork; from Wheeler 1932, Fig 16, no 46. (7) A bronze brooch, probably late 5th century, with both 'Roman' and 'Teutonic' affinites, from Wheeler 1932, Fig 15. (8) Two 'Proto-hand-pins' from St Oswald's, Gloucester; drawn by Andy Jones. (9) Ring brooch from the river Thames at Kempsford, Gloucestershire; taken from Dickinson 1982, p 65 no 55; late 4th to early 5th century.

harvest yield to a crucial extent. Civil war must also have had its effect. There were late Roman barbarian raids in 367–8, by Scottish and Irish pirates. Some of these may have come up the Bristol Channel, both then and in the following century. They may have been the reason why a large number of Britains emigrated to what is now Brittany in the late 400s, reducing the population further. With the fall in population went changes in agriculture – it is not known which was the cause, which the effect. Elsewhere in the country, some marginal land passed out of cultivation and went back to forest, and this may have happened in some parts of Gloucestershire. In the Oxfordshire Thames Valley, across the Cotswolds, the 5th century was a time when settlements on the low-lying gravels were abandoned. This was because the labour intensive system of the 5th century B.C. to the 4th A.D. was able to support 'a rich but difficult environment' based on complex drainage systems. A fall in population, and other economic changes whether or not connected with the end of imperial rule, meant that methods of farming changed. Cultivation on the higher slopes would have accelerated the flooding of the drainage systems on the lower terraces.

None of these changes were caused by Anglo-Saxons. Only in the late 400s did large groups of wealthy Saxons settle in the Thames valley, two being just within the Gloucestershire border at Lechlade and Fairford. During the 500s Saxon settlements advanced up the dip slope of the Cotswolds, reaching Cirencester and the heights above the Stroud valley at Chavenage. But there was little Saxon settlement in the Vale, which must have been occupied by a powerful British kingdom, one of a number in the west of Britain at this time. There was another, for instance, in the Upper Severn Valley in the Shropshire area, known only from later Welsh poetry.

The historical record of the capture of the Severn Valley is contained in the Anglo-Saxon Chronicle under the year 577:-

> In this year Cuthwine and Ceawlin [of Wessex] fought against the Britons and killed three kings, Conmail, Condidan, and Farinmail, at the place which is called Dyrham, and they captured three of their cities, Gloucester, Cirencester, and Bath.

The Anglo-Saxon Chronicle is not reliable history for these early times, but this entry, with its catalogue of British names (possibly genuinely 6th century), is convincing; for one thing it is very likely that the sub-Roman British kingdoms would be centred on the Roman towns. The battle of Dyrham may have been fought near or at the old Iron Age hill fort on Hinton Hill; the site commands a view of the Severn Estuary. For the first time an Anglo-Saxon army had penetrated the kingdom from coast to coast, and separated the British of Cornwall from those of Wales. Even

The ramparts of the Iron Age fort of Hinton Hill, where the battle of Dyrham may have been fought in 577. The place commands a view of the whole Severn Valley with the Severn Estuary and the hills of Wales in the distance. Here for the first time the Saxons viewed the west shore of Britain.

without the annal of 577, one cemetery at Bishops Cleeve, near Cheltenham, shows that around 550 or so Anglo-Saxon influence had reached the Severn Valley. This was the beginning of the end of Romano–British Gloucestershire.

2
The Anglo-Saxons Take Over

By 600 Gloucestershire was part of the Anglo-Saxon world. The name 'Anglo-Saxon' is given to a group of Germanic people who migrated west from north-western Europe in the 5th century. They were a mixed race, deriving mainly from Saxony (north Germany), and Angeln (south Denmark) but they also included Jutes (from north Denmark), Frisians (north Belgium and Holland) and Franks (from north-east France). Some 'Anglo-Saxons' had already come to Britain in the late 4th century in the pay of the Roman authorities. Tradition has it that, when the Roman armies no longer defended Britain, Saxons continued to be employed as mercenaries, but subsequently rebelled against their employers. By the 470s they had taken over a substantial part of south-east Britain.

The Anglo-Saxons come in two sorts: 'Anglian' and 'Saxon'. The two terms can also mean a linguistic division, defined by dialect, and it also has a political meaning, describing those from Anglian or Saxon areas of England. Most Gloucestershire Anglo-Saxons are actually Saxons, and we may call them that for short. We don't know what the Saxons called themselves, but Pope Gregory, in the famous story where he inquired the race of some boys in the Rome slave market, was told they were 'Anglians', and certainly that word later became the name of the race, 'English'.

Because the Anglo-Saxons conveniently laid their dead in the ground, and placed with them objects they had used and valued in their lifetime, the pagan Saxon burials of Gloucestershire are easily recognisable. Many of them were grubbed up without much ceremony in the 19th century by Victorian antiquarians. Only some of the objects ended up in museums; many found their way into antique shops, where they may still occasionally appear (it is not only excavation and metal detectors that produce 'finds'). So, much of what we know about the pagan Saxons derives from objects buried with them.

Although by the 500s most Anglo-Saxons buried their dead in the ground, their earlier custom had been cremation, and those Anglo-Saxons of conservative disposition are occasionally found in cemeteries, their ashes placed in pottery urns.

Studying people by objects, which is what archaeologists do, is not

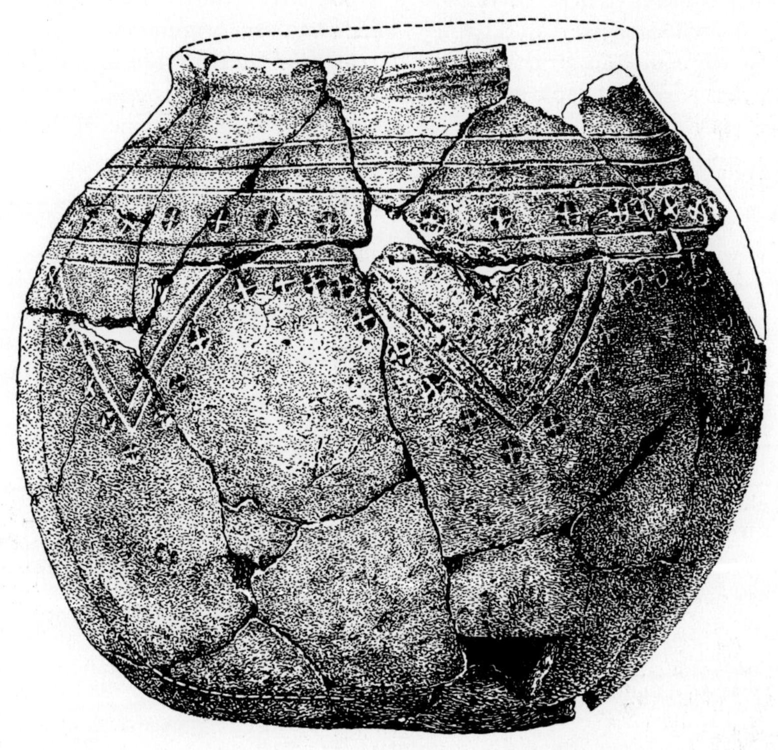

An Anglo Saxon cremation urn from Burn Ground, Hampnett (about 21 cms high). The first Anglo-Saxons cremated their dead, and placed the ashes in urns like these. Reproduced from W. Grimes, Excavations on Defences Sites, *HMSO. Copyright HMSO; by permission.*

always satisfactory. Dividing people into groups according to the objects they use can have peculiar results. Not all people with French saucepans in their kitchens are French, and we cannot be sure that all people using Anglo-Saxon objects are racially Germanic. Some of these 'Anglo-Saxon' people could, for example, be Celts using Anglo-Saxon dress fashions, or in Saxon employ, or (in the case of women) married to Saxons. Still, advertising being less powerful among the Anglo-Saxons, if we do find concentrations of people using Anglo-Saxon objects, we can at least assume strong Anglo-Saxon influence, especially if the objects are military weapons, and therefore used by men, who are more likely to be traditional about such things.

The earliest Anglo-Saxon cemeteries in Gloucestershire appear in the Thames Valley, where there was a very early Anglo-Saxon kingdom centred on Dorchester-on-Thames. This kingdom originated at the very end of the Romano-British period. Cemeteries at Lechlade and Fairford show that wealthy people using Anglo-Saxon objects were established there in the very late 400s, and in the 500s there were Anglo-Saxons at Kemble

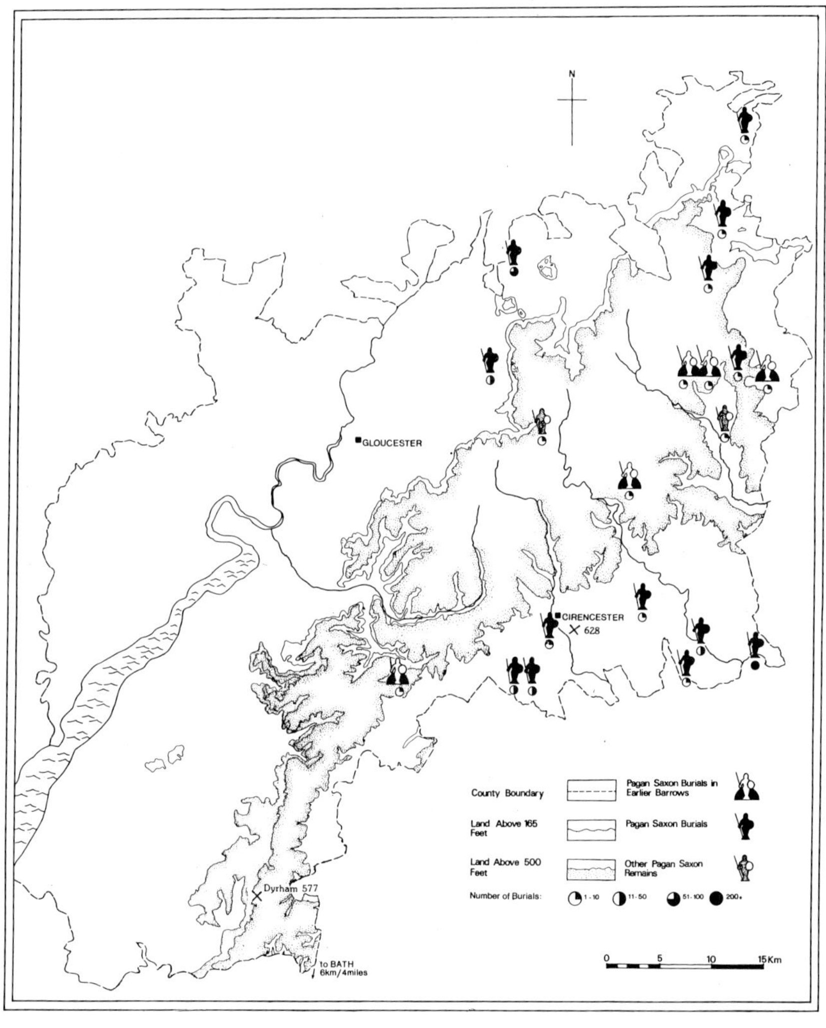

Map of Pagan Anglo-Saxon burials in Gloucestershire. This shows how far Anglo-Saxon influence had reached by about 600. Drawn by Brian Cummings.

and Cirencester, up the Windrush Valley near Stow-on-the-Wold, and in the Stroud Valley at Avening and Chavenage. No Anglo-Saxon burials have been found in the central Cotswolds except for a group in Withington. There is one cemetery in the Severn Vale at Bishop's Cleeve near Cheltenham.

Beyond Gloucestershire to the north there was another settlement of Anglo-Saxons. The Avon Valley above Tewkesbury was settled by a group of people whose equipment shows they had links with Anglo-Saxons in East Anglia; they were 'Angles', whereas the Thames Valley people were 'Saxons'.

There are not a great many Anglo-Saxon burials in Gloucestershire, and a few of the burials on the Cotswolds may not represent pagan Anglo-Saxons at all. The Withington burials consisted of three crouched skeletons, two with Anglo-Saxon bone combs, possibly 7th century. The spiral-headed pins found with burials at Bourton-on-the-Water and Stow-on-the-Wold are objects used both in Celtic and Anglo-Saxon areas of Britain. The man buried at Leckhampton, usually counted as an Anglo-Saxon, wore an extraordinary object on his head which has no parallel in Anglo-Saxon or Celtic archaeology, and cannot yet be counted as an Anglo-Saxon helmet.

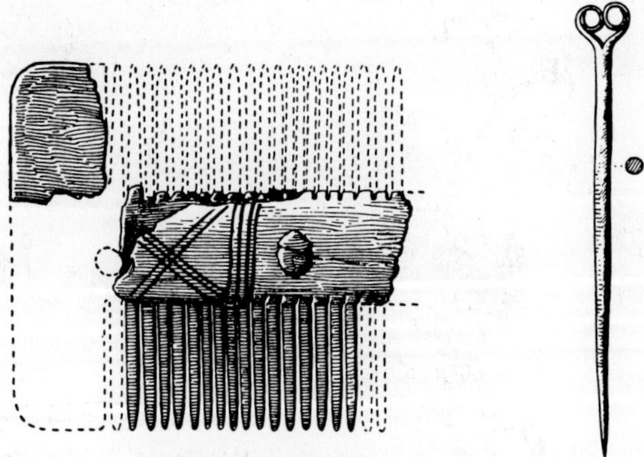

Bone comb found with Anglo-Saxon burials at Foxcote, Withington; spiral-headed pin found at Stow-on-the-Wold. Reproduced from TBGAS 58 (1936), p 157–70.

The majority of Gloucestershire's pagan Saxon cemeteries are in the East Cotswolds. The most westerly burials, technically, are those at Chavenage, near Stroud. The Bishops Cleeve cemetery had connections with those of the Thames Valley; it was discovered only in 1968, and is the only archaeological evidence that any Saxons at all penetrated the Lower Severn

A pair of saucer brooches, a star saucer brooch, and ornamented disc from Anglo-Saxon graves at Bishops Cleeve. Photo: Ashmolean Museum, Oxford.

Valley. There may be more Saxon cemeteries to be found in the vale, but this is unlikely. The Gloucester area in particular should have produced some by now: the extensive housing estates which surround the town on all sides have all been watched as they were constructed, and not a single pagan Saxon has come to light. The cemetery at Bishops Cleeve seems so isolated that it may be a group of Saxons fighting under Celtic kings, or settled by treaty, rather than representing a 'conquest'.

Most Anglo-Saxon burials in Gloucestershire were laid out in flat cemeteries. Much further east, some Anglo-Saxons preferred to build a mound over their burials, the most famous being those in the great cemetery of Sutton Hoo, in East Anglia. Gloucestershire Saxons instead were content to use the Bronze Age burial mounds built more than two thousand years before.

Mounds which the Anglo-Saxons used for burial were often described by them as a *hlaw* – a word which survives today on the map, e.g. Whitelaw, Blakelow. These names ending in *hlaw* may indicate pagan Saxon burials and can be added to maps to plot the area of pagan Saxon burial sites. They agree on the whole with the distribution of pagan burials except for an odd group of names in the Dean: Bledisloe, Hagloe, and Botloe. If these represent pagan Saxons, then they were a long way from their fellows. Della Hooke suggests they too may have been mercenaries fighting under the Celtic banner. Excavation at Bledisloe Tump has found no Saxon burials, but since the Tump appears to have been erected in the 12th century, the Saxon name presumably refers to another site, now lost. At no Dean *hlaw* is there a burial-mound surviving.

Saxon burials show what men and women used in their lifetimes. Many men and women were buried with an iron knife – an essential piece of equipment whether hunting or cooking. Women and men liked to wear bright, florid jewellery. Strings of brightly-coloured beads were worn on necks and wrists. Weapons of war are also found; usually iron shield bosses, and the heads of spears or daggers. Swords are very rare; they were carried only by the nobility, but were also highly valued, and were perhaps usually passed on to heirs rather than being buried with the body.

The biggest Gloucestershire Anglo-Saxon cemetery was at Fairford. Anglo-Saxon objects and skeletons have been dug up there since the 1820s. It produced the round gilt brooches appropriately called 'saucer brooches', big square-headed brooches, and some imported things like a glass Frankish 'claw beaker' and a splendid buckle which might have come from Kent. There are the usual Anglo-Saxon shield bosses and spears, and also a few swords, and bronze bowls, both indicators that people of high status were buried here. At Kemble there were two Anglo-Saxon cemeteries, and recent discoveries by Cirencester Museum show that one of them covered several acres.

The barrow burials could also be richly furnished. A barrow near Chavenage was levelled in 1847 and found to contain a central grave, with 7 more burials, all of adults, round the edge of the barrow. Some of the burials contained iron shield bosses, spear-heads, and iron buckles. The only objects to survive today are a bronze ring, a gilt saucer brooch, some flat annular brooches, and some beads. There are also some unusual earrings, of very thin silver. The date of these burials appears to be late 6th century; it is nearly the last in the series of cemeteries which all (except for Lechlade) cease to be used about 600. At Oddington, near Stow, a barrow was opened in the 19th century, and many skeletons found 'with several

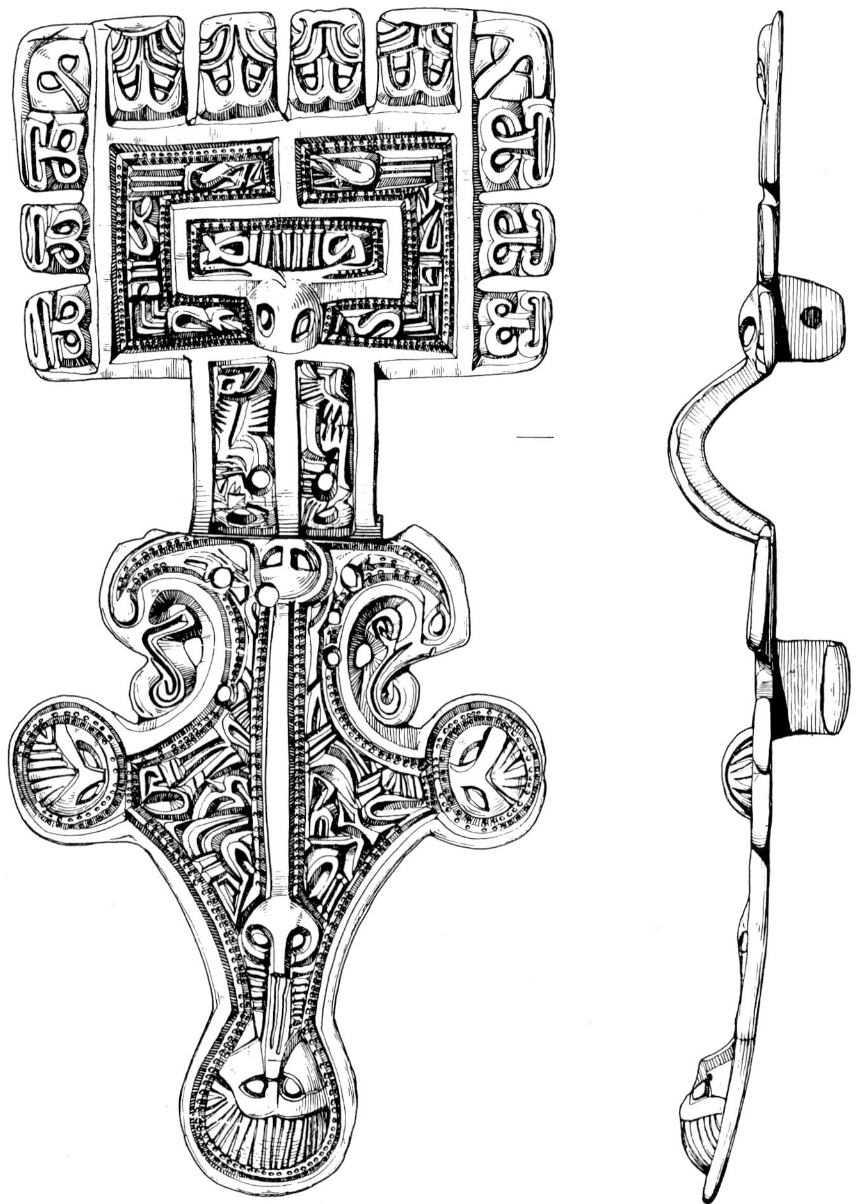

Square-headed brooch from Anglo-Saxon grave, Fairford. These were used to fasten a cloak, and were worn with the square part downwards. Scale 1:1. Copyright, Ashmolean Museum. Drawn by Frank Gardiner.

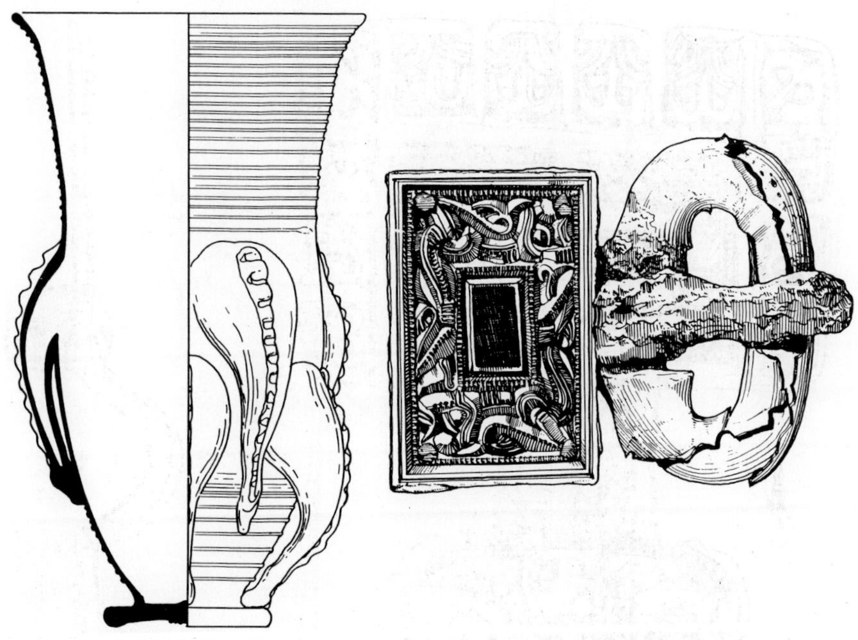

Objects showing the luxurious nature of some Anglo-Saxon graves at Fairford. Belt-buckle from male grave. The buckle is gilt-bronze, with a garnet slab in the middle. The oval loop is covered in sheet silver. The buckle may have been made in Kent in the 6th century. Scale: actual size. Copyright, Ashmolean Museum, Oxford. Drawn by Frank Gardiner. Glass claw-beaker, probably imported from Kent or Gaul. Scale 1/2. Ashmolean Museum, Oxford.

remains of personal ornaments and habiliments of war'. The objects are all lost, although an illustration was made showing spears and a shield boss; also a saucer brooch exactly like some from Fairford.

Because most Gloucestershire Anglo-Saxon burials were found in the 19th century, the objects have often been lost. Modern techniques not only conserve finds better but also obtain fuller information from the bodies themselves. The cemetery at Lechlade was excavated by the Oxfordshire Archaeological Unit in 1985. There were 217 burials, and 32 cremations. The cemetery began to be used in the early 500s; perhaps three burials belong to the late 400s. This cemetery is unusual in Gloucestershire in having burials dating to the 600s – most pagan Saxon burials cease c. 600. The cemetery had separate areas for men and women. Most of the women had worn characteristic bronze saucer brooches or the smaller button brooches, one on each shoulder, holding up a woollen or linen tubular dress. Amber and glass beads were favoured, and bronze pins. Everyday objects were iron knives, sometimes bronze bowls or buckets. Rich goods

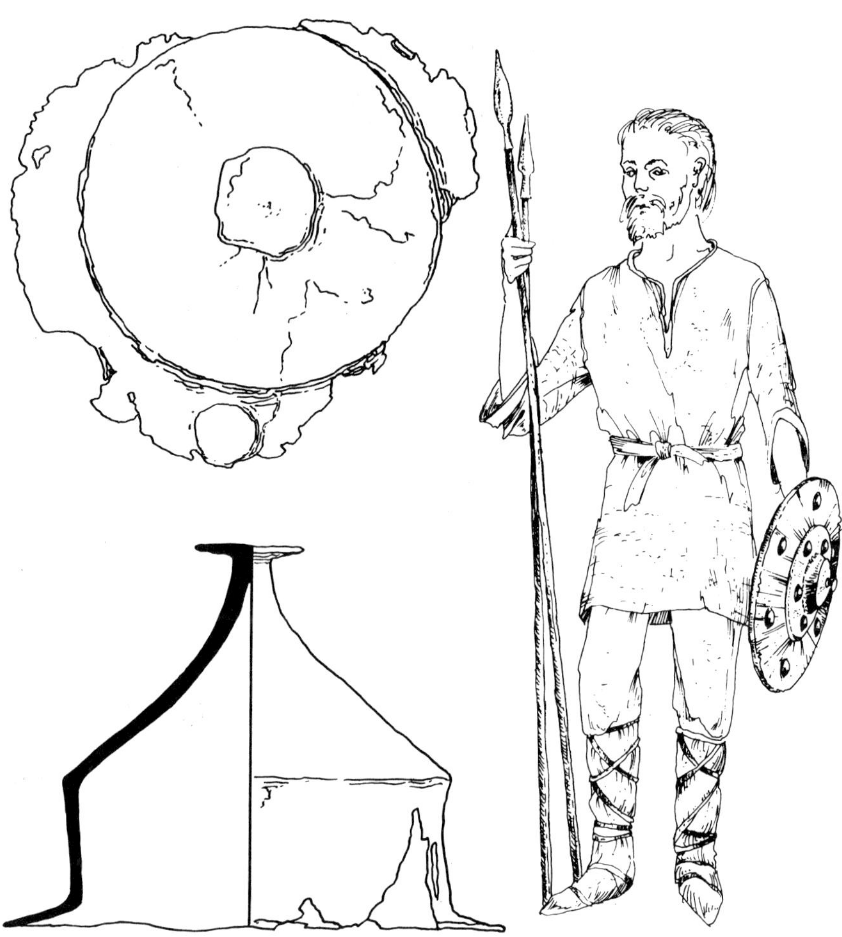

Early Anglo-Saxon shield-boss from Fairford. The boss would have formed the handgrip at the centre of a leather-covered shield. Scale 1/2. Ashmolean Museum, Oxford. Reconstruction drawing by John Lange of an Anglo-Saxon warrior. Oxfordshire Excavation Unit.

with children showed that wealth (and so status) was, as one might expect, inherited. One grave was exceptional; that of a young woman about 18 years of age. The excavators named her 'Mrs Getty'. She was buried in a wooden coffin (in itself a rarity). Behind her skull was a circlet of glass beads which had held back her hair. There was a saucer brooch on each shoulder; traces of the woollen cloth they had held were still visible on the back of the brooch. A massive square-headed brooch held her cloak together. Thickly spread across her chest were amber beads and a string of blue glass beads; by her waist were more beads which had been in a bag.

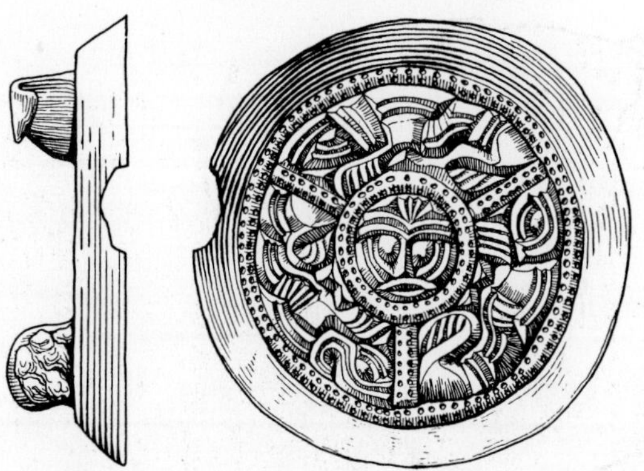

One of a pair of Anglo-Saxon saucer brooches from Fairford. These were worn one on each shoulder. They are similar to those found at Bishops Cleeve. Ashmolean Museum, Oxford.

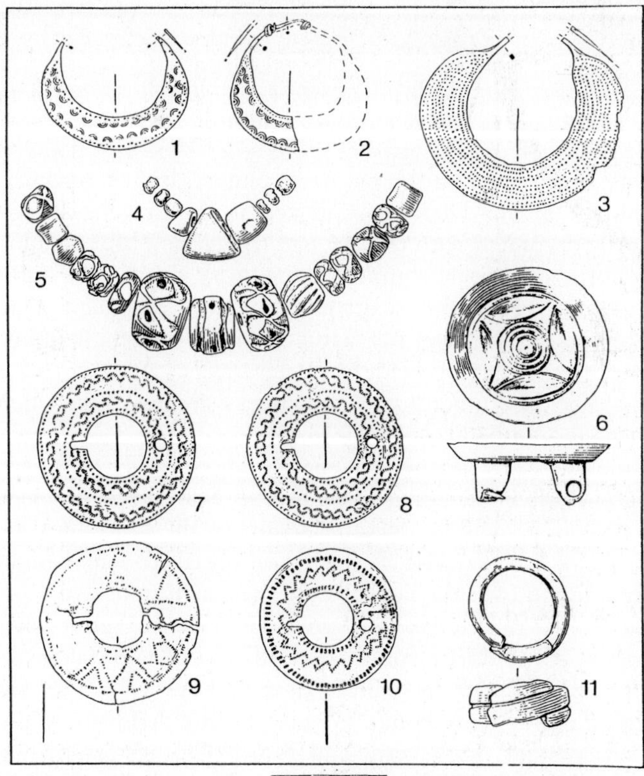

Pagan Saxon objects from a barrow at Chavenage. The objects probably date to the very end of the 500s. Nos 1–3: silver earrings; nos 4–5: coloured paste beads; no 6: gilt saucer brooch; nos 7–10; annular brooches. Scale full size. Copyright Ashmolean Museum.

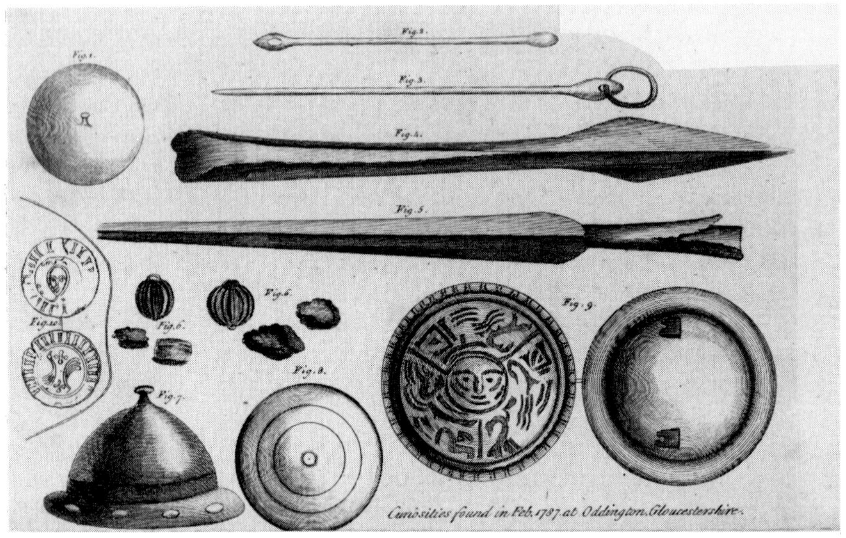

Pagan saxon objects from Saxon burials found in a barrow at Oddington. From Archaeologia, 34 (1851); reproduced from print in Gloucester Collection, 208.3.

There were silver rings on the woman's fingers, bronze pins in her dress, and a cosmetic brush. There were objects in the grave too; a wooden or leather bottle decorated with circular and triangular bronze plaques; a bone spindle whorl, and a bone comb. A large ivory ring by her waist was the stiffener of a bag. From her waist hung an iron 'chatelaine' – a bunch of key-like objects symbolising her status as mistress of the household.

The men's graves at Lechlade were fewer, because the area excavated turned out to be the women's area . The men were not of such high status as the women; the husband and male relatives of 'Mrs Getty' are probably buried somewhere else nearby. The men had been buried with spear, shield, knife, and in clothing including a belt-buckle. Some graves included a bowl or bucket. This item is the Saxon version of the Celtic devotion to the cauldron, magic or otherwise. Some Saxon burials contain hanging bowls, like the one found over the face of a skeleton at Kempsford.

It is not only cemeteries that provide evidence about Anglo-Saxon settlement. Ancient documents include dialect Anglo-Saxon words and place-names from which the pattern of dialect speech in the early Anglo-Saxon period can be worked out. Gloucestershire divided into three dialect areas. That west of the Severn, and North Gloucestershire west of the Cotswolds, both spoke different Anglian dialects; the south of the county, and the south-east Cotswolds spoke a West Saxon dialect. This presumably represent the two different Saxon influences, one from the Midlands (Anglian), the other from the Thames Valley (West Saxon).

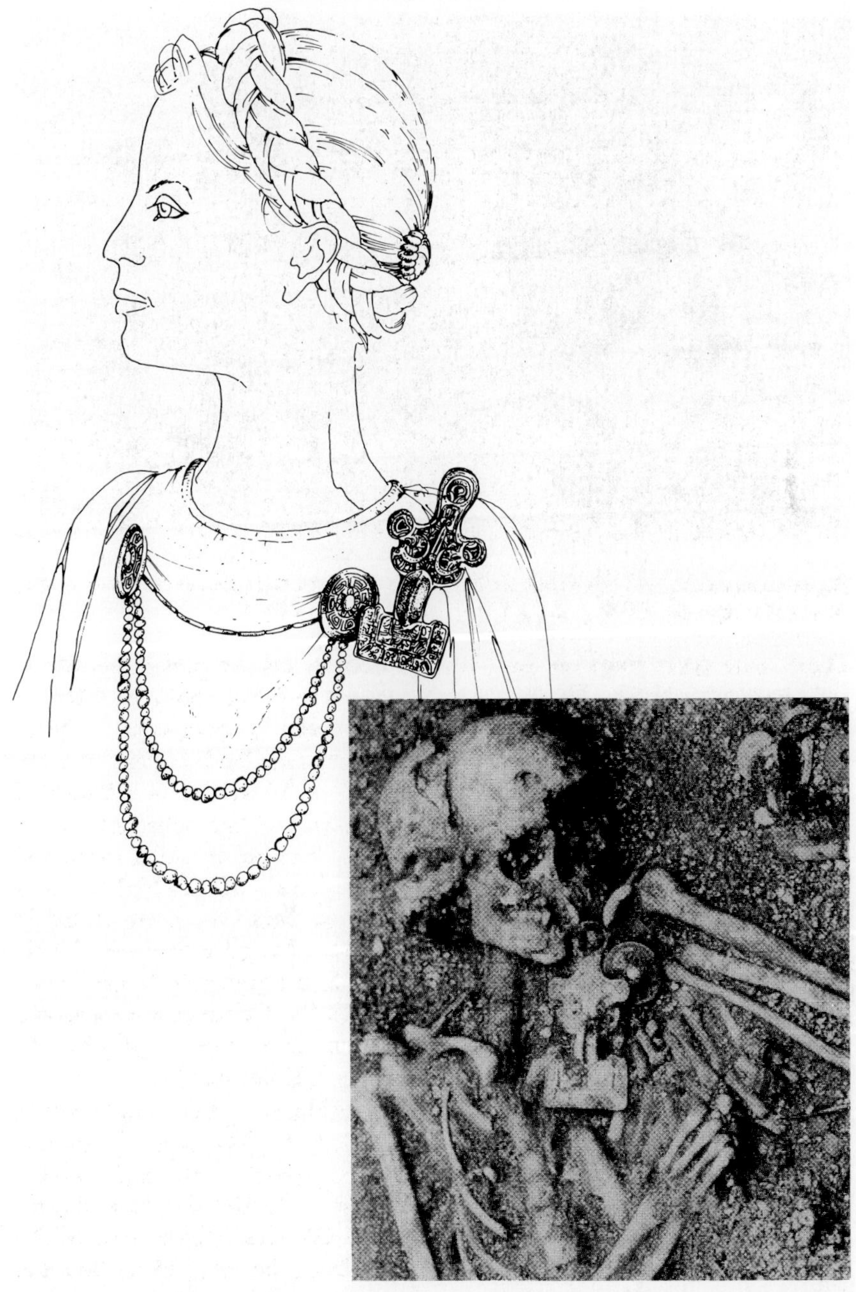

Photograph and reconstruction drawing of the young Saxon girl buried in the Lechlade cemetery, in all her finery. Drawing by John Lange. Copyright, Oxford Excavation Unit.

The Kempsford Cauldron. This was found over the face of a skeleton, about half a mile NNW of Kempsford church. It had been used as a cooking pot before it went into the grave. Such cauldrons were valuable Anglo-Saxon trade objects, and were made in the Rhineland.

Place-names are useful in many other ways. The names of farms, fields, woods, and streams survive from the past, and anyone can check the origin of their local place names by simply turning to the work of the English Place Name Society, whose four Gloucestershire volumes give nearly every name on the map and many, mentioned in old documents, which are no longer used. A majority of Gloucestershire names are Anglo-Saxon, but there are many British words and also many mixed names, evidence of Anglo-Saxon and British struggle for understanding. Our Saxon and our Briton stand beside a hill; the Saxon asks its name (by pointing), The Briton says it is a hill (*pen*), so the Saxon calls it Pen Hill (hill-hill). There are plenty of these hybrid hames in Gloucestershire; for instance Churchdown, which is the British *crouco* (hill) with Old English *dun* (hill). Not all British names occur only as hybrids, of course. Kemble is from a British word related to Welsh *cyfyl*, 'border', Dorn from – *duro* – 'gate' or 'fort'. A number of natural landscape features retain their British names to this day, like the rivers Avon, Churn, Coln and Windrush. North of Bredon, just outside the Gloucestershire boundary, are two villages called Comberton, from the

Skeleton of Anglo-Saxon warrior, 7th century, from the cemetery at Lechlade. He was buried with spear, 'seax' (sword) and iron-bound bucket. By his side is a girl with a necklace of gold, silver, garnet, and amethyst. Photo: D. Miles, Oxfordshire Archaeology Unit.

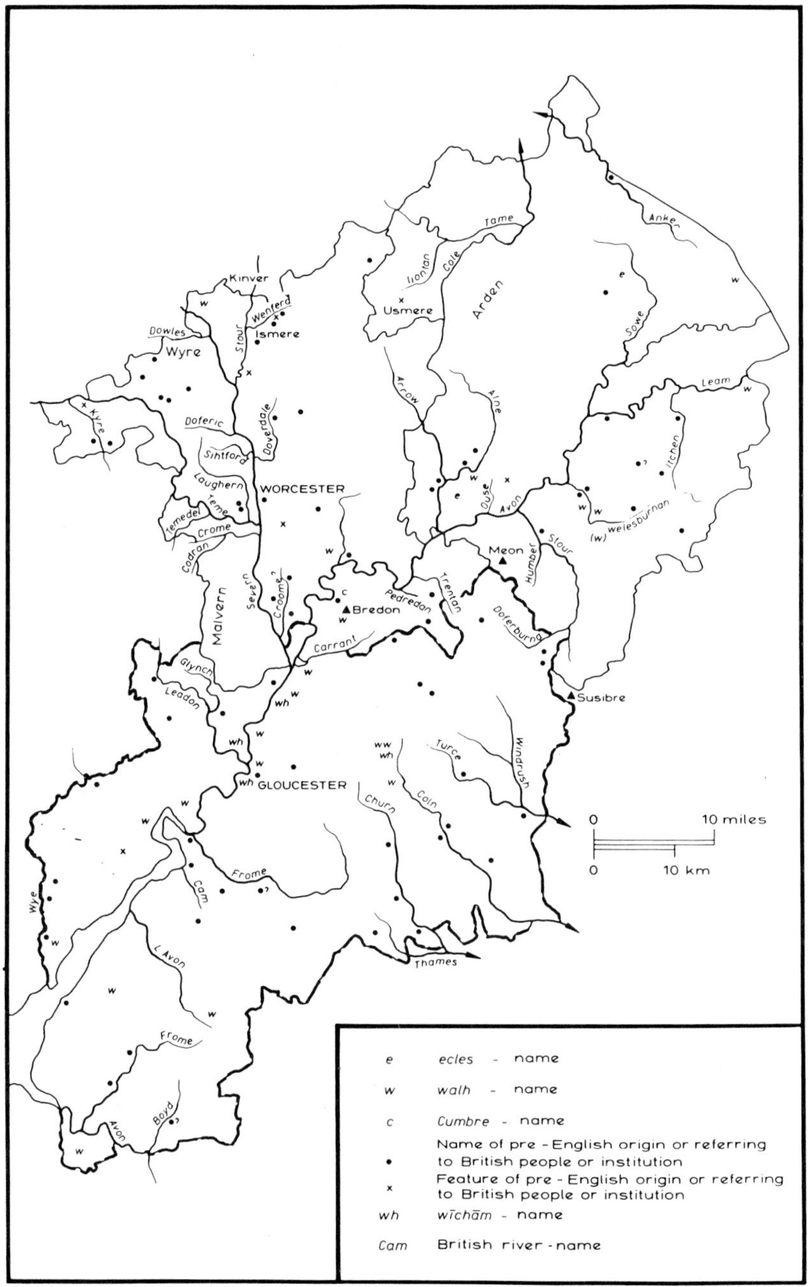

Place-name evidence of Celtic survival in the Kingdom of the Hwicce. Reproduced from Della Hooke, The Anglo Saxon Landscape: The kingdom of the Hwicce, *(Manchester University Press 1985), Fig 6, p 33.*

name the British gave to themselves – *cumbre*. It means 'comrades' and is also, of course, the name the Welsh still use (*Cymru/Cymric*).

The words the British used included some Latin, and some of these have survived. An important one is *ecclesia* church, which occurs as *eccles* in place-names. Gloucester and Cirencester are the Romano-British names Glevum and Corinium with Anglo-Saxon *ceastor* (meaning a fort or walled place). There are also a number of names in *-wicham*, deriving from the Latin *vicus*. *-Wicham* names were apparently an English name for a Roman settlement.

Evidence of British survival, especially in the area just close to Gloucester, comes from a number of place-names like Walham and Wallsworth which derive from Old English *wealh*, 'Welshman', later 'slave'. This 'slave' meaning once led to the conclusion that *wealh* names indicated enclosures of British kept in servitude, but it may have been applied to the British simply because they occupied most of the lower levels of society and were, therefore, slaves – as most of them always had been.

The real puzzle in Gloucestershire is why there are so few British place names surviving, given the large number of British speakers who inhabited Gloucestershire in the Roman period, and the apparently small number of Saxon invaders. Anglo-Saxon speech has penetrated the whole language, down to the everyday items of use, the fields, the small streams and woods which nearly all, today, carry Anglo-Saxon names. This can be contrasted with the tiny handful of Norman French words imported as a result of the invasion of William the Conqueror. However numerous the British may have been, there can be no doubt that the Anglo-Saxons were the leaders of society.

The annal of 577 states that the Anglo-Saxon conquest of the kingdoms of Gloucester, Cirencester, and Bath was by West Saxon leaders. This fits in with the archaeological evidence, which shows that most of the Gloucestershire Saxon cemeteries were related to a West Saxon kingdom in the Thames Valley. It also fits with the evidence of ancient dialect, which shows that the south and south-east of the county spoke West Saxon dialects. Yet politically, judging by the Chronicle entries, the west-Saxon conquest of Gloucestershire was short-lived. An annal of 628 states that Cynegils and Cwichelm (kings of Wessex) fought Penda of Mercia at Cirencester, 'and afterwards came to terms', that is, they surrendered. This is the famous Penda, who had become or was soon to become king of all the central Kingdom of Mercia, and, from 651, Northumbria also. He was the last of the pagan English kings. From Penda's time onwards, perhaps from 628 onwards, Gloucestershire was part of a small kingdom which was subject to Mercia. The kingdom was named after its rulers, a people called the *Hwicce*. The area of the Hwicce included the whole of Worcestershire, south-west Warwickshire, and Gloucestershire except for the Forest of Dean. Some

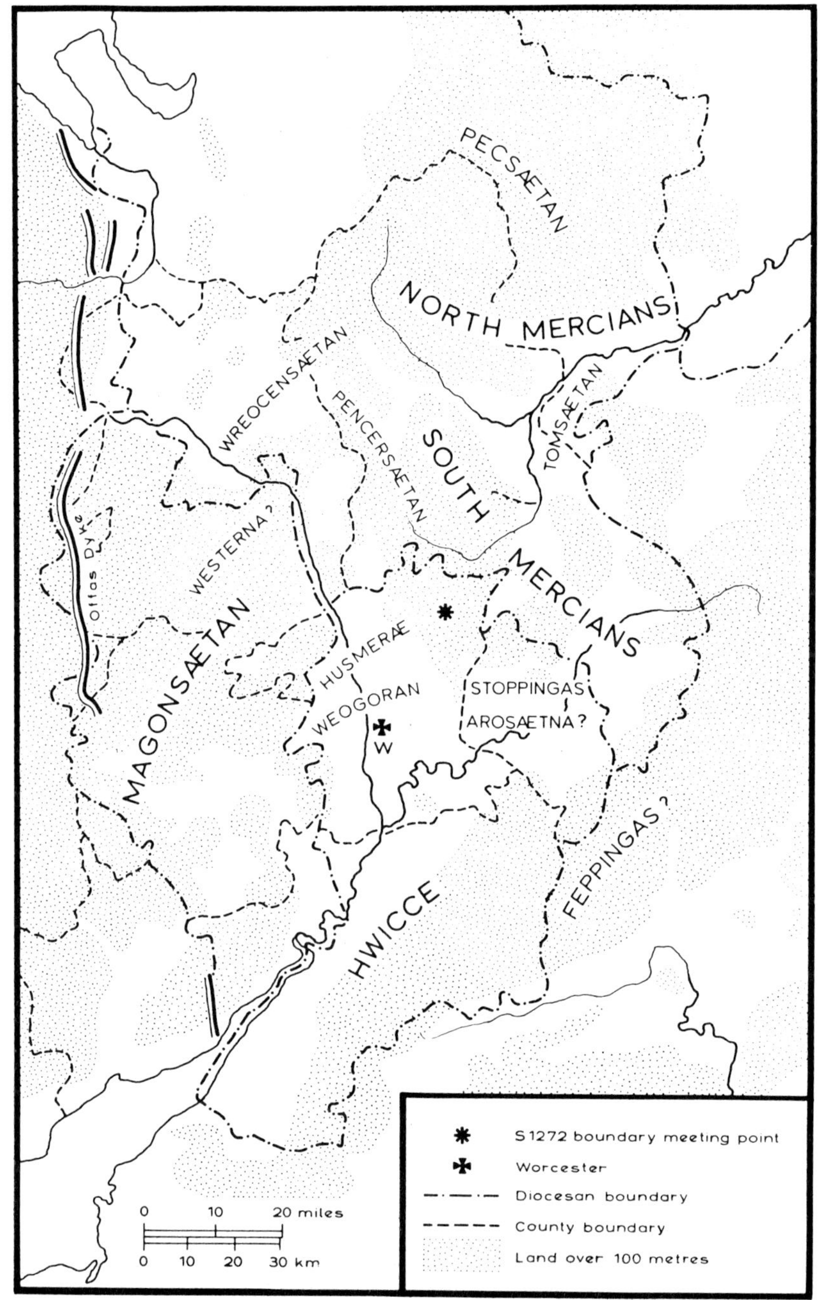

The Kingdom of the Hwicce and the other kingdoms of western Mercia in the 7th century. Reproduced from Della Hooke, The Anglo Saxon Landscape: The kingdom of the Hwicce *(Manchester University Press, 1985) p 7, fig 2.*

place-names betray the Hwiccian kingdom: high land near Cutsdean in the north Cotswolds was known as *mons . . . Hwicciorum* in the 8th century; Bredon was *in provincia Hwicciorum*. Wychwood, in Oxfordshire, derives from *Hwicca wudu*, as it was called in an 9th century charter. It is also possible to map the extent of the Hwicce area by plotting from charters what land their nobles had to give away. The southern boundary originally included Bath, since its monastery was founded (c. 675) by Osric, under-King of the Hwicce. In the late 7th century, the diocese of Worcester was created, coterminous with the kingdom. Even in the 10th century, Bishops of Worcester styled themselves *episcopi Hwicciorum*. The boundaries of the Hwicce survived as the diocesan boundary to the 16th century (the boundary, like the later county boundary, did not then include Bath which in the 10th century passed under the control of Wessex).

The origin of the Hwicce has been much debated. The kingdom was not all settled by the same sorts of Saxons. The northern part (now Worcestershire) was originally settled by Angles derived from the Cambridge area, who had moved west down the Avon valley; the southern part (i.e. most of Gloucestershire) was, as we have seen, settled by Saxons from the Upper Thames Valley (Oxfordshire). The Avon valley Angles were much more numerous, judging by the archaeology, than the Saxons in the lower Severn valley, and it may have been these Angles who were the original 'Hwicce', who formed the tribe's royal family, and who subsequently extended their power over all Gloucestershire. The area around Worcester, the town which became the episcopal centre of the Hwicce, had very little Saxon settlement. Worcester may have been the centre of another Celtic kingdom, like Gloucester, Cirencester, and Bath, and may thus have retained its importance under Anglo-Saxon rule.

Some of the leaders of the Hwicce might have been Anglo-Saxon nobles from the Northumbrian area: Professor Finberg and others argued that the nobility of the Hwicce won their kingdom with the help of Northumbrian princes. There were also some ecclesiastical connections pointing the same way; the conversion of central England began under Northumbrian priests. An estate at Fladbury in Worcestershire had once belonged to Osryth, daughter of Oswy of Northumbria.

The name 'Hwicce' itself is peculiar. Its derivation is unknown, although it is a very ancient type of folk name. The English Place Name Society is cagey, and says, 'it may well go back to the pre-migration period'. Margaret Gelling thinks it may be a topographical name, meaning 'chest', relating to the shape of the land at the Malvern Hills, but there is linguistic evidence that the Hwicce were originally Angles from the Northampton-shire area, and they may have brought their name with them. The name Worcester is also of pre-Saxon origin, from a tribal name which also survives in the name of Wyre Forest.

The earliest recorded Hwiccian princes were Eanfrid and Eanhere, who were joint rulers over the Hwicce around the mid 600s. The next known were Oshere and Osric, also joint rulers. It was not uncommon for Saxon kingdoms to be divided between two or even more rulers; perhaps in this case because the kingdom derived from two tribes (Anglian and Saxon) and so fell naturally into two divisions.

There are hints that the leaders of the Hwicce had dangerously high aspirations for their province. Osryth, who was Queen of Mercia, wife of Ethelred of Mercia, was assassinated by the leading Mercian nobles in 697. Osryth was of the Northumbrian dynasty, a niece of the warrior saint King Oswald, but she was also related to the Hwiccian ruling family. Her kinsman Oshere died suddenly at about the same time, and they may have been conspiring together to restore the Hwicce to independence.

The family continued, however to be the principal ruling power of the region throughout the 700s. They were not kings but viceroys, or sub-kings, semi-independent rulers who granted land with the consent of the Mercian kings. Although later, after about 800, the Hwicce were governed only by 'ealdormen' (the Anglo–Saxon equivalent of an earl), and so had slipped a little further down the heirarchy of kingdoms, in the 700s they were great princes. Their life and style was a reflection of that of the Mercian kings. They too would have held feastings and assemblies in their halls, gone hunting, heard the harpists recite *Beowulf* and similar poems, worn magnificent clothes and jewels, maintained a glittering retinue. The arts were supported by their patronage.

The leaders of the Hwicce were Christian by c. 660, and the kingdom was a bishopric after 675. There must already have been Christians among the subject people of the Hwicce in the 700s. However, their brand of Christianity plainly did not count, for the Hwiccian nobility saw it necessary to found new monasteries (they called them 'minsters'). By 800 there were well over a dozen in Gloucestershire. It might appear from this that the Hwicce had a commendable regard for the Christian souls of their subjects. The minsters were communities of priests (sometimes of priests and nuns) who carried out missionary activities and provided Christian services for a wide tract of countryside. The Hwicce were no doubt pious in intention, but there were other motives for founding monasteries. One was that land granted to a minster enjoyed certain tax advantages. Another was to provide a suitable occupation for relatives, women as well as men, and monasteries seem to have been seen very much as the personal property of a noble family, who expected to be able to bequeath it to their relatives. The well-connected inmates of a monastery would have power and influence in the community, supporting the interests of the founder. The monasteries were endowed not only with land but with precious art objects including books, and with painted carvings in wood and stone. In Gloucestershire all this is lost except for a few fragments of stone carving at Berkeley and Lypiatt, but once the churches would have been resplendent with gold, silver, and colour, not forgetting magnificent embroideries, for which the English were famous.

Whatever the various motives, a great deal of land passed into church hands during the 8th century; Dr Taylor has calculated that, by the end of the 8th century, about a quarter of all the land in Gloucestershire had passed into ecclesiastical hands – a fact which reflects not so much the power of the church as the influence of the secular leaders, the viceroys of the Hwicce and the king of Mercia.

Gloucestershire at this time had another set of rulers whom we should not leave out. These were the princes of the lands across the Severn and the Leadon. The southern part of what we call the Forest of Dean apparently remained under Welsh control until well into the 700s, for in about 703 King Morgan of Glywysing granted the church of Tidenham to a Welsh bishop called Berthwyn. The rest of the Dean was in the kingdom of the Magonsaetan. The Magonsaetan were, like the Hwicce, a sub-kingdom of Mercia, and just as the boundaries of the Hwicce were preserved in the medieval diocese of Worcester, so the boundaries of the Magonsaete were preserved in the diocese of Hereford (created c. 675). The territory comprised west Gloucestershire, Herefordshire, and south Shropshire. We know very little about the Magonsaetan, mainly because documents at Hereford happen to have survived less well than those at Worcester. But there can be no doubt that the Forest of Dean had different origins from the rest of Gloucestershire (Gloucestershire men from both sides of the river will tell you that the other side is different, though it may not be the finer points of dialect that they have in mind). The ancient Anglo-Saxon dialect of the Forest of Dean area was a Mercian one, but it was different from the more East Midlands version spoken in north Gloucestershire. The more Midland speech of the Dean probably derives from its take-over in the 600s by the Mercian Magonsaetan, whereas the Hwicce, as we have seen, who settled north and north-east Gloucestershire, derived from the east midlands. Even in this century, the recorded dialects of Gloucestershire have been observed to divide along the Severn in this way.

It is in the Forest of Dean that we find one of the greatest monuments of the Anglo-Saxon past: Offa's dyke. Offa (757–796) was the greatest of the Mercian kings, and much more than just a local despot. He corresponded in equal terms with Charlemagne, and the charters of his reign show increasing sophistication of administration. His coinage, based on the Frankish system of 12 pence to the shilling, and twenty shillings to the pound, proved an enduring memorial. His centre of operations was Tamworth, Staffordshire, where he maintained a palace. He cooperated with, one might say manipulated, the church authorities, even the Pope, for

Offa's dyke, overlooking the Wye Valley above Tintern Abbey, near 'Devils Pulpit'.

his own ends, and was able to found a Mercian archbishopric at Lichfield.

In Gloucestershire he negotiated a precise western frontier and marked its line with a dyke. To build this work, Offa must have been able to conscript labour in tens of thousands. The two dykes, Offa's Dyke and Wat's Dyke, stretch from north to south, marking the frontier between Mercia and Wales. The dykes between them are about 149 miles long, and their length is greater than Hadrian's wall and the Antonine wall put together. The rampart of Offa's dyke was about 24 ft above the bottom of the ditch (which is on the English side); the ditch was about 6 ft deep. Even today, after 1000 years of weather erosion, the dyke is still impressive – a monument to the efficiency of the Anglo Saxon state.

3
Vikings!

> 789. There came for the first time three ships of Northmen [to Portland] and then the reeve rode to them and wished to force them to the king's residence, for he did not know what they were; and they slew him. Those were the first ships of Danish men which came to the land of the English.

> 793. In this year dire portents appeared over Northumbria and sorely frightened the people. They consisted of immense whirlwinds and flashes of lightening, and fiery dragons were seen flying in the air. A great famine immediately followed those signs, and a little after that in the same year, on 8 June, the ravages of heathen men miserably destroyed God's church on Lindisfarne, with plunder and slaughter.

The Anglo Saxon Chronicle

Already in Offa's lifetime the first raids of the Danish pirates, the Vikings, were being made on English territory. For the next century the raids continued. It was a period of dynastic insecurity and national weakness for Mercia, and its eastern area in particular was vulnerable to Danish attack. Repton, Derbyshire, revered monastery and burial place of Mercian kings, was occupied by a Danish army in 873 and Burgred, King of Mercia, fled to Rome. From 874 the Danes appointed their own King of Mercia: Ceolwulf, a thegn of Burgred's, on the understanding that the kingdom should be at their disposal whenever they might wish to occupy it. Three years later they did claim the eastern half of the Mercian kingdom, though Coelwulf continued to rule in the west. In spite of being a Danish 'quisling', Ceolwulf reigned as a legitimate king and his charters were recognised as valid by other Saxon rulers.

The Hwiccian province was, however, relatively remote from Danish attack. In 845 Danish ships came up the Bristol Channel but reached no further than the Bridgewater area, where they were driven off. In 877 the Danes were at Exeter, and having fought Alfred of Wessex and called a truce, they moved up to Gloucester later in the year and 'built booths in the streets'. They were defeated again in 878 at Eddington and spent the next

A group of Vikings, as represented by The Dark age society, Regia Anglorum.
Photo: Regia Anglorum.

winter at Cirencester. In 880 they retired to East Anglia and 'shared out the land'.

In 893 another Viking army had returned from the Continent, obtained reinforcements from East Anglia, and passed up the Thames and Severn valleys towards Chester.

> Then Ealdorman Ethelred and Ealdorman Æthelhelm and Ealdorman Æthelnoth and the king's thegns who then were at home at the fortresses assembled from every borough east of the Parret, and both west and east of Selwood, and also north of the Thames and west of the Severn, and also some portion of the Welsh people. When they were all assembled, they overtook the Danish army at Buttington on the bank of the Severn, and besieged it on every side in a fortress. . . . Then when they had encamped for many weeks on the two sides of the river, and the king was occupied in the west in Devon against the naval force, the besieged were oppressed by famine, and had eaten the greater part of their horses and the rest had died of starvation. They then came out against the men who were encamped on the east side of the river, and fought against them, and the Christians had the victory. And the king's thegn Ordeah and also many other king's thegns were killed, and a very great slaughter of the Danes was made, and the part that escaped were saved by flight.

Buttington is on Offa's Dyke, in the upper reaches of the Severn, a few miles west of Shrewsbury. It is interesting that the Welsh, in this crisis, helped against the Vikings. Other evidence suggests that at this time the Welsh were gaining ground in Gloucestershire; a grant of land at Tidenham by Hywel, King of Glywyssing, between 855 and 885, shows that the Welsh had won back land east of the Dyke. A hundred years later in 956, Tidenham was again English.

The mention in the account of the Buttington victory of 'the men from every borough' emphasises that the towns had taken on a new role in the struggle against the Danes. They now operated as defended and fortified centres from which attacks could be made. Eighth-century Mercia was one of the earliest regions to use towns in this way, refortifying them and laying out their plans in regular grids. Certainly the Danish attacks spurred the Kings of Wessex, who led the resistance to the Danes, to great efforts of urban reorganisation. It is Alfred of Wessex who is credited with the foundation of dozens of fortified towns in the south, some using the defences of Roman centres, as at Winchester, some built anew in earth and timber, as at Cricklade.

Alfred's success and the terms of his treaty with the Danes had left the western half of Mercia in English hands. In the late 900s it was under the overlordship of Wessex, under the rule of Earl Ethelred. His ancestry is not known, but his position was a strong one, for he was married to Æthelflæd, eldest child of Alfred. Her brother was Alfred's successor to the throne of Wessex, Edward the Elder. Æthelflæd's mother had been a Mercian princess; an advantage in ruling over a people who had once formed an independent kingdom and who might well view the overlordship of Wessex with resentment, regarding their 'rescue' from Danish power as anything but liberation.

Æthelflæd, 'Lady of the Mercians', is one of the most interesting characters on the stage of Gloucestershire's history. Though it was technically her husband who was ruler of Mercia, he was considerably her senior and in failing health for about ten years before his death in 911. It is an indication of the high status that women could hold in Anglo-Saxon society that from about 902 to her death in 918, Æthelflæd ruled Mercia in her own right. One of her principal tasks was to complete a series of garrison towns. Three were founded before 900 at Worcester, Hereford, and Gloucester. Winchcombe was also defended at about this time. Æthelflæd built many more in the West Midlands between 910 and 918.

A crucial part of these campaigns was the organisation of shires, each shire being a region which contributed to the military fortifications of a central town. Gloucestershire was now created, though smaller than the Domesday county, for it had a partner shire, that of Winchcombe. The head towns of these shires were key points in these west midland campaigns, and there is also evidence that Gloucester, over and above its new status, was a place for which Æthelflæd and Ethelred had special regard. The town was rebuilt within its Roman walls, with a new grid street plan. It already had a mint, another mark of its status, and it had a royal manor house or palace north of the city, which Æthelflæd must have visited. Gloucester also acquired a new minster church, built by Æthelflæd. In 914 she brought to it the relics of Saint Oswald of Northumbria. These relics were claimed from Danish territory in Bardney, Lincs, an area to which Edward had led an expedition in the same year. Æthelflæd died in Tamworth, the traditional capital of Mercia. Yet both she and her husband were buried at Gloucester: Ethelred in 911 and Æthelflæd in 918. The Anglo Saxon Chronicle (Mercian Register), which ought to know, says she was buried 'in Gloucester in the east chapel of St Peters church'. It is by no means certain that this referred to St Peter's Abbey, and St Oswald's minster (which had only 9 years before received St Oswald's relics) may once have been dedicated to St Peter.

Gloucestershire was thus equipped to deal with Danish attacks. The campaigns of 892–95 had left the Kingdom of Wessex in a strong position, with the Danes confined behind their own frontier in East Anglia and in the eastern half of Mercia and Northumbria. Alfred died in 899 and his kingdom passed to his son, Edward 'The Elder'. In 910 the Danish armies who had settled in Northumbria broke their truce with King Edward, and went raiding in central and south-west England; 'the fields of the Mercians are wasted on all sides by the aforsaid disturbance' (says the chronicler Æthelweard), 'right up the the River Avon, where begins the boundary of the West Saxons and the Mercians'. From there they crossed the Severn 'into the western districts', presumably south Wales and the Forest of Dean, 'and there obtained by plunder no little booty'. They then returned, 'exulting in their rich spoils', crossing the Severn 'at a place which is called *Cantbrycg*'. This is not Cambridge in Gloucestershire but a miss-spelling for *Cuatbricg*, Bridgnorth, which makes much better sense with what followed. The Danes were met by an army from both Mercia and Wessex, quickly summoned by King Edward, and the Danes were defeated at Wednesfield (near Tettenhall, Wolverhampton), and three Danish leaders were killed. Perhaps it was part of the same Danish campaign which, in the same year, 910, brough a naval force of Vikings from Britanny. This force 'ravaged greatly by the Severn', but it too was defeated.

Æthelflæd and Edward followed up their success by pushing on with their policy of fortress building; by 915 the West Midlands area was studded with fortified towns including Bridgnorth (912), Tamworth and Stafford (913), Eddisbury and Warwick (914), Chirbury and Runcorn (915). In 917 Æthelflæd captured Derby and early in 918 she gained control of Leicester 'and the greater part of the [Danish] army which belonged to it was subjected'.

The success of the fortress policy was soon to be demonstrated in the Severn estuary. In 914 a Danish force, led by two earls Ohter and Hroald, dashed up the Severn from Brittany

> and ravaged in Wales everywhere along the coast where it suited them. And they captured Cyfeiliog, Bishop of Archenfield [west Herefordshire]. . .and King Edward ransomed him for 40 pounds. Then after that all the army went inland, still wishing to go on a raid towards Archenfield. Then the men from Hereford and Gloucester and from the nearest boroughs met them and fought against them and put them to flight and killed the earl Hroald and the brother of Ohter, the other earl, and a great part of the army, and drove them into an enclosure and beseiged them there until they gave them hostages, [promising] that they would leave the king's dominion. And the king had arranged that men were stationed against them on the south side of the Severn Estuary, from the west, from Cornwall, east as far as Avonmouth, so that they dared not attack the land anywhere on that side.

Two attempts by the Danish fleet to get ashore were beaten off; the Danes remained beseiged on Steepholme Island until hunger forced them to retreat to Ireland.

This campaign makes it clear that the burhs were by now well organised for defence. There is a contrast between the Viking incursion of 910, which apparently took everyone by surprise, and which came overland from York, and the attack of 914 when everyone was well alerted, even though a sea advance might be supposed to be more sudden than a land-based one. There were most probably coastal watch-towers and beacon fires whose efficiency had kept the Severn clear of Viking attack through many previous Viking raids.

By the time of Æthelflæd's death in 918, western Mercia had ceased to be Danish. The independence of the Mercian kingdom was, however, at an end; Æthelflæd was its last semi-independent ruler. On her death Edward the Elder took care that there should not continue to be a Mercian dynasty; Æthelflæd's daughter Ælfwyn 'was deprived of all authority in Mercia and taken into Wessex'. She is not heard of again, and probably ended her days in a nunnery. The future Kings of England were to be descended from Alfred's sons, and Gloucestershire, as part of Mercia, was to be ruled by ealdormen (earls) as part of the English kingdom.

Athelstan (924–54) was to be one of the most powerful kings of Wessex and of England. He had been brought up in Mercia, in the court of his aunt Æthelflæd. He seems to have been literate from childhood, unusual in one of noble birth. His travels about his kingdom show that he visited central England and Gloucestershire quite frequently, unlike his father Edward, whose itineraries were confined to Wessex. Athelstan was born out of

Athelstan presents the charter to the New Minster at Winchester. A drawing by Heather Brown, based on the New Minster Charter, BL Cotton MS Vespasian A. viii, f.2b.

wedlock and came to the throne after the death of one of his younger rivals; Athelstan's experience and mature years (he was 30) obviously recommended him to his nobles who elected him 'with great unanimity'.

Athelstan was to rule over more of England than any of his predecessors. He made an alliance with the Viking kingdom of York, having defeated a great Scottish/Viking alliance in the north. He also gained to some extent the subjugation of the Welsh. Already his grandfather Alfred had made agreements with the southern Welsh kings, and Æthelflæd too had made expeditions against the Welsh. Athelstan, according to William of Malmesbury, forced the Welsh to meet him at Hereford, and to submit to him, and the annual tribute was 2000 pounds of gold, 300 of silver, 25,000 oxen, as well as hunting dogs and hawks. According to a tenth-century Welsh poem, this tribute was paid at Cirencester.

In the campaign against the Welsh, both Gloucester and Hereford were important centres for military musters, as they were a century later. Athelstan, indeed, died at Gloucester, and he must have made other visits. He was buried at Malmesbury Abbey which he had enriched along with many other religious houses; William of Malmesbury commented:

> There can scarcely have been an old monastery in the whole of England which he did not embellish either with buildings or ornaments or books or estates.

After Athelstan's death his half-brother Edmund came to the throne at the age of 18. He had to once more subdue the kingdom of York, which he did successfully, but his reign was short. While on a visit to one of his royal manors at Pucklechurch, in Gloucestershire, his bailiff was attacked by a robber. Edmund leapt to his man's defence, but was killed. He had reigned less than six years and was buried at Glastonbury. The kingdom went to his brother Eadred, who survived only nine more years. The Rev. C. S. Taylor credited him with the transfer of Bath to Wessex. The kingdom was then shared for a time between the brothers Eadwig (West Saxons) and Edgar (Mercians), until the former died, leaving the whole kingdom to Edgar. With his accession there began an era of exceptional stability and prosperity for the English kingdom, which was later looked back on as a golden age.

The late tenth century was certainly a time of tremendous creative energy. The towns founded as fortresses in Edward the Elder's reign were supported by royal laws, growing in size and economic strength. Edgar was also patron of a great monastic revival, and with this went a great increase of art and literature. The reform of the monasteries, begun under Athelstan and continued under Edgar, involved the creation of a standard monastic rule, the *Regularis Concordia*; the reform and re-endowment of monasteries, both with land and with precious objects and books; and the promotion of learning. In Western Mercia, Worcester was reformed by Bishop Oswald, and new communities were established at Deerhurst, Winchcombe, Pershore, Evesham, and Westbury-on-Trym.

In Edgar's thirtieth year, a ceremony of coronation was held in Bath on Whitsunday 973. The solemn ceremony took place against the backcloth of the faded glory of the Roman city, restored to life not long before in the era of fortress-building. Soon afterwards, in 975, Edgar died, leaving a grieving

The 'Three Shire Stones', on the Fosse Way north of Bath. This was once known as Eadred's stone and may have been so named when King Eadred (946–955) created a new hundred around Bath and transferred it for the first time from Mercia to Wessex.

nation and a succession crisis which was to affect deeply the subsequent history of the country.

The reform of the monasteries had inevitably involved the end of the system by which powerful men regarded monasteries as family property. The ending of such secular control offended a good many nobles, among them Ælfhere, ealdorman of Mercia. At the death of Edgar, Ælfhere seized much monastic property, sacking Evesham and threatening Winchcombe. The Abbot of Winchcombe, who had been close to Bishop Oswald, fled abroad. On the death of Ælfhere in 983, the monks were able to return. But few monasteries of the region were reformed in the late 10th century, no doubt due to Ælfhere's influence.

Edgar's son Edward was still only a teenager on his father's death. Edward had the support of the monastic reform party, and the anti-reformers including Ælfhere may have been among those who plotted Edward's death. Edward was murdered at Corfe in Dorset in 978, and the throne passed to his half-brother Ethelred, nicknamed Unræd, 'No counsel'. The name does not mean that the King was unprepared, only that he received bad advice. His reign was a disaster, but it was not all his fault. He had problems which Edgar had never had to deal with, for Danish armies, this time much better organised, often under the leadership of the Danish royal family, were again threatening England. Ethelred's policy was usually to buy off the invaders, but ultimately even the payment of tens of thousands of pounds of silver could not prevent Danish armies from raiding extensively in England. Again, most of the raids were confined to the south and east, though in 997 the Danes came up the Severn estuary to Cornwall, Devon, and south Wales. All Ethelred's attempts to deal with the Danes, by mustering armies, building ships, or buying off the Danes, were fruitless. In 1006 all the armies of Wessex and Mercia (including Gloucestershire)

> were out on military service against the Danish army the whole autumn, yet it availed no whit more than it had often done before; for in spite of it all, the Danish army went about as it pleased, and the English levy caused the people of the country every sort of harm, so that they profited neither from the native army nor the foreign army.

The utter demoralisation of the English is expressed in the Chronicle entry for 1010:

> and when [the Danes] were in the east, the English army was kept in the west, and when they were in the south, our army was in the north. Then all the councillors were summoned to the king, and it was then to be decided how this country should be defended. But even if anything was then decided, it did not last even a month. Finally there was no leader who would collect any army, but each fled as best he could, and in the end no shire would even help the next.

By 1011 the Danish army had overrun the whole of east and south-east England; Gloucestershire, though not occupied, was threatened on all sides, and would have had to pay its contribution both in tribute and in men for the army.

In 1013 many of the eastern counties surrendered to Swein of Denmark; later in the year, at Bath, King Swein and his army received the submission of 'the western thegns'. When King Ethelred died in 1016, his kingdom was in chaos. Half of it was occupied by the Danish King's army: his queen and two sons (Alfred and Edward) had fled to Normandy. King Swein had died the year before, but his military success had been continued by his son Cnut.

Ethelred's son Edmund (Ironside) made valiant efforts to redress the military balance; five times he raised the English levies, sometimes with success, but ending in defeat at Ashingdon, in Essex.

Gloucestershire was still relatively unaffected by the fighting, so it was to Gloucestershire that King Edmund went. Cnut followed him there and the two kings assembled with their followers on either side of the river Severn, near the monastery of Deerhurst. From here they travelled to 'Alney Island', which may have been in the river near Deerhurst or which may have been the meadowland of that name beside Gloucester. Cnut and Edmund agreed to share the kingdom. In Gloucester Museum is a stirrup of the early 11th century, which could have been lost on this occasion. But before long Edmund too had died, in London, 'and Cnut succeeded to the whole kingdom'.

During the Danish campaigns the ealdorman of the Hwicce was Leofwine. Leofwine may have been dead by 1017; in the same year his son Northman was killed and another son Leofric became ealdorman of the Hwicce in his place. A more famous character was the ealdorman of Mercia, Eadric, known as Eadric Streona. Eadric twice changed his allegiance. He went over to Cnut in 1015 and joined forces with him. The two, with their armies, crossed the Thames at Cricklade and turned to Warwickshire, devasting Mercian territory as they went. They would have passed along the Fosse Way, through Cirencester and Stow on the Wold and so northwards. Since this was Leofwine's territory, rather than Eadric's, perhaps they were political opponents, though it was not unknown for a ruler to devastate his own lands. After the succession of Edmund in 1015, Eadric seems to have thought better of the new king, and transferred allegiance to him. But at Ashingdon, the final Danish victory, Eadric left early in the battle, taking his Hereford levies with him. He was a prime mover in arranging the meeting between Edmund and Cnut at Alney, persuading Edmund to parley rather than fight on. On his succession, Cnut created him earl of Mercia; but after only a few months had him murdered.

The reasons for Eadric's changes of policy are not known, but we should

An 11th century stirrup of Viking type from Gloucester Museum. Photograph: Gloucester City Museum.

remember that the Chronicle's account of Eadric's chequered career is partisan, being written down in Cnut's reign, between 1016 and 1023, when Eadric had already been disgraced. Eadric's principal act from the Gloucestershire point of view was in 1017, when he combined the two shires of Gloucester and Winchcombe, thus creating the administrative area of Gloucestershire that was to survive, with minor modifications, for 856 years.

Cnut began by killing off a number of rivals, and marrying his predecessor's wife, Emma of Normandy. He went on to do his best to be a pattern-book English king. He was a friend of the church, supporting monastic reform. He made full use of the local government system of shire and hundred, exacting heavy taxes just as Ethelred had done. His greatest innovation was to create the four great earldoms of Wessex, Mercia, Northumbria and East Anglia, and put them under the control of his own men, mostly Danes.

The earldoms and their holders were to dominate politics for the next fifty years. The greatest of the earls was Godwin of Wessex, an ambitious personality whose credit rating is hardly improved by the reputation of his father Wulfnoth, a thegn who had abandoned the service of King Ethelred to take up piracy. Godwin's power was growing under Cnut and during the short English reigns of Cnut's two sons. After Ethelred's son Edward regained his father's throne in 1042, Godwin was the most powerful man in the land next to the King himself. He held the earldom of Wessex; his daughter was married to the King; by 1050 his sons Swein, Harold, and his nephew Beorn held other southern earldoms. Swein was earl of West Mercia in 1043, and was therefore known – indeed infamous – to the men of Gloucestershire. It is testimony to the influence of his father that he managed to extricate himself from his various scrapes. Having seduced the Abbess of Leominster, to the scandal of all, Swein judged it wise to leave the country. On his return from Denmark, where he had also got into trouble, he treacherously murdered his own cousin Beorn, and was exiled, but Godwin's power was such that he was able to recall Swein and re-establish him in the earldom of West Mercia.

King Edward, known as the Confessor, is often thought of as a milk-and-water character. Though he may have inherited from his father Ethelred a tendency for erratic decision making, he was far from being a nonentity. Nor did he neglect kingly pursuits; that is, he spent much of his time hunting, often in the Forest of Dean, and holding Councils, often in Gloucester. It was in Gloucestershire, in 1051, that events occurred which show him in his forceful aspect.

Early in the year, on the death of the Archbishop of Canterbury, Edward had appointed a Norman, Robert of Jumièges; not an appointment satisfactory to the Godwin family. In the same year Edward received a visit from

William of Normandy – at which Edward and William must have discussed the matter of the succession. All this shows that the King was not always influenced by Godwin. In the autumn of 1051 the King was at Gloucester. The King's cousin, Eustace of Boulogne, was in Dover where he got into a squabble with the locals. Men on both sides were killed and Eustace and his men went to Edward at Gloucester to complain. Edward ordered Godwin (in whose earldom Dover lay) to harry Dover as a punishment. Godwin refused. Pressed further, he responded by assembling an army in Gloucestershire near Beverstone – an army, says the Chronicle, 'ready to do battle against the King'. King Edward was able to muster at Gloucester the troops of Mercia and Northumbria. The armies, when it came to it, chose not to fight, for

> some of them thought it would be a great piece of folly if they joined battle, for in the two hosts there was most of what was noblest in England, and they considered that they would be opening a way for our enemies to enter the country and to cause great ruin among ourselves.

This sounds something like patriotism; at least the leaders seem to have had a higher goal in mind than their own regional squabbles. Whatever the sentiments, they were the saving of King Edward. Godwin had lost face; he was driven out, he and his sons deprived of their earldoms, and his daughter Edith, the king's own wife, packed off to a nunnery.

Next year the Godwins were back: Godwin was able to raise military support for his own return and once again the opposing forces were reluctant to fight. This time it worked to Edward's disadvantage. Robert of Jumièges, seeing his enemy triumph, fled, and an English (schismatic) Archbishop of Canterbury, Stigand, was appointed. The king lost some of what he had gained. On the death of Godwin in 1053, the earldom of Wessex and the mantle of family power went to his second son Harold. Harold was now Earl of Wessex, and the earldom included Gloucestershire in its extent. He was often in that county, for he had an enemy to deal with: Gruffydd ap Llywelyn, who had become overlord of all of Wales, and who was in the 1050s making frequent raids across the border. In 1055 the Welsh attacked Hereford. An English army gathered against them fled (it was, the Chronicle says, fighting on horseback and unused to it); the Welsh

> went back to the town and burnt it with the glorious minster. . .they stripped and robbed it of relics and vestments and everything, and killed the people, and some they carried off.

The English were enraged and immediately collected a huge army from all over England which was assembled at Gloucester. The town of Hereford was refortified by Harold, and the Welsh army made peace. It took several more campaigns (in one of which the bishop of Hereford, Leofgar, fought and was killed) before the Welsh king was killed and his head taken to King Edward

> and the figurehead of his ship and the ornaments with it.

Much of south Wales thus passed under English control, and thence into Norman hands, appearing in Domesday book as recently annexed land.

Meanwhile King Edward still had no declared heir, and was far enough from considering Earl Harold; indeed he sent him to Normandy on embassy to Duke William, probably to discuss the Duke's taking the English throne. But in 1066 when the King died, Harold saw his chance and seized the kingdom of England. The subsequent history is well known: his victory at Stamford Bridge against Harold Hardrada of Norway (the other claimant), his defeat at Hastings, and the accession of William, whose own brainchild, Domesday Book, has recently celebrated its 900th birthday.

Domesday Book makes a suitable end to this account of Saxon Gloucestershire. It provides us with an inventory of the country and the county at a point about twenty years after the Norman Conquest, giving estate values and owners in the time of Edward the Confessor and comparing them with those of 1086. It is a mine of information about the thousands of estates which had once been in the hands of Anglo Saxon nobles. Their transference to Norman power meant modifications, but no major differences, to the lives of ordinary people. The system did not greatly change, either; and Domesday Book itself, the product of William's organising Norman mind, could not have been made without the administrative framework of centuries of Anglo-Saxon rule.

4
The Land

The lives of the kings and earls, though often the stuff of history books, were the lives of a small minority of the population. The wealth which the great enjoyed came from one source – the land – and from the agricultural work of the vast majority of their countrymen.

The land of Gloucestershire in Anglo-Saxon times consisted largely of settlements based on mixed-arable farming in a countryside which had long since been cleared of its original native woodland, though in some areas, such as the north Cotswolds, woodland had grown back in the centuries after the Roman period.

We learn most about early Anglo-Saxon landscape by a study of the charters which recorded land transactions from the late 600s onwards. The survival of these is patchy for Gloucestershire, but there is still a surprising number. Many estates were named after their owners: Bibury was the estate of Beaga; Tredington that of *Tyrdda*. Estates were reckoned in 'hides'. A hide was probably originally the unit of land necessary to support one family; in the Latin of the charters it was described as *cassati* or *manentes* or sometimes *tributarii*. The early grants were usually between 20 and 50 hides, occasionally more than 100 hides. Since a hide was an assessment unit, rather than a precise area of land, it is impossible to say how much land it represents; assessments for Gloucestershire hides have varied from about 30 to about 120 acres. Where these estates are locatable on the ground, the earliest charters are seen to be concerned with large tracts of land, perhaps 20 square miles. Later estates tended to have become sub-divided, and to be much smaller.

Many of the charters, especially later ones, describe the boundaries of the estate in precise terms. Boundaries followed features such as streams or Roman roads, which have often survived; others have become fossilised as parish, hundredal, or other administrative boundaries. Many boundaries still await solution. It is possible to do this with a large-scale map, but better still to follow the boundaries on the ground. The task can be tackled by anyone with a copy of Grundy's *Saxon Charters* (and the landowners' permission, though many boundaries are followed today by public footpaths). The Anglo-Saxon estate of Stoke Bishop, an estate of 12 hides in

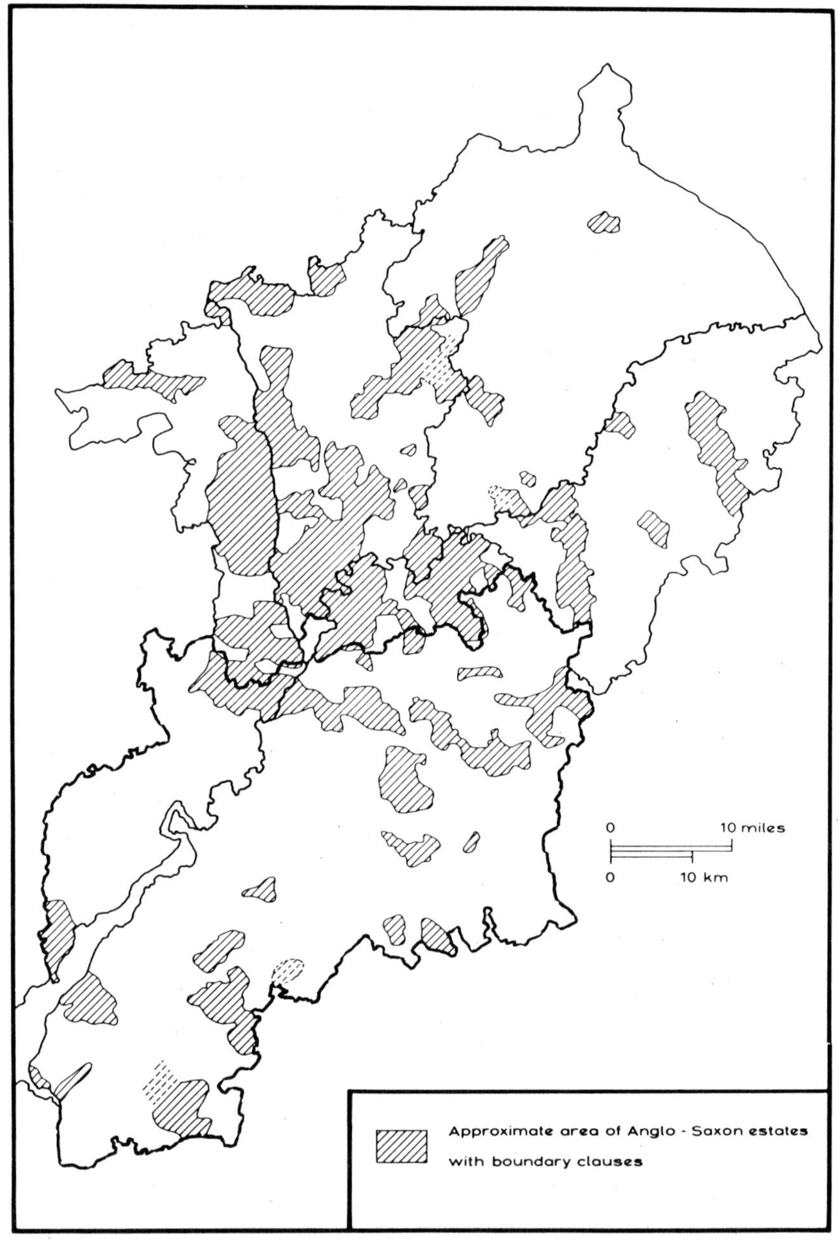

Surviving Anglo-Saxon charters with boundaries. Reproduced from Della Hooke, The Anglo Saxon Landscape; The Kingdom of the Hwicce, *Manchester University Press 1985, p 51, Fig 12. The heavier line is the boundary of Gloucestershire.*

a charter of 883, approximates to the medieval parish which survived until the 19th century. An estate of 8 hides at Blockley was granted between 727 and 736 to the Bishop of Worcester: its boundaries ran thus,

> On the south [this property] includes a great part of the hill; on the east it is enclosed by the King's highway; on the north it is girt by flowing waters; the west bounds it with certain marshes.

The grant can be identified on the ground with the parish of Batsford and the eastern half of Blockley. This early grant is a noticeable contrast to the later ones; it gives fairly vague limits (the hill, the marshes), and suggests a relatively unpeopled landscape. By contrast, later grants are immensely detailed. An example (which has not been fully solved) can be taken at random. The survey is of an estate at Pucklechurch; it dates to 950 and its boundary is described as follows –

> First from Stone Ford to the Appletree on the Hoar Stone
> So to Waterhen's Pond
> From Waterhen's Pond to Goose Pond to Stone Bank
> From Stone Bank to the Gate of the Deerleap
> From the Gate of the Deerleap along the Enclosures
> From the Enclosures to the Oaktree
> From the Oaktree to Queen's Bridge
> From Queen's Bridge to King's Ride
> From King's Ride to the Stone of the Eadwald Family
> From the Stone to Muca's Tree
> From Muca's Tree to the Appletrees
> Then straight to Muddy Brook. . .

and so on.

The immense detail describes features which have usually vanished, and it is the general topography which guides our steps. But the charter for this very reason provides us with a sight of the late Saxon countryside. It is densely settled, packed with fences, hedges, stone walls, constructions such as deerleaps. Even where the landmark has gone, it may be remembered on the modern map by a field name. One example of a charter whose boundaries have been worked out is at Deerhurst, where a grant of unknown date concerns a large tract of country between Cheltenham and Tewkesbury, on either side of the river Severn.

Some of these detailed later boundaries can be seen to zig-zag in and out between cultivated fields. There is an example of this at Donnington, dated 889:

> From the Dyke on the Hill to the Fox Earth
> From the Fox's Earth to the other Steep Slope

By the Steep Slope to the Blind Spring
From the Blind Spring to the Stone
From the Stone to the Headland of a Ploughland
By the Headland to the Furrow
Along the Furrow to Horsedown Slade
From Horsedown Slade to the Swamp where the Hassock Grass grows
From Hassock Swamp to the End Furrow
From the End Furrow to the Watercress Spring
Along the Watercourse of Watercress Spring to the High Street
From the Street to the Two Stones
From the Two Stones to the Watercourse of the Green Barrow

and so it continues, including many more references to ploughlands, headlands, and furrows. This estate is small, compared to some earlier ones, and it subdivided an already intensely cultivated landscape.

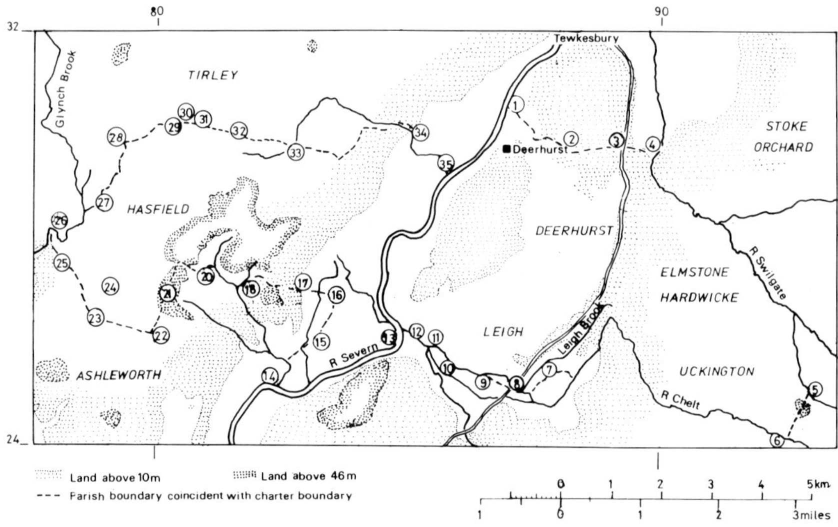

The Anglo-Saxon boundaries of an estate at Deerhurst. The circled numbers are the marker-points given in the charter. (1) From the Severn to the enclosures on the boundary. (2) Wanta's pit. (3) Willow Hill [Salter's Hill]. (4) The Tyrl [The Swilgate]. (5) Along the stream to Hawk Hill. (6) Arle [the River Chelt]. (7) Along Arle to Punt's pear tree to the Deep Rivulet [Leigh Brook]. (8) Tor's Mere. (9) Eagle-clearing to the Boundary Spring. (10) The Deep Rivulet. (11) To Linden-Lea to Arle. (12) Rucche's Pill. (13) The Severn. (14) The Bracken-burn. (15) Pudda's Brook. (16) The wold. (17) Hill Spring. (18) Hill Lea. (19) Ash Moor. (20) The gate of Wide Combe. (21) Frost Ridge. (22) East Lea. (23) Corse Marsh. (24) Little Hill. (25) Harridge. (26) Glynch Brook. (27) Bird Brook. (28) Pasture Ridge. (29) Thorn Field. (30) Dudd's Acre. (31) The bare moor. (32) Elves' Seat. (33) Reedy Burn. (34) Cumberworth to the burn called An. (35) The Severn. (36) Along the river again to the enclosures on the boundary.

Ploughing with an ox team. A drawing by Heather Brown. Based on the Harley Psalter, an 11th century copy of a 9th century document.

The estate of Woodchester was described in a charter of between 716 and 745; it consisted of an area approximately the same as today's parish of Woodchester. The estate is cited as 'three cassates of wooded country', which would be a good description of the same area today. The estate was in dispute in 896, and the matter was settled at a Council in Gloucester, in the presence of Earl Ethelred of Mercia, and an assembly of the great men of his kingdom.

> . . . Earl Ethelred summoned together at Gloucester all the Mercian council, the bishops and the earls and all his nobility; and this he did with the cognisance and leave of King Alfred. . . .Then Bishop Werferth informed the council that he had been robbed of nearly all the woodland belonging to Woodchester, which King Æthelbald had given to Worcester. . . .then all the council declared that justice should be done. . .

To settle the dispute, a thegn, Ecglaf, was ordered to ride the boundaries with the local priest, Wulfhun,

> . . .and Ecglaf led Wulfhun along all the boundaries, as Wulfhun read out from the old charters, how they had been determined of old by the grant of King Æthelbald.

There is something very appealing in this picture of the officials setting out, charter in hand, to check the boundaries just as a surveyor would do today.

Another sub-division of the landscape was the hundred. These administrative units survived into medieval and post-medieval times, by which time some were new, some very ancient. Each hundred had its royal estate centre ('vill') to which the estates paid the rents and services, and the fact that a similar system was in used in Celtic Wales in the middle ages

Hatherop Barrow, near Coln St Aldwyn's. Barrows, already ancient in Saxon times, were often the site of hundred meeting places. This barrow, probably the meeting place of Brightwell's Barrow hundred, is in the classic position for a hundred meeting place: at a crossroads, in an elevated position, and on a parish boundary. Such meeting places were probably very ancient, and could be pre-Saxon, even pre-Roman. Photo: Mick Sharp.

probably hints that the hundredal arrangement was a pre-Saxon Celtic system.

All the people in a hundred attended hundred assemblies. These, in an illiterate society, were absolutely essential for issuing laws of military orders, or dispensing justice. The antiquity of the system is shown by the hundred meeting places themselves; many are remote and rural, making use of prehistoric landmarks such as standing stones (Greston, Tibblestone, Dudstone, Whitstone, Bagstone, Edderstone) or burial mounds (Brightwells Barrow, Blakelow, Letberg, Botloe, Bledisloe) or else named after natural features such as trees, fords, and streams. A classic site for a hundred meeting place was an elevated position on a crossroads, near the boundaries of parishes; this would be neutral territory, equidistant for the people coming from their various settlements. Some hundreds, obviously later creations, were named after and created out of estates; Tewkesbury and Deerhurst are two of these.

The lords of Anglo–Saxon estates did not own the land in the sense in

The Tibblestone, a standing stone at Teddington Hounds crossroads, which once marked the meeting-place of Tibblestone Hundred. The name means 'Theobald's Stone' and commemorates an early local landowner whose name is also preserved in nearby Teddington.

which we mean the word. All land was held on lease from the king and rent was paid both in produce and in military service. There were two sorts of land, folkland and bookland. (The village of Buckland was once 'Bookland'). Folkland passed from a holder to his family; bookland was conveyed by charter, and the holder could convey the land to whom he chose (with royal consent of course). Holding by bookland was originally an ecclesiasicial privilege, as is shown by the number of charters which are concerned with church land. Later on, bookland was granted to laymen as well. Some people have claimed that holding bookland meant immunity from rents, but this cannot be so, as some bookland paid quite heavy rents.

The earliest grant showing rents being paid 'to the royal estate' is one by Offa of Mercia to the church of Worcester, dated 793–796, of land at Westbury and Henbury. The rent was:

> two tuns full of pure ale and a coomb full of mild ale and a coomb full of Welsh ale, and seven oxen six wethers and 40 cheeses and six long *theru* [no-one knows what these were] and 30 ambers of unground corn and four ambers of meal.

The rent was obviously in non-perishable goods – note the large quantities of ale! – and the royal estate buildings would have to have large store-rooms and animal pens to accommodate them all. Rents were due a couple of times a year, and these must have been busy ones for the royal steward – checking off the quantities, arranging for their storage. Paying in money would obviously have been simpler, and by the time of Domesday book these rents had at least partly been commuted to money, but in early days the king must have done much travelling from one royal vill to another to eat up his rents. The rents were reckoned in a quantity known as the 'ferm of one night' – the amount needed to feed and house the king and his company for 24 hours.

Some of the burdens on the land were severe; for instance, the minster at Blockley paid a large sum of money to be free of the burden of

> feeding and maintenance of all hawks and falcons in the land of the Mercians, and of all huntsmen of the king or ealdorman except only those who are in the province of the Hwicce; likewise even from the feeding and maintenance of those men whom we call in Saxon *walhfaereld* and from lodging them and from lodging all mounted men of the English race and foreigners, whether of noble or humble birth.

Walhhaereld means 'Welsh expedition' and may refer to soldiers who patrolled the Welsh border. The charter, of 855, records that Bishop Ealhun of Worcester purchased his exemption for 300 shillings – a very considerable sum in the 9th century. It was obviously well worth the money to get out of feeding and housing so many royal servants and soldiers. Charters of exemption are rare, and it is likely that most estates went on paying to the king considerable rents in both food and hospitality.

There were some duties which were never exempted. From 770 and probably before, any exemptions from royal dues made three exceptions, the duties of military service, bridge work, and fortress work. Land granted by Uhtred, sub-king of the Hwicce in 770 was

> free from every tribute, small or great, of public matters, and from all
> services whether of kind or ealdorman, except the building of bridges
> or the necessary defences of fortresses against enemies.

These were obviously essential; bridge maintenance was vital to the road network, and the bridges, usually of timber, but occasionally perhaps surviving Roman stone bridges, were liable to be damaged in winter floods, impairing the efficiency of the road network. The importance of military service to any king goes without saying. From an early date it was established that every 5 hides of land should support one soldier (it is doubtful whether full peasant levies were often, if ever, called up). The fortress work has interesting implications: archaeology suggests that already in Offa's time fortified urban centres such as Tamworth and Hereford were being built; some such obligation would also, of course, have provided Offa with the men to build his great Welsh dyke.

Any working agricultural estate needed access to all the different types of land; meadow, pasture, woodland, and arable. Meadow land, for cutting and storing hay, was essential; there was more meadow land near rivers on the low-lying land, and communities often had access to this even though it might be some way from their settlements. For grazing, many earlier estates had common land, rough unused scrubland where animals could graze. Later, grazing was in short supply and might be some distance from a settlement. The swineherd or cattleherd would have to drive the animals to and fro, or even go out to live on the pasture with the animals for a time. Animals would also be pastured in stubble in the village fields, when the crops were in. This was convenient and economical and also manured the field, but it had to be carefully controlled, or the animals would stray and eat garden crops or crops not yet harvested.

Woodland was also used for pasture, though this too had to be carefully watched; too much grazing destroyed the young trees.

Woodland was vital, providing timber for houses, and for making utensils and tools, fuel for cooking and warmth, charcoal for iron-making, coppiced branches for making hurdles, baskets, wattle fences, and many other uses, such as fodder for pigs, who ran wild in the under-growth. Woodland also provided game, small and large, from wild boar and deer down to hare and pigeon. Some estates, lacking sufficient woodland, had woodland rights elsewhere, sometimes at a considerable distance – such arrangments probably reflect the much earlier situation when estates were more extended.

The woodland was very carefully managed. Indiscrimate felling of trees was carefully controlled. After felling the roots were allowed to grow up again into coppices, to make a supply of slender branches. Areas of woodland were kept fenced by *haga* which meant a hawthorn hedge. 'Haga'

Lime woodland on the Cotswold scarp at Cranham. Woodland was an important and renewable Anglo-Saxon resource. Felled trees rapidly grow new shoots from the stump, like many in this illustration, creating in a few years a dense crop of poles for fencing and housing. Cranham woods were there in Anglo-Saxon times and have been continuously exploited since.

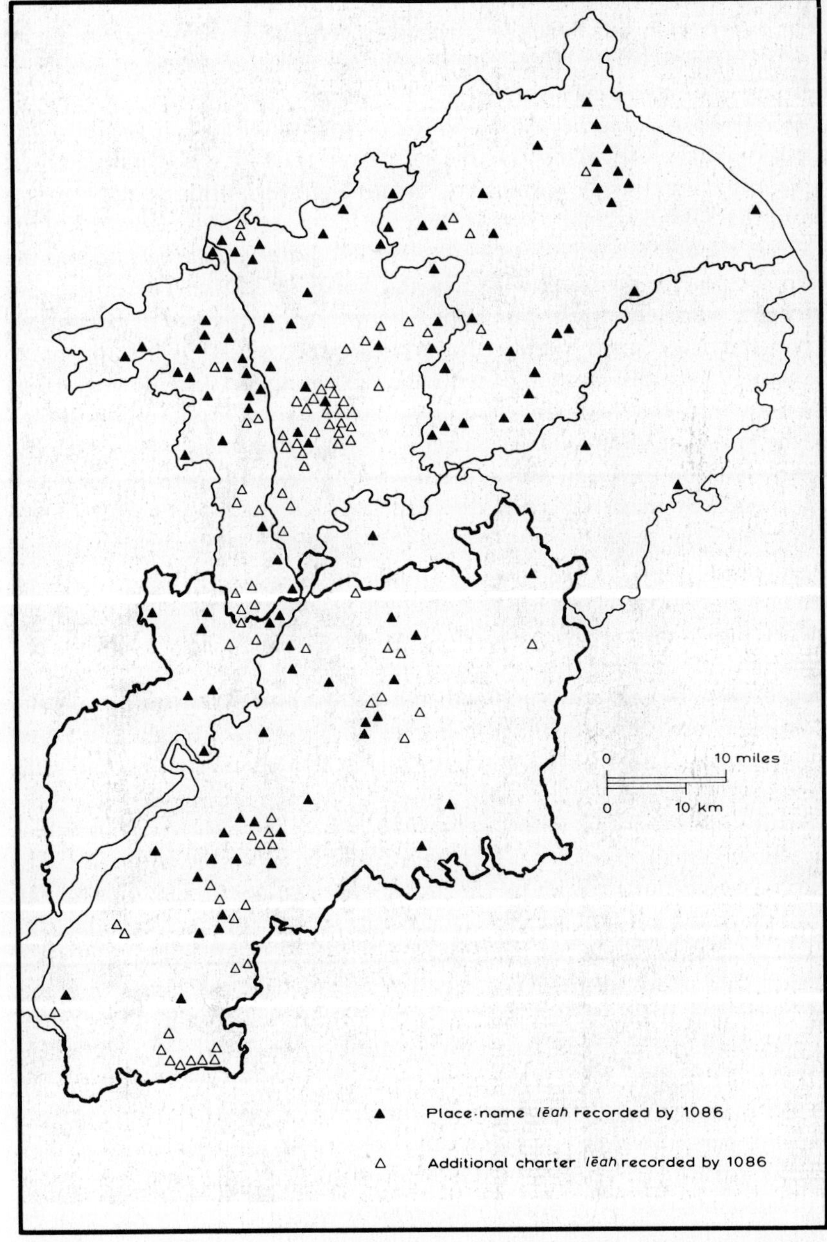

leah *place-names. The term implies a woodland clearing, and its presence probably indicates areas of Anglo Saxon woodland. Reproduced from Della Hooke,* The Anglo-Saxon Landscape: The Kingdom of the Hwicce, *Manchester University Press 1985, fig 10, p 48.*

were also enclosures for keeping or driving game, especially deer: the word often survives in place-names. Examples are 'the Haw' (*haga*) in Tirley parish; 'Haywardsfield House' in Stonehouse parish (from *haga, geat, feld,* meaning 'gate to an enclosure').

Woodland in the earlier Anglo-Saxon period is indicated by the term *leah* in place-names. Originally this meant a large tract of woodland; later the name implies a clearing within woodland. The distribution of these names shows that Gloucestershire was among the less densely wooded areas of the Hwicce, though woodland was still plentiful, and was concentrated on the scarp face of the Cotswolds and in the Forest of Dean. There was also extensive woodland in the Forest of Kingswood, north-east of Bristol.

For the late Saxon period the woodland is noted down for us in Domesday. The distribution of woodland in Gloucestershire was similar to that shown by the *leah* map, though we might expect more to be recorded for the Forest of Dean, and it is generally agreed that there was a good deal of woodland in the Dean which did not get mentioned, perhaps because it was owned by manors a good distance away. Though some of the Dean was arable land, the proportion of arable was much lower than elsewhere in the county; in 1086 the Dean had 1 plough-team per square mile, as opposed to 3 or 4 elsewhere. Much of the rest of the Dean may have been woodland pasture rather than dense woodland, and it was well-used by the various industrial enterprises connected with iron-making. There may have been pockets of truly ancient woodland; the 13th century roof of Blackfriars, Gloucester, used more than 150 oak trees with a straight trunk 50 ft (15m) or more high. These were Dean oaks in a near-natural state; probably the last remnants of the Wild Wood.

Finally, we must look at the arable fields which grew the crops on which the whole system depended. Here we encounter enormous difficulty. The truth is we do not know how the arable was organised. The first Saxons probably found a 'Celtic' system of agriculture, with the landscape looking much as it does in Devon and Cornwall today: small fields, few large villages, and many scattered hamlets. Fields would be individually owned, the cultivated fields (called the 'infield') being well-manured and some rougher land (the 'outfield') used for pasturing animals. The outfield might occasionally be cultivated as the need arose. We do not know how or when the Celtic system was superceded. By the medieval period in many parts of England, particularly the midlands, another system had been adopted. This was the 'open-field' system, or the 'Midland system'. The arable land was all divided into two (later often three), enormous fields, in each of which the villagers owned individual strips, not in bundles but scattered about. Crops were grown in rotation, and one of the fields was left fallow every second year (or third year in the case of the three-field system). This meant that cattle were able to graze on the fallow field, and manure it at the same time.

Ridge and furrow around the deserted village of Lower Ditchford, north of Moreton-in-the-Marsh. The clustered village with its strip-fields used to be seen as an Anglo-Saxon importation, but it is now thought the strip-field system, and perhaps villages too, originated in the late-Saxon period, or later. Cambridge University Collection: copyright reserved.

Experts discuss endlessly how this extraordinarily complex arrangement came into being. It might have been the result of deliberate reorganisation in late-Saxon times, or have roots in pre-Saxon times, a result of the slow development from the Welsh system of partible inheritance. Some argue that it resulted from a time of declining population, others that it occurred during a period of increasing population. Whatever the mechanism by which it came into existence, this system was general in Gloucestershire by the 12th century, and most recent studies have concluded that the system was a late Saxon or even post-Conquest development. At Frocester, Mr E. Price has found some evidence that the medieval ridge-and-furrow, indicating the strip-fields, came into being in the 10th century. Before that, however, there is evidence of a slightly different layout, still in a series of ridges, though what sort of social or tenurial organisation this implies is unknown.

Remains of both the 'Celtic' and the 'open field' systems of arable farming can be seen in the countryside. The remains of small fields, often called 'Celtic fields', can be seen particularly on marginal land on upper slopes where they have not been obliterated by later cultivation. The remains of strip-fields, on the other hand, are everywhere. The ploughing of these strips, with a team of up to 8 oxen, turned the furrows into the centre of the strips and so created great ridges, often with a slightly S-shaped curve, which become particularly visible under light snow or in low evening light. They can be distinguished, not only from the distinctive slight curve but also because they disappear and re-emerge when they encounter motorways, railway lines, and 18th-century roads. The medieval strip-fields were a part of the landscape until the 18th century, when the open fields were 'enclosed' into compact fields. Some of the strip-fields of Upton St Leonards were only enclosed in 1897, and survived long enough to be photographed in use. Now modern farming methods are uprooting the 18th and 19th century hedges and returning the landscape to a more medieval open-field appearance.

Another change in the landscape which probably went with the creation of the 'midland system' was the creation of villages. These, with their Anglo-Saxon names, are often thought of as extending back into the Anglo-Saxon past, and being founded by the first Anglo-Saxon settlers. This is probably not true, and the settlements in Domesday book, which today have the same names as a thousand years ago, may then have applied, not to a village, but to a collection of scattered hamlets, a 'township'. It was probably in the late Saxon period, and sometimes even later, that the landscape with the nucleated villages was finally formed. At Upton in Blockley, for instance, excavation showed that the peasant long-houses around their village green date only to the 12th or 13th century. Elsewhere in the country, for instance at Wharram Percy, Yorkshire, the replacement of scattered hamlets by villages happened only in the 9th to 10th century, with the strip-fields being laid out at about the same time. No Gloucestershire villages other than Upton (which is deserted) have been archae-ologically excavated, and indeed it is hardly possible to dig up a whole living village, but the Wharram evidence should at least caution us not to assume that the network of villages we see today looked similar in Anglo-Saxon times.

Though we cannot be sure what the villages and their fields looked like, we know a little about the crops grown. These included barley, oats, wheat, rye. hemp, flax, woad, beans, and vines – there was a vineyard in Stonehouse by 1086, and in the early 12th century William of Malmesbury commented on the vineyards of the Severn Valley. Fruit and vegetables were also grown. Honey was gathered wild in the woods, and bees were also kept in hives. Cows, oxen, and sheep were all important; cows for milk and cheese, the oxen for draught animals. Poultry were kept. Pigs were the commonest domestic animals, and herds of them ranged free in the woodlands, where they interbred with the wild boar. Anglo-Saxon cattle were rather small, not much larger than Iron Age cattle, and a little smaller than the present-day Chillingham breed.

Sheep farming became a major industry during the Saxon period. Sheep were kept for wool, meat, milk, and dung, while their fat made tallow candles. The Cotswolds, as early as the 8th century, provided extensive sheep runs, and a famous letter of Charlemagne to Offa of Mercia (796) mentions the import to France of woollen cloaks, which some enterprising exporter seems to have been economising on:

> Our people make a demand about the size of the cloaks, that you may order them to be such as used to come to us in former times.

Sheep are surprisingly few in Domesday book, but it is clear that many were omitted from the record when the final version of the survey was made. There must have been many thousands of sheep in Gloucestershire.

Horses were used more as mounts than as draught animals on the farm. Riding horses are often mentioned in documents because they were used by men doing messenger-service.

Cats were kept for catching mice, but the Saxons were not apparently sentimental about them, as their skins were used for warm cloaks. Dogs were highly prized. English hunting dogs were famous and were often given as diplomatic presents. William of Malmesbury's description of the Welsh tribute to Athelstan included as many dogs as the King chose:

> which could discover with their keen scent the dens and lurking places of wild beasts.

It is possible that in the sheep runs of the Cotswolds sheep-dogs were used.

Fishing, in coastal and estuarine waters, was very important, and on the Severn by the 11th century there were 18 places with fisheries. These made use of basket-weirs, probably rows of tapering baskets set in a row of stakes across the river. Rods for making these were part of the rents paid by workers on an estate at Tidenham. Another sort of weir, a hack-weir, was a barrier of wattle set across the current to produce an eddy in which fish could be caught from a boat. The fish included eels and salmon, and at Tidenham there were rarer, much valued, catches of herring, porpoise, sturgeon, and other sea-fish. In the 11th century, Tidenham paid as rent 1 mark of gold, 6 porpoises, and 30,000 herrings. There were 65 fisheries in this manor alone, providing fish for the markets as well as for ecclesiasical Fridays and Lent; there would also be salted and dried fish for the winter months.

The landscape was not without mechanisation and industry. Water-mills were a useful part of the Anglo-Saxon economy and a prominent part of the landscape, involving the elaborate diverting of streams for the mill-leet. The mill-ponds were also used as fish ponds. The earliest reference to a mill was at Stoke Bishop in 883. A 9th-century mill excavated at Tamworth was a very sophisticated structure, but it may not have been unusual and there were probably many such in Gloucestershire. By the time of Domesday Book there were over 180 mills, many being on the Cotswold scarp with its swift streams.

Anglo-Saxon extractive industries played a small part in the landscape, but they were essential to the functioning of the economy. Salt was vital for the preservation of food, and by the time of Domesday Book, many places in Gloucestershire owned salt-rights in Droitwich: Tewkesbury, Stanway, Thornbury, Sodbury, Mickleton, Rockhampton, and Gloucester. There may have been an industry at Awre, manufacturing salt from the saline estuary, but the other places owned shares in the Droitwich industry which entitled them to salt, measured in horse-loads.

Lead-workings are mentioned in a charter for Stoke Bishop in 883; the lead could have travelled by boat up the Severn. One use for lead was for making the huge pans in which brine was boiled to make salt. Iron was manufactured in many places; Gloucester paid part of its rent in iron rods 'for nails for the King's ships'. The manors of Alvington and Pucklechurch also paid renders in iron. Iron ore was probably smelted in the Forest of Dean, where iron deposits and wood for charcoal were to hand. The Dean, far from being a remote place, must have been very busy, with miners, iron smelters, charcoal burners, and smiths.

Though in the early Saxon period building stone was not much quarried, by the 10th century it was extensively used, especially for churches. Quarries on the Cotswold face in Gloucestershire were used; the evidence still survives in the number of late Saxon church buildings. There are references in charters to quarries, usually on the Great Oolite, just on top of the Cotswold Scarp, and the old ridgeway roads were close by to transport the stone. Sand must have been extracted too, for use as filler in the Anglo-Saxon wall plaster which completed the church interiors. Sand pits are sometimes mentioned in charters.

No description of the landscape would be complete without some mention of the network which bound it all together – the roads. The whole landscape was criss-crossed with roads, lanes, and tracks, and most of those which we see today were there already in the Anglo-Saxon period. The

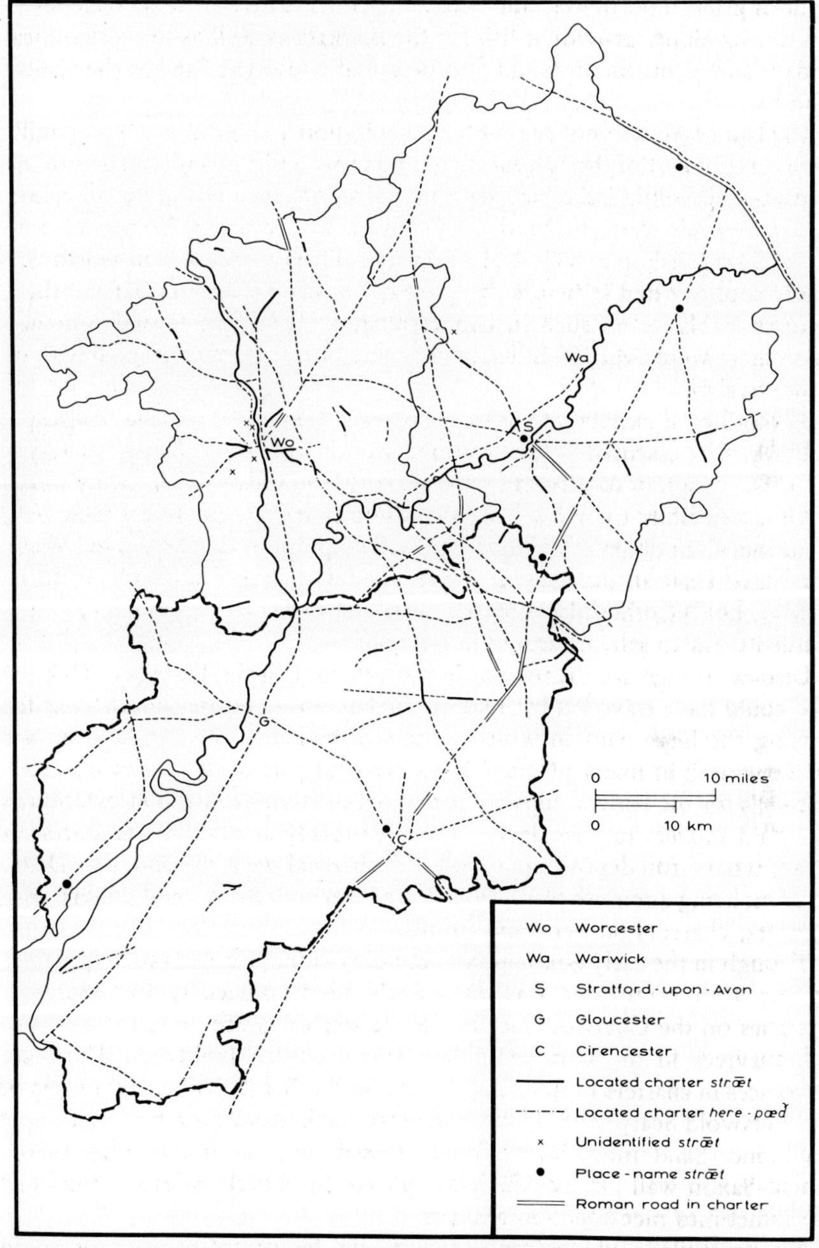

Anglo Saxon routeways in the west midlands; the charter evidence. Roman roads are often mentioned in charters, but there were many minor roads as well, some of them paved. Reproduced from Della Hooke, The Anglo-Saxon Landscape, The Kingdom of the Hwicce *(Manchester University Press 1985), fig 36, p 146.*

The Roman road, 'Ryknild Street', in Gloucestershire. Roman roads were much used by the Saxons. Photograph: Mick Sharp.

principal roads were, of course, still the great Roman highways, such as the Fosse Way and Ermin Street, well-surfaced with pounded gravel. The Saxons gave names to these roads and sometimes borrowed the British names. *Fosse* is a British borrowing of the Latin for 'ditch', and the *Foss Way* was named after the prominent ditches on either side of these Roman roads. The Roman road leading from the east to Cirencester was named *Akeman Street* after the Saxon name for Bath (*Acemannes ceastor*). Roman roads were vital throughout the Saxon period, and were probably still in reasonable condition. They were possibly even maintained by the Saxon kings, whose special tax, raised for military service, work on fortresses, and work on bridges, must imply that roads were also repaired.

In fact, we know that the Anglo-Saxons travelled about a great deal, either in wagons or on horseback. The Viking armies were exceptionally mobile and can hardly have been riding through rough country; they were using the Roman and pre-Roman roads. One Anglo-Saxon word for a road was *straet*, which seems usually to refer to a Roman road, and roads and tracks are frequently mentioned as the boundaries of charters. In the later period, as towns (*ports*), became important market centres, the name *port*

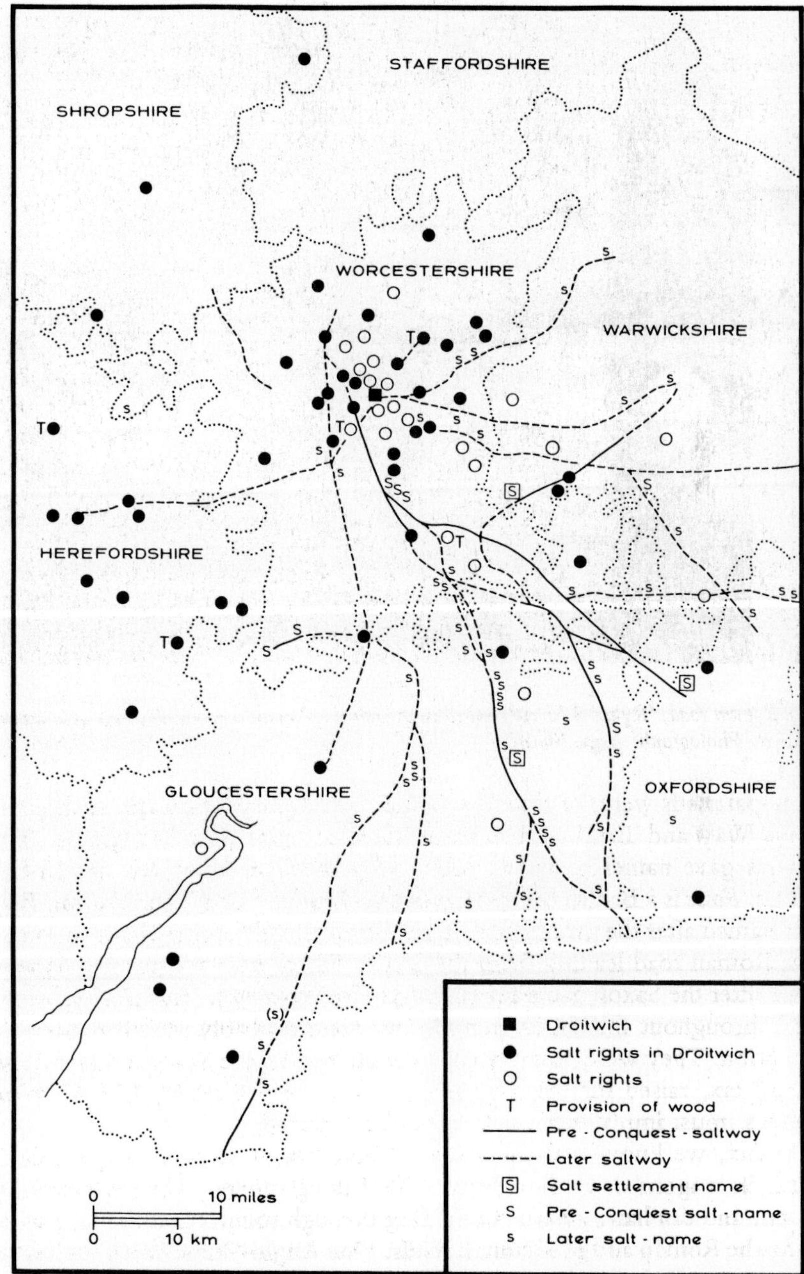

The salt industry and salt roads in the west midlands. Reproduced from Della Hooke, The Anglo-Saxon Landscape, the Kingdom of the Hwicce *(Manchester University Press 1985), fig 31, p 125.*

The salt road, the 'White Way', north of Chedworth woods. The many salt names for roads in Gloucestershire betray the pack routes by which salt was conveyed to all parts of the west of England. Photograph: Mick Sharp.

straet was attached to the routes which led to them. The *port straet* of Teddington leads westwards to the town of Tewkesbury; another *port straet* on the boundary of the estate at Withington led north to Winchcombe.

The Anglo-Saxon economy frequently demanded the transport of essential commodities over considerable distances. Salt was carried from Droitwich, by pack horse or waggon, to the markets of central England; the salt routes often carry names which betray their origin, such as 'Salt way' or 'White Way'. In Gloucestershire some of the saltways can still be traced on the OS map. One entered the county near Dumbleton in the north of the county, passed through Hailes, up Salters Lane to the top of Salters Hill, along the Salt Way past Hawling and Chedworth, past Saltway Farm, east of Coln St Dennis, down to Coln St Aldwyns and Lechlade. Another more easterly route passed through the Guitings, Sherborne, and Eastleach, also to Lechlade. Another went from Tewkesbury to Gloucester, another along the Cotswold ridge to the south-west and Somerset. All these routes avoid today's villages, and they also by-pass the major Roman settlements; they are of considerable antiquity, being pre-Saxon, and probably pre-Roman.

Wood as fuel for boiling brine at the saltworks was also essential, and by the late Saxon period was having to be transported considerable distances. The lead and iron mined in the Forest of Dean had to travel to many destinations; newly-quarried stone, though taken by water when possible, must have travelled at least part of the journey by road. In the records of duties owed, the number of men who had to do carrying service, either with horse, or horse-and-waggon, shows that it was commonplace to move goods from place to place. The very rapidity with which the Domesday survey was carried out may be testimony to the fact that the roads were maintained to a sufficient standard to allow the Commissioners rapid passage. Many of the roads were, like the saltways, far more ancient than the Roman ones. From the network of footpaths and field roads, which enabled the workers to reach their plots of land, to the drove roads which brought cattle long distances to market, and the direct Roman roads of 500 years before, the Saxons had a system of communications which is still substantially intact today.

5
People

We are entitled to ask how much the political dealings of great men affected the lives of ordinary people. The answer is, not much. People were busy winning a livelihood from the land (or from the river); occasional devastations of heathen and sometimes Welsh armies would cause local disruption, but battles and raids were localised events, affecting only a few of Gloucestershire's 50,000 or so people. Nearly all people were farm labourers of some kind; one quarter of the population were slaves – a higher proportion than many other English counties, probably because the county is so near Wales, whose Celtic customs included a high number of slaves.

If we were to be transported back into the 10th century, and given no choice of our status on arrival, we should have a 95% chance of being a peasant and a 25% chance of being an enslaved one. Anglo Saxon society was hierarchical and pyramidal; a very small aristocracy lived from the labour of a great many peasants. There were of course a number of grades of men in society. At the top were the handful of great men, the king and his ealdormen (the Danes and 11th century English called them jarls or earls), then came the thegns, or landholders, equivalent to the knights or lords of the manor of later society. Below them were the grades of agricultural workers; *geneat, cottar* (cottagers), *gebur* (or 'boor', equivalent to the Norman villein) and slave. There is no evidence that the peasantry had ever been free, though in some areas of the country they had more freedom than others. Every man's loyalty was twofold; to his superior in society and to his community. In his daily life each man was bound by a complex series of duties or services known by long custom. Records of these duties have occasionally survived.

For instance there is an account of the services due by tenants on the estate of Tidenham in about 1060. The estate had two great rivers, the Severn and the Wye, on two of its boundaries, and fishing was very important. There were 30 hides, and a number of settlements: Stroat, Milton, Kingston (now Sedbury), Bishton, and Lancaut.

> . . . throughout the whole estate 12 pence is due from every yardland
> and 4 pence as alms. On every weir within the 30 hides every alternate

fish belongs to the lord of the manor, and every rare fish which is of value – sturgeon or porpoise, herring or sea fish – and no one has the right of selling any such for money when the lord is on the estate without informing him about it. From Tidenham much labour is due. The *geneat* must labour either on the estate or off the estate, whichever he is bidden, and ride and furnish carrying service and supply transport and drive herds and do many other things. The boor must do what is due from him – he must plough half-an-acre as week-work and himself fetch the seed from the lord's barn, and a whole acre for church dues from his own barn. For weir building he must supply 40 larger rods or a fother of small rods, or he shall build 8 yokes for 3 ebb tides, supply 15 poles of field fencing or dig 5, fence and dig 1 pole of the manor-house hedge, reap 1½ acres and mow half an acre, and work at other kinds of work, always in proportion to the work. He shall give 6 pence after Easter and half a sester of honey, at Lammas 6 sesters of malt, at Martinmas a ball of good net yarn. On the same estate it is the rule that he who has 7 swine shall give 3 and thereafter always the tenth, and in spite of this pay for the right of having mast [fodder for pigs, usually acorns] when there is mast.

Another document which dates to the 11th century is called the *Rectitudines*, or *Rights and Conditions of Men*. This is a 'handbook' of what each class of society, in general, had to do. The document emphasises that customs varied from place to place, and that estate owners should make sure they know the local customs; nevertheless the duties usually expected of a 'gebur' were heavy.

On some estates the custom is that he must perform week-work for 2 days in each week of the year as he is directed, and 3 days from the feast of the Purification [2 February] to Easter. If he perform carrying service he need not work while his horse is out. At Michaelmas [29 September] he must pay 10 pence for *gafol* and at Martinmas [1 November] 23 sesters of barley and 2 hens, and at Easter a young sheep or 2 pence. And he must lie from Martinmas to Easter at his lord's fold as often as it falls to his lot; and from the time when ploughing is first done until Martinmas he must each week plough 1 acre, and himself present the seed in the lord's barn. Also [he must plough] 3 acres as boon work, and 2 for pasturage. If he needs more grass, let him earn it as he may be permitted. Let him plough 3 acres as his tribute land [probably the lord's land] and sow it from his own barn, and pay his hearth-penny. And every pair of boors must maintain 1 hunting dog, and each boor must give 6 loaves to the herdsman of the lord's swine when he drives his herd to the mast-pasture. On the same land to which the customs apply, a farmer ought to be given for his occupation of the land 2 oxen, 1 cow, 6 sheep, and 7 acres sown on his rood of land. After that year let him perform all the dues that fall to him, and let him be given tools for his work and utensils for his house. When death befalls him let the lord take charge of what he leaves.

Thus well over half the working week of six days was taken up with work on the lord's land, and there were other services as well as various taxes to be paid. It was, however, a position of great psychological security: the worker's status and duties were fixed; his position in society established. His house and plot of land was provided for him, ready stocked with beasts, tools and household utensils. When the boor died, the lord took all this back. Even a slave had a strip of land for raising crops, and the laws of Alfred show that time was allowed to slaves to sell anything they could earn 'in any of their leisure moments'. It was not unknown for a slave to save up and buy his freedom.

Other workers mentioned in the *Rectitudines* were the bee-keeper, the swineherd, the cowherd, the keeper of the granary, the woodward, the hayward, and the beadle. The beekeeper had to collect and harbour the wild bees in the woods, but he might also keep bee hives. Swineherd and cowherds were obviously necessary, especially the swineherds, for since most Anglo-Saxon pigs seem to have run wild in the woods, it would be a full-time job keeping track of them and catching them when necessary. The woodward managed the woodland, the hayward watched grazing animals to make sure that they did not damage crops. The *Rectitudines* say that the hayward's land should be near the pasture, so that his crops were first to suffer if he neglected his duties! Little Boy Blue in the nursery rhyme was a hayward. The beadle's task was to watch for malefactors, and to raise the hue and cry if any crime was committed. He was to have lighter work than other men, to enable him to be more watchful.

There were in all communities a small number of specialists who had a rather higher status in society. One of these was the miller. There was a mill in up to half the villages of the 11th century, and most of them probably had a long ancestry. The mill enabled the production of flour on a commercial scale – a useful asset when even a small monastery must have consumed dozens of loaves a week, and when rents were often paid in bread. The manor of Kings Barton by Gloucester in 1066 paid 3,000 loaves for the king's hunting dogs. It is perhaps no coincidence that the manor had two mills. The miller was able to collect a levy on the flour he produced for the villagers; and though he had heavy rents to pay, he made a good profit.

The smith, too, was important for every settlement; it was he who mended the ploughs, harrows, and many other implements, shod the oxen and the horses, or fixed new bindings to the wooden spades.

Each family would have had a small plot of land round their cottage, on which to grow some vegetables and herbs, and to keep the family pig. A pig fended for itself, ate scraps, and when killed provided a winter's worth of bacon and pork fat. The keeping and killing of the pig, as described in the late 19th century in Flora Thompson's *Lark Rise*, was an aspect of medieval life which had not changed for over a thousand years.

Firewood was an everyday necessity. Gathering fallen wood on the commons would have provided some of it, the rest was gathered or more likely purchased, from whoever owned the woodland rights. The firewood would have been in the form of bundles of faggots, not logs. The woodward had the right to any trees blown down by the wind.

Hunting would have helped to vary people's diet. In Cnut's day every man was entitled to hunting 'on his own land', and the king's hunting was preserved 'on pain of full fine'. The vicious punishments of William I's day were still in the future. No doubt these hunting rights did not extend to ordinary people; nevertheless we can be sure that the odd hare or pigeon would find its way into the pot. They would be a welcome change, for the diet of the average Anglo Saxon, though nutritious and high in fibre, was by our standards monotonous. It consisted very largely of wholemeal bread, either wheat or rye, and garden crops such as beans and leeks. In the autumn there would be plenty of fruit, particularly apples, cherries, sloes, elderberries, and blackberries. A 9th century pit in Gloucester was full of apple pips, suggesting collection of apples on a large scale, for making cider, or for preserves or even dried apple rings.

To understand the Anglo-Saxons, it helps to know what they wore. Anglo-Saxon dress fashions in general had actually changed very little from Romano-British days. Men and women wore a version of the tunic (short for men, long for women) over a sleeved undershirt. Many illustrations, for instance the Bayeux Tapestry, show the tunics tucked high up for awkward jobs like wading through rivers. In colder weather the legs were covered in stockings or leggings, and a cloak was added. The clothes were pinned together with a variety of brooches, small buckles, or bone pins. For the pagan Saxon period, when people were buried with their finery, jewellery has survived; there is much less for the Christian centuries when such things were passed on to heirs. Chance losses from the past occur occasionally, like the decorated 9th century strap-end from Abbeydale, Gloucester. Most

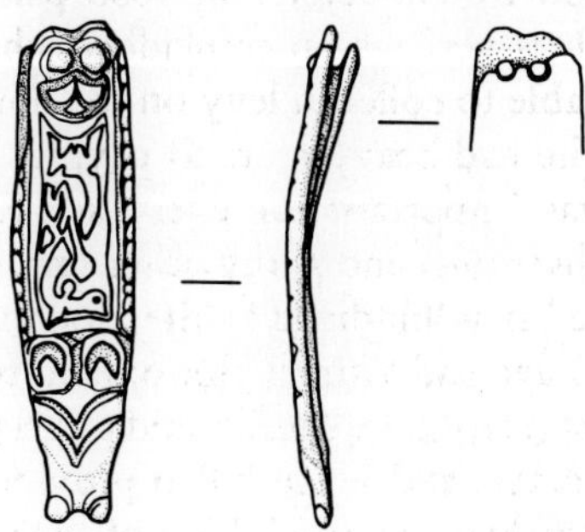

9th century strap end found by John Smith at Abbeydale, Gloucester. Drawn by P. Cracknell, Gloucester Excavation Unit.

men carried a knife, a few noblemen a sword, or in the later period, a short sword with an angled back known as a scramasax. Though no late-Saxon swords have survived in Gloucestershire, there is a 9th century sword scabbard from Gloucester; also two 10th–11th century scramasax sheaths.

Clothes would have been of linen or wool, especially wool, the cheapest and most versatile of coverings. Much of the cloth worn was probably dyed in bright colours and woven patterns. The cloth was made in the home, and the spinning, weaving and making up of cloth took up a large part of women's time. Spinning in particular, done by hand on a weighted stick, needed to be done constantly to keep up with the demands of the weavers, and young women with no husbands and families to occupy them had to spend much of their time spinning, so that the term 'spinster' passed into official language to describe an unmarried women. Weaving was done in the home and nearly every house would have had its loom, a simple affair with timber uprights and clay weights. By the 9th century the horizontal loom, for making cloth in larger and longer quantities, was also in use in some places. Bone weaving pins for tamping down the threads in weaving are often found on archaeological sites.

The main difference in clothing between humble and noble people would be in the type of materials. For warmth, for instance, the humble had

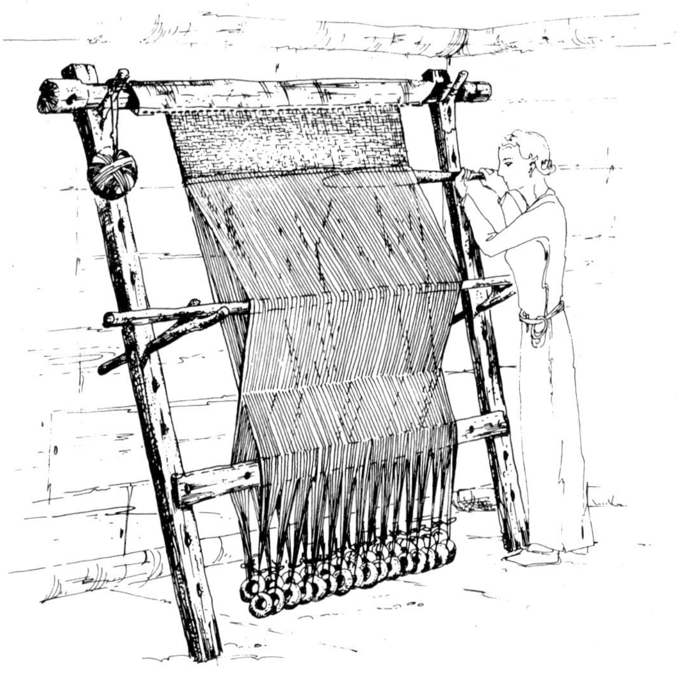

A Saxon loom: Drawing by John Lange, Oxfordshire Excavation Unit.

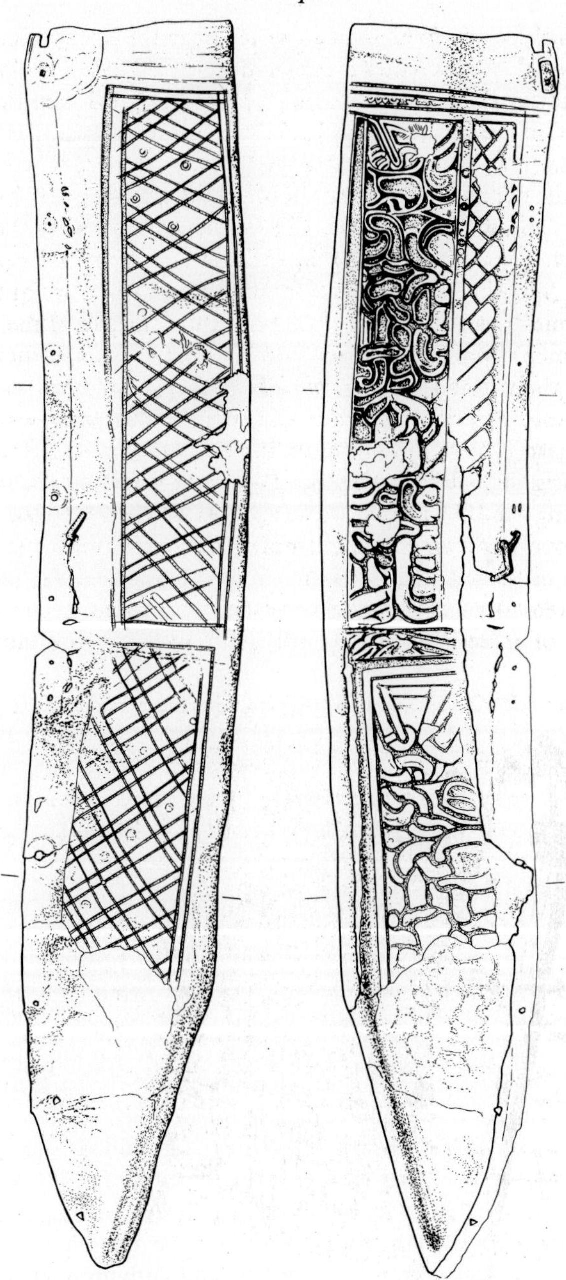

*10th–11th century Scramasax sheath from Gloucester. Drawn by Richard Bryant.
Length: 41 cm.*

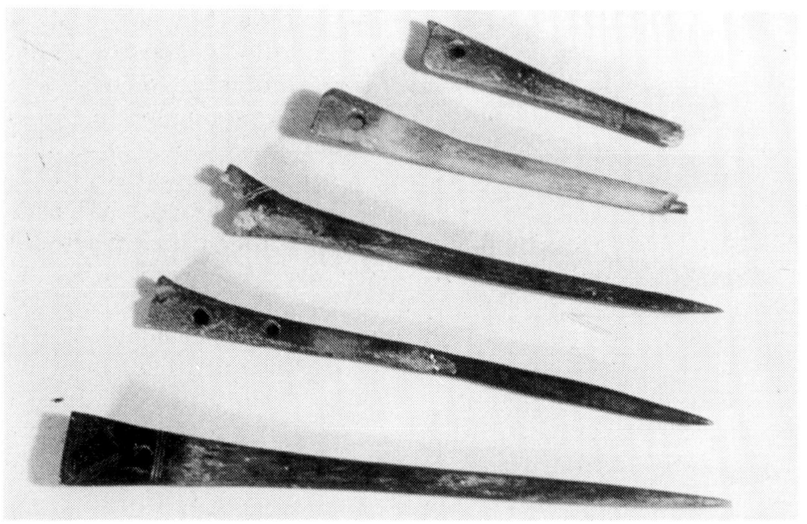

11th century bone pins from Gloucester. Such pins were commonly used in weaving, for beating down the cloth. Photo: Ashmolean Museum.

sheepskin but the rich used furs. Wulfstan, Bishop of Worcester, always simple in his dress, was laughed at by the Norman, Geoffrey Bishop of Coutances, for wearing only wool; Geoffrey urged him to put on sable or beaver or wolf, or at least cat-skin, as more fitting to his station in life. As a cleric, Wulfstan would have worn long robes, though as late as the 9th century the short tunics were still worn in many monasteries.

One fashion which did change was length of hair. The laws imply that unfree women had to wear their hair shaven or short; freewomen wore their hair long, tied up in a variety of ways; bone combs and beaded nets are known from the early Saxon period, and later there were not only combs but leather tie-backs with a bone pin pushed through two holes. Men's hair fashions altered quite drastically over the centuries. When the Vikings first appeared on these shores, their hair was shaven short at the back and shaggy at the front; imitation of this pagan punk was condemned by the church. By the time of Domesday Book it was the Viking-descended Normans who still wore their hair shaven up the nape of the neck; the English wore their hair long and were sneered at by the Normans for effeminacy. This long hair was now in its turn disapproved of by the church: Wulfstan of Worcester used to sneak up behind young men and with his pocket knife cut off a chunk of their flowing locks, demanding that the victim adjust the length of the rest to match.

In a few years we shall know much more than we do now about the physique of the Anglo-Saxon, the age at which he died, and the diseases from which he suffered. Excavations now carefully preserve in polythene bags the debris of the Anglo-Saxons, and the remains of various beetles and parasites are very informative. Ordinary living conditions seem to have been very insanitary, although in the upper levels of society and in the monasteries baths were not unknown, and were given up as a penance. Investigation of 10th century houses in York show that everyone had lice, and that very many people suffered from intestinal parasites ; quite severe infestations of worms appear to have been usual. The houses at York were apparently knee-keep in filth and crawling with all sorts of vermin ; a picture emerges of 'rotting wooden buildings with earth floors covered by decaying vegetation, surrounded by streets and yards filled by pits and middens of even fouler organic waste'. The towns may have been worse than the countryside, and in any case there is a suggestion at York that people actually lived in rather more comfortable conditions on the upper floors.

Anglo Saxon skeleton from St Oswald's, Gloucester. Such remains, carefully examined by medical specialists, can tell us a great deal about our Anglo Saxon ancestors. Photo: Gloucester City Museum Excavation Unit.

Skeletons give information as well. In Gloucestershire, over 500 skeletons from the late Saxon minster of St Oswald's at Gloucester are being examined. Already we know that a high proportion of people suffered from the various forms of arthritis; that tuberculosis of the bones sometimes occurred, and that the average height of the Saxon population was the same as that of the Roman and medieval people – that is, small, by today's standards, perhaps 5ft 7ins (1.7m) for men and 5ft 2in (1.57m) for women. We have become much taller in the last 100 years.

As for mortality rates, the information is not available yet, but we can get a good idea of the way of life in Anglo Saxon times by going back to the situation in pre-industrial England. Peter Laslett and the Cambridge Group for the History of Population have produced figures, culled from parish records, about life in that time. In highly conservative agricultural societies it is likely that conditions did not greatly change for hundreds of years, so it is not so wild to see the 15th and 16th centuries as a distant echo of life in Anglo-Saxon England. It is likely, for instance, that Anglo-Saxons did not live in large extended families. A couple could not set up together until they had a house and a plot of land, which meant that marriages were often delayed, and that most families, like ours today, consisted only of parents and their children. Because of late marriage, and late sexual maturity, fewer children were born in each marriage, and because of the high child mortality rates, not all these survived. However, child mortality rates were possibly not as high as is sometimes stated; rather less than a fifth of babies born might die before their first year; perhaps a quarter of all children born might not survive their 10th year. In addition, many children might live away from home; children of lowly households worked as servants in the larger ones. Even in noble households it was common for the children to be bought up in the household of other nobles, where they learned social graces such as how to wait at table. Bishop Wulfstan of Worcester had a number of wealthy young nobles in his household, who, as one might expect, took a poor view of Wulfstan's insistence that they behave humbly to the poor people who were looked after at the monastery.

Small families are confirmed by a remarkable document from the estate of St Germain, near Paris, dating to between 809 and 839. This document lists all the families which worked on the estate, and gives details of their families. The average size of the family was 5.79 people – but there were a number of joint heads of households in these figures, due to the system of partible inheritance, so the average number of people in each family was less than 3. There were few children – most of them were probably out at work as servants– and there was also a conspicuous absence of grandparents. People married late, between the ages of 20 and 30. Other documents, for instance from Marseilles in the early 800s, show that peasants married in their late 20s. All this would contribute a small family size. Once past the dangerous years of childhood, many people could expect to live to their full three score years and ten, though, because of the risks of childbirth, women were more likely to die young than men.

Anglo-Saxon children are not often mentioned in the sources; they were not children for long. In Cnut's laws 'every man over twelve years of age' was to swear the oath against theft or accessory to theft. In the laws of

Athelstan, 'any man over 12 years old' could be killed if found guilty of theft. Twelve was the age at which a child officially became an adult, and children over that age would do their share of the work of the village. Many of them, as mentioned already, especially the girls, would work as servants in the more prosperous households. It is likely, as in third-world countries today, and until recently in our own history, that quite small children would also work.

Anglo-Saxon houses were of timber. The very word for 'to build' in Anglo-Saxon was *timbran*. There was a long tradition of timber construction, inherited from the Celtic as well as the Anglo Saxon past. The early Anglo-Saxons often made use of squalid-looking huts sunk in the ground; these pit huts (the archaeologists call them grubenhäuser or sunken-featured buildings) may have been work huts, or might have been floored to make them more habitable. One of these was found at Bourton on the Water, in Gloucestershire, in the 1930s; it had a stone seat and posts for a loom. No one now believes that all Saxons lived in these scruffy buildings, and in other parts of the country other buildings have now been found, built of timber, but with wall-posts and wattle panels. Covered in daub, these huts would be well insulated, and the smoke from the central fire, filtered through the thatched roof, helped keep down vermin and simultaneously cured the hams.

The houses of noblemen were also of wood, but on a grander scale. It was customary for a noble to live in a great hall, where he could hold courts,

A model of an Anglo-Saxon hut from Bourton on the Water. Photo: Gloucester Museum.

feasts and assemblies. These halls would have looked not unlike medieval barns which still survive in the countryside today. At Tewkesbury, when the site of the District Offices was excavated, under the medieval manor-house were found the massive post-sockets which represented the great hall of the Anglo-Saxon lord of Tewkesbury. Though the lord's personal servants and his armed men might sleep in the hall, the lord would have a special apartment at one end of the hall, or sleep in a separate building, the *bur* (origin of the word 'bower') which was also the women's and children's quarters.

We tend to envisage cooking as always making use of a cauldron, but there were many different methods, often outside the house. Ovens would be made of baked clay and turf, and there would also probably be bakeries with more permanent ovens. Even the humble cauldron was not just a

The late Saxon hall excavated at Tewkesbury. The ranging poles work the position of the wall-posts. Photo: Alan Hannan.

stew-pot; bags with puddings and meats could be cooked together in the manner of a modern steamer.

Nearly all domestic utensils were of wood; plates, spoons, bowls, furniture, churns. The disappearance of all wooden objects is the reason why Anglo-Saxons have often seemed poor in equipment. Bone and horn were also extensively used for everyday objects. Very rarely the objects used by the Saxons are found preserved. A 9th century manure heap at the centre of Gloucester contained a great variety of wooden objects; and in a pit of the 11th century were pieces of wooden furniture and a large collection of bone pin-beaters.

We should not make the daily life of the Anglo-Saxon appear too gloomy. The lice and parasites were a fact of life, everyone was used to them. Everyday life for the average man and woman did consist of hard physical labour which took up all the daylight hours. But there was immense security as well; each person had a place in society, and knew that place and its tasks. Each year followed the established and familiar agricultural round, the ploughing, sowing, tending, and harvest. As the festivals came round (festivals, like Easter and Christmas, which the church had wisely adapted from pagan agricultural festivals and which were immeasurably ancient), they were celebrated with the appropriate church service and with the appropriate feasts. For life was not all work, and the lord had his part to do . The *Rectitudines* mention that the lord had to provide 'winter provisions, Easter provisions, a harvest feast for reaping the corn, a drinking feast for ploughing, reward for haymaking, food for making the rick, at wood-carrying a log from each load, at corn-carrying, food on completion of the rick.' The highlights of the agricultural year were marked by a great communal feast, with the lord providing, and everyone joining in. These were surely very merry events with plenty of telling and singing of riddles and jokes. (The 'Exeter Book', in which Saxon riddles have survived, displays a very earthy sense of humour which we can still appreciate). In medieval times these meals still continued, when they were known as the 'bene feast' (from Latin for 'giving' – nothing to do with beans!).

There were less riotous times for leisure as well, for Sundays were, by law, days when no man was allowed to demand work from his men. By the 11th century nearly every community had its church, and many, perhaps most, people would assemble for Sunday Mass, to listen to the mysterious Latin service, and occasionally to hear a sermon. Sunday, too, was a time for games, even for dicing and board games which have been played from time immemorial. The wealthy had gaming pieces like the chess-man from the East Gate site, Gloucester; ordinary people made do with boards scratched on stones and coloured pebbles, or counters clipped from scraps of pottery.

Wooden objects from late Saxon levels in Gloucester. Above is a 9th century churn paddle: this would have been fixed to a long handle and pumped up and down in a container. (A churn such as this was the subject of a lewd Anglo-Saxon riddle.) Below are a wooden bowl and a cup from 11th century levels in Gloucester.

Late Saxon gaming-piece from Gloucester.

These apparently self-contained communities were not cut off from the outside world. The doings of great men, and all local gossip, would travel by word of mouth. Each freeman had to attend the hundred court every four weeks, and could pick up news to take back to the community. Pedlars would come by the village, conveying news as well as trinkets. Every six months, when the shire court was held, the sheriff himself would attend with his servants and a veritable feast of rumours and news would filter back to the villagers. Some of the freemen of the village did riding and carrying service, and would be asked to convey goods or messages considerable distances. They, too, could bring back news. The markets, held in the towns, and the less frequent but more widely attended fairs, were also major social and business occasions. There were also exceptional occasions, as when villagers turned out to witness a trial by ordeal, or gathered to pursue a thief, because the beadle had raised the 'hue and cry'.

There were also a considerable number of hardy souls who went on pilgrimage. Pilgrimage to religious places of importance was a favourite Anglo Saxon pastime, a sort of equivalent of modern pop festivals, with much of the same feeling of community and excitement. Well-to-do people travelled even abroad (St Boniface in the 8th century advised ladies against going on pilgrimage, as too many of them lapsed from virtue on the way). Poorer people made local pilgrimages, making use of the road network to visit the famous shrines of the English (or even earlier) saints; St Alban, St

Welcoming guests at the family hearth. A drawing by Heather Brown,

Oswald at Gloucester; St Augustine at Canterbury, St Aidan and St Patrick at Glastonbury, St Columba at Iona. Once there, pilgrims thronged the churches, visited the shrines, and purchased souvenirs, such as a piece of cloth which had touched the sacred relics, or, if they were rich, a fragment of some original relics in a costly container. The Protestant churches have discarded this reverence for relics, but it seems to have seeped into secular matters instead; plenty of people make journeys to the house of (for example) Elvis Presley with much the same expectations.

Most people must have been passed over by the stormy events recorded in the Chronicles. Personal violence was, however, more common. Fights crop up frequently in the laws. Perhaps this had something to do with the quantities of ale that were drunk, and the fact that most men carried a knife. Injuring another man, even accidentally, was liable to be answered in kind; the blood feud was deeply entrenched in society, even though many kings attempted to legislate against it. Wulfstan of Worcester, visiting Gloucester in the late 11th century, encountered five brothers who were pursuing a vendetta against the man who had accidentally slain their brother. They refused all efforts to make them accept the *wergild* instead. The most violent of the brothers went mad – a visitation seen as a divine punishment for not accepting Wulfstan's peacemaking efforts.

The holding of the hundred court every four weeks and the more rare holding of an ordeal were major events for the community. At the court, an accused man appeared and defended himself against the charge by solemnly swearing his innocence and by getting other men to support him, also by swearing an oath. There was little attempt to get at facts or weigh the evidence; there would have been no employment for a detective in Anglo-Saxon England. The testimony of a group of men who knew each other and were known to the community, and their conviction of divine justice, were considered sufficient to provide a just result. If the man was held to be guilty, or if he could not find the right number of men to swear to support him as 'oath helpers', he had to pay the penalty (usually a fine) or go to the ordeal. The nature of this was decided by the accuser. In the ordeal of water, the accused was thrown, fastened on a rope, into a convenient pond or river; if he floated he was guilty. In the ordeal of hot water, the accused had to take a stone from the bottom of a cauldron of boiling water; in the ordeal of iron, he had to carry a heated iron bar a certain distance. In both cases the accused was cleared if after three days his hand had healed. The ordeal seems unfair to the 20th century mind; to the Saxon, it was simply a system which allowed maximum scope for divine intervention.

The ordeal was sacred, and took place in a church to the accompaniment of elaborate rituals. The accused, in those small communities where everything was known to everyone, must often have been guilty, and usually would admit it; no-one would have expected God's intervention in his favour if he knew himself to be in the wrong. In most cases, the guilty man was punished by a fine, and the profits of justice would go to the lord of the court, either local magnate or king. A compensation was also paid to any injured party, on a scale which was graded according to a man's status in society. Killing a nobleman was much more expensive than killing a slave. If the fine were very heavy, the guilty man might have to go into slavery to the man he had injured.

On the whole the earlier laws were not unduly severe. In the laws of Ine of Wessex (688–694), thieves were liable to the death penalty, but could pay their *wergild*, the worth appropriate to their rank in society, instead. Only persistent offenders, and then only if of *ceorl* status, were mutilated by having a hand or foot struck off. If a man who had been enslaved for some crime ran away, he had to be hanged. But first he had to be caught, and it is likely that, as in later medieval England, escape was common, and crime often went unpunished. In many cases the wrong-doer would simply escape to another part of the country, perhaps to live in hiding with other outlaws. Such gangs of men hovered on the edge of medieval life for centuries to come.

So much of our knowledge about Anglo-Saxon people has to be pieced together from different scraps of information. Often we wish we had just one biography of an ordinary person, to fill out our view of the past. No writer, of course, ever turned his pen to the humdrum activites of the peasant; they are a completely silent majority. We have to be content with accounts of the lives of greater men, and for Gloucestershire there is the man already frequently referred to in this chapter, Bishop Wulfstan of Worcester. His *Life* was written by his own prior, Colman, not long after his death, and it was translated from the original Anglo-Saxon by William of Malmesbury between 1124 and 1143.

Wulfstan was born in about 1008, into a landholding family at Itchington in Warwickshire. He was educated at Evesham Abbey; later he was attached to the household of Brihteah, Bishop of Worcester, and went on to become deacon and priest. For a while he was a priest in the Gloucestershire church of Hawkesbury. Subsequently he became a monk at Worcester, and in 1062 he was elected Bishop of Worcester. He was a man of character, a stern disciplinarian and supporter of reform, yet with a real sympathy and care for the poor and the nobleman alike. Earl Harold Godwineson would ride far out of his way to visit Wulfstan, and when the Conquest put King William on he throne, Wulfstan remained in office, becoming the last Old English bishop. He died in 1095.

As a monk, and a conscientious one, Wulfstan was particularly aware of his duty to common people and to the poor, and he was a great travellor and preacher in his diocese. Consequently his life was full of events concerning the people of Gloucestershire. In one incident, Bishop Wulfstan was confirming children at Gloucester – Coleman says he confirmed 2000 to 3000 in one day. At midday he was persuaded to retire to eat with the monks while more children were lined up to receive the bishop's blessing. Outside a large crowd of waiting people filled the cemetery. Getting bored, a young man started to clown about, imitating the bishop and signing the children's foreheads with mud. The people, laughing, joined in. But divine vengeance intervened; the young man went suddenly mad and fell down in a fit, beating his head against a wall, and finally tumbled into a well. The people exclaimed at the miracle. The young man, after Wulfstan forgave him, recovered from his madness, though he later died from his injuries. This crowd of people, men, women and children, filled with curiousity, inclined to superstition and hysteria, and yet always ready to be turned to fun and laughter, is a rare glimpse of the people of Anglo-Saxon England.

6
Christianity and the Church

ROMAN CHRISTIANITY AND ITS POSSIBLE SURVIVAL

Christianity was an official religion of Roman Britain from 313, but we do not know how widespread it was. It is difficult to assess the presence of any religion when the only evidence is material – that of buildings and objects. For example, the Christian ('chi-ro') symbols carved on stones at Chedworth Roman villa tell us that Christians were there; they cannot tell us how many, or how they were organised, or where they worshipped. The great lead baptismal tanks from Bourton-on-the-Water, similarly, can only suggest Christian use (some examples from elsewhere in the country have Christian symbols on them); we do not know how many Christians they represent. The ring from Barnsley Park inscribed with a figure of the Good Shepherd probably belonged to a Christian, and, since it is not a costly object, is unlikely to have travelled far from its original owner. At Cirencester was found a Christian word-square scratched on Roman wall plaster. The documentary evidence for the 5th century, slight as it is, suggests a number of states and kingdoms that were, in the words of Professor Charles Thomas, 'officially, nominally, and perhaps historically Christian ones'. In Gildas' time, in the mid 500s, Christianity was evidently the accepted religion, even if it was not generally practised; Gildas castigated the rulers in the Severn valley area for all sorts of sins, but does not include paganism. It is often said that Christianity was strongest in the upper classes of society. When Germanus of Auxerre came to Britain in 429, he encountered Christians who were richly dressed and surrounded by crowds of followers. Christian symbols, mosaics, and meeting rooms, where found in Britain, are in the wealthy towns and villas. It is also true that it is villas and towns that have been most investigated, so the Christianity of humble people may have passed us by.

The Anglo-Saxon settlements of the 500s brought new pagan religions to Gloucestershire, but they seem to have had little influence. There are no place-names in Gloucestershire which provide evidence for Anglo-Saxon pagan religions. Moreover the actual numbers of Anglo-Saxons entering the kingdom seem to have been small, judged by the numbers of people in their cemeteries. Indeed there are hints that Christianity might have survived in Gloucestershire until the early 7th century. In 597 the Roman missionaries led by St Augustine had landed in Kent. In 603, according to the Venerable Bede, 'Augustine summoned the bishops and teachers of the nearest British province to a conference at a place still known to the English as Augustine's Oak, which lies on the border between the Hwiccas and the West Saxons'. In Bede's time the border was approximately the southern border of Gloucestershire: the Oak may have been Aust, where the modern road bridge now crosses to Wales, or it may have been The Oak, Down Ampney, on the Wiltshire border. The phrase, 'nearest British province' presumably refers to South Wales or Dumnonia, since Gloucestershire was by then Anglo-Saxon rather than British, but it is clear that there was Christian influence in the locality. There is evidence in Gloucestershire, at St Mary de Lode, Gloucester, and at Frocester, St Peter, that some churches had origins in 5th–6th century burial grounds, oriented east-west and so possibly Christian. The Roman temple at Uley appears to have become a Christian church in the post-Roman period. Twelfth-century legends refer to a 5th century bishop of Gloucester called Eldad, or Aldate; there was a medieval church in Gloucester dedicated to St Aldate.

There were also Celtic saints close to Gloucestershire. The southern Forest of Dean area had by 700 an important church at Tidenham; and there was a chapel at Lancaut. Lancaut is named after St Cewydd, a 6th century Welsh saint, founder of Aberedw and Dyserth and Llangewydd (near Bridgend). He was the Welsh rain-saint, an equivalent of St Swithun. There is in the Dean the place name, 'St Briavels'; Briavel being a Welsh personal name which often occurs in early charters. Nearby, at Hewelsfield, is a circular churchyard which some people think indicates a Welsh origin. At Beachley, in the Severn estuary, close to the Roman ferry on the west side, and now dwarfed by the motorway bridge, there is a tiny tidal islet once inhabited by a Welsh hermit called St Tecychius. St Tecychius was a disciple of St Tatheus, a 7th century Irish saint. At Oldbury on Severn, the church, a 19th century structure dedicated to St Arilda, a Saxon saint, is perched on a small natural hill – a very likely site for an early Celtic chapel.

There are one or two dedications in Gloucester churches to Roman saints, such as the lost dedication to St Pancras in Marshfield parish. The chapel of St Blaisius, at Blaise Castle, near Bristol, is on the site of a post-Roman cemetery.

In the 5th century a number of Christian monuments, standing stones with inscribed memorials to the dead, usually in Latin, were set up in parts of Wales. None have ever been found in Gloucestershire, but one curious stone from St Briavels ought to be mentioned. It is a Roman altar reused in post-Roman times, when it had an inscription cut into it. The inscription

A Roman altar from St Briavels, Forest of Dean; it carries an unreadable inscription, and looks like an attempt to copy a 5th-6th century Christian memorial stone. Photo: Gloucester Museum Excavation Unit, Mick Sharp.

appears to make no sense but it could be an illiterate copy of a Christian memorial stone.

If there was Christianity surviving in Gloucestershire in the 6th century, it might explain why most pagan Saxon burials cease about 600, with the exception of those at Lechlade. It is possible that the Saxons soon began to bury their dead in Christian churchyards, which were in different places

Cross-pendant from the Anglo-Saxon cemetery at Lechlade. Some of the Lechlade Saxons may have been Christian in the 7th century.

from the pagan burial sites. Any Christian influence can hardly have come from St Augustine's single visit. A British Christianity might either have survived from Roman times, or have been reintroduced from South Wales, or even from Ireland. The 7th century burials at Lechlade, the only Saxon ones of this date known in Gloucestershire, do show the traces of Christian influence. There was a dramatic change in orientation, when burials began to be laid east-west. One 7th century grave contained a pendant shaped like a cross, which could be Christian. But perhaps it was political and social pressures which caused the burial practices and burial places of the Anglo-Saxons to change.

ANGLO-SAXON CHRISTIANITY AND THE EARLY MONASTERIES

Though some Christianity probably already existed in Gloucestershire when the Saxons took over, the new rulers were less likely to be influenced by their own subjects than by their peers and lords. Christianisation of the Anglo Saxon princes had begun in Mercia in Penda's time: though heathen, he placed no ban on missionaries, who were operating in his area two years before his death. Many of these missionaries derived from the Celtic churches, in particular from Iona, an Irish monastery in the Western Isles of Scotland, rather than from the Roman missions of Kent. King Peada was baptised in 654, and this must have had an important effect, for the attitude of the ruling monarch was crucial to the success or otherwise of any mission. The first Bishop of Mercia, Diuma, a Scot, was appointed in the same year that Peada was baptised. We are not told if his authority also covered the area of the Hwicce.

By the end of the 600s, when the kingdom of the Hwicce had been formed and its Anglo-Saxon aristocracy established, the Hwicce were Christian. Bede says that Eanfrid and Eanhere, princes of the Hwicce in the mid 600s, were Christians, 'as were their people'. Oshere and Osric were also Christians and it was during Osric's rule that a bishopric for the Hwicce was created, with its seat at Worcester, in 675. Not surprisingly, the bishopric had the same boundaries as the kingdom, for spiritual and secular

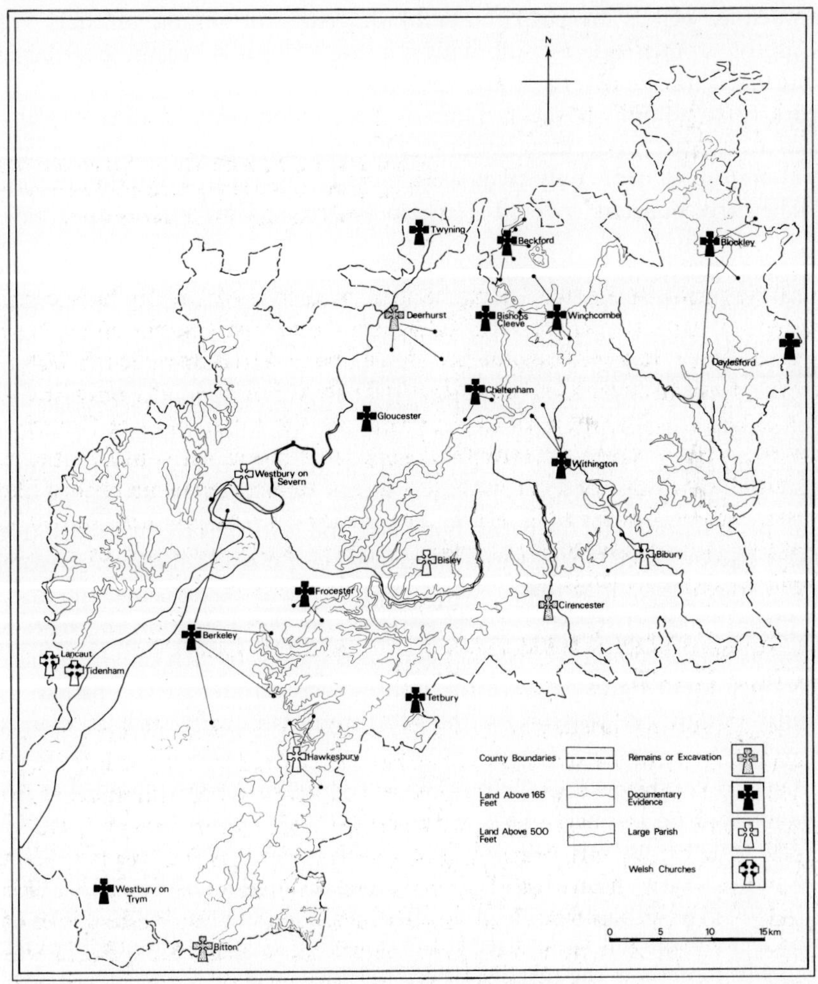

Anglo Saxon minster churches. A map by Brian Cummings.

power were closely bound together. This boundary, as the see of Worcester, survived with only some modification until the 16th century.

The Christian princes of the Hwicce showed their devotion by founding a great number of monasteries, or 'minsters' as the Anglo-Saxons called them. The founding of a minster had many advantages. Their intention was, of course, pious, to pray for the souls of the founder and his family, to give alms, and to spread the Christian faith in the large area around the minster, known as its parish. Another, less worthy, purpose was the establishment of a career structure for members of the founder's family. Many of the principal officials of the minster would be aristocrats, and would be related to the founder. Places could be found in minsters for women as well as men, for the Frankish system of 'double minsters' – a house of women side by side with a house of men – became popular in England. The women, the nuns, obviously were not allowed to do pastoral work or to administer the sacraments, so a community of men was also needed to carry out these duties. The monasteries at Gloucester and Withington, to name only two, were initially this type of double minster.

The early minsters covered a large territory, and the priests must have travelled considerable distances to carry out their duties of preaching and teaching. Before there was a network of subsidiary chapels, teaching would have been in the open air, next to some prearranged landmark. In places, preaching crosses were set up, of wood, and exceptionally of stone. 8th-century standing crosses are well-known in Northumbria; there, however, the crosses are in churchyards and are presumably memorials. In Gloucestershire there is one, whose remote position must indicate it was a preaching cross. This is the 8th century Lypiatt cross, whose battered stone shaft stands on the main road from Bisley to Stroud. For well over a century, it has marked the parish boundary and it still has the letters BP (for Bisley Parish) carved on it. Originally, however, it stood at the cross-roads at Stancombe Ash, near Bisley, where it probably marked the meeting place of Bisley hundred. Damaged though it is, the decoration on the shaft is recognisable as having consisted of canopied niches, in each of which there was once a tall figure. Above the figures were further carved panels. A similar design can be seen on the Northumbrian shafts such as that at Bewcastle.

There is every sign that many of the early minsters were regarded as the private property of the founder, so that the minster would inevitably have a parish which coincided with the area of the lord's power. It is noticeable that nearly every hundred had a minster in it. Not all hundreds are ancient, but some probably represent early estates, or jurisdictions. Some minsters, like Cheltenham and Bisley, are at the centre of a compact hundred which probably represents the minster parish.

By the time Bede wrote his *Ecclesiastical History* in 731 a great many

The Lypiatt Cross, the worn remains of an 8th century preaching cross. In each side were canopied panels with biblical figures. Photo: Mick Sharp.

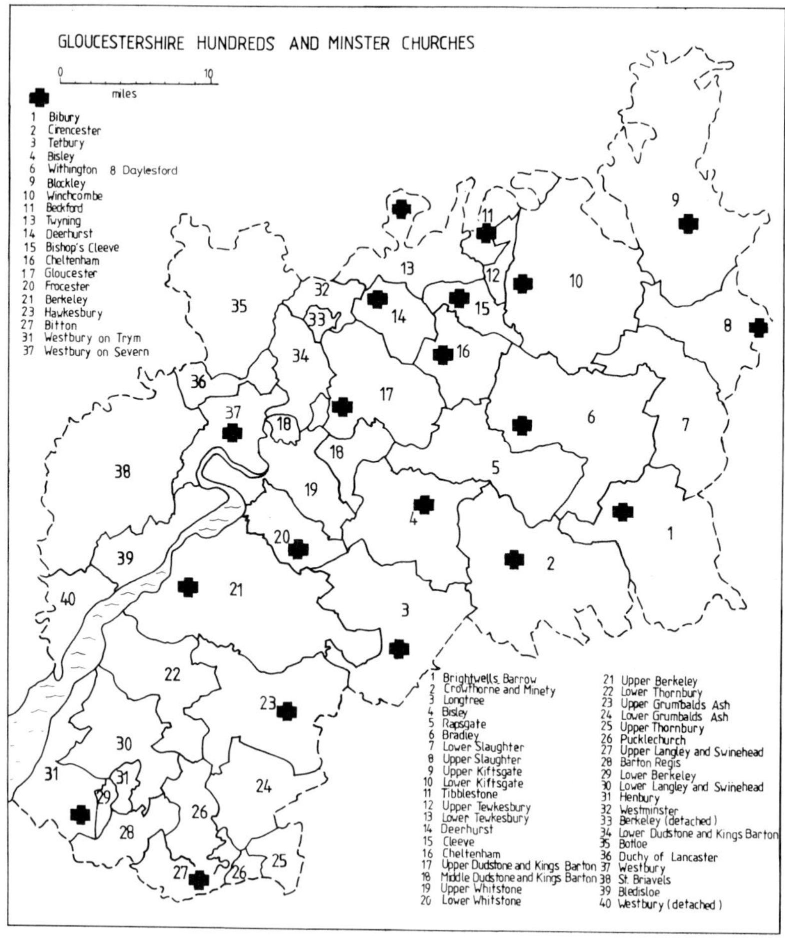

Minster churches in relationship to hundred boundaries. Map drawn by Brian Cummings.

minsters had been founded. Not all these maintained irreproachable standards. Some indeed were created as a tax-dodge; they were only founded to gain 'bookland' privileges. Bede complained in a letter to Archbishop Egbert,

> thus, having usurped for themselves estates and villages, and being henceforward free from divine as well as from human service, they gratify their own desires alone, laymen in charge of monks; nay, rather, it is not monks that they collect there, but whomsoever they may perchance find wandering anywhere, expelled from true monasteries for the fault of disobedience. . . . With the unseemly companies of these persons they fill the monasteries which they have built and . . . are now occupied with wives and the procreation of children.

nuns expcted to maintain something of their former life-style. In 873–5 a Papal edict demanded that English clerics give up 'the lay habit, voluminous but also short' and instead wear long robes 'after the Roman manner'. Obviously many or most clerics went about in secular dress. Church councils frequently condemned such practices as clerics dressing in rich clothes, going hunting, carrying arms, and allowing in their monasteries such unsuitable activities as performances by poets, harpists, and musicians, and the staging of horse-races on religious festivals. The activities of the great hall have simply been transferred to the monasteries.

As for the celibacy of the clergy, it is very likely that Bede took a more high-minded view than his contemporaries. Certainly after a couple more centuries, all the minsters were regarded as being staffed by secular clerics, that is priests rather than monks, who often maintained wives and families, much like the clergy of an Anglican cathedral today.

This situation continued until the 10th century, when some monasteries were reformed, and Benedictine monks substituted for the secular priests. There was bitter resistance to reform on the part of the nobility, for it represented an invasion of their privileges and a loss of property. Ælfhere, Ealdorman of Mercia, fought a determined battle against monastic reform, and his policies were continued by his son. It may have been due to him that the impetus of reform in western Mercia soon petered out. The last monastery to be reformed in the Anglo Saxon period in Gloucestershire was one of the oldest, the monastery of St Peter at Gloucester, which became Benedictine in 1022.

Little has survived of the buildings of any of the early minsters, though one or two, Bibury for instance, have impressive late Saxon remains. Deerhurst is the only church which can be said to have fabric surviving from the 8th century, and there are fragments of 8th century architectural sculpture from Berkeley. Without the evidence of the charters, we would not know of the existence of most of the minsters, though they can betray themselves in other ways. The early minsters had large parishes, later separated into smaller ones, and the original, larger units can still be distinguished on parish maps. Later historical documents help, too. Minsters tended to have dependent chapels which later became churches in their own right; sometimes the evidence for their dependency survives, for example as payments of 'soulscot' to the mother church.

Two of the earliest minsters, founded by Osric, were placed in the ancient towns of Bath and Gloucester, and the choice of Roman towns is significant. All archaeological evidence shows that the towns were ruinous and decayed, but they obviously had symbolic importance for the Anglo-Saxons.

At Bath, in 675, Osric founded a double minster and placed at its head Abbess Berta, who may with some colleagues have come from a group of

St Peters, Gloucester. A reconstruction by Richard Bryant of the area of the 7th century monastery. The monastery was staffed by two communities, one of men and one of women; the reconstruction shows separate enclosures for each. A procession leaves each enclosure towards the church whilst a group of people listen to a sermon beside a preaching cross. Copyright: the Dean and Chapter of Gloucester Cathedral.

Even when the monasteries were rather more worthy than this, it was inevitable that, since they were staffed mainly by aristocrats, the monks or monasteries in the Paris area – a reminder of the importance of Frankish influence in the founding of these English monasteries. In 681 the Abbess was an Englishwoman, Bernguida, but her deputy, Folcburg, was a Frank. By 757–8 Bath was an all-male community. At that time the monastery was under the control of the Bishop of Worcester. In 781 the monastery came directly under the control of Offa of Mercia, who also strengthened his southern border by the purchase of 30 hides south of the River Avon south of the city. By 796, when Ecgfrith of Mercia issued a charter to Bath, the monastery had become simply part of the royal estate.

It was in the 10th century, perhaps in the reign of King Eadred (946–955), that Bath was transferred from Mercia to Wessex; by the early 11th century, Bath was outside the borders of Gloucestershire, and had presumably been transferred from the diocese of Worcester to that of Wells. The site of the early minster at Bath was possibly close to the sacred spring, among the ruins of the Roman temples. Perhaps the author of the famous Anglo-Saxon poem 'The Ruin' was a monk of Bath Abbey.

The church at Gloucester was also a double minster. It was founded in 679, also by Osric, and its first abbess, Kyneburg, was Osric's sister. The monastery was endowed with the land of 'three hundred tributaries', or three hundreds – a considerable tract of land.

It would seem logical that Cirencester, the greatest of the three Roman cities of the region, should also have had a minster. All the documents referring to a pre-conquest minster at Cirencester are forgeries, but excavations have uncovered a Saxon church 179 feet long and 52 feet wide, with nave flanked by side chapels, an eastern apse, a crypt, and a western porch. It is constructed of re-used Roman stone. There is no dating

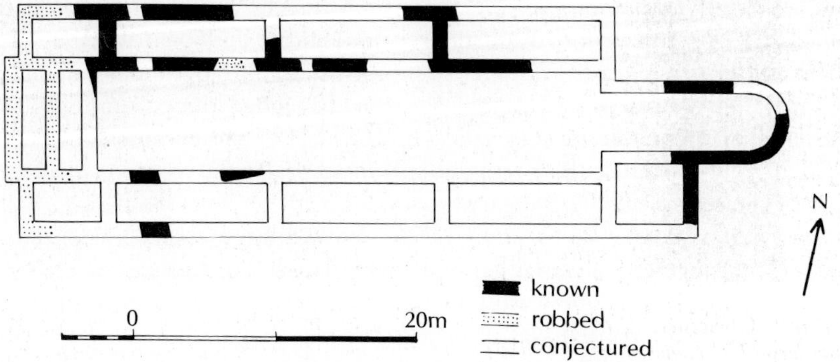

A plan of the Saxon church at Cirencester, excavated in 1965. After D. Brown in McWhirr (ed.) 1976.

evidence for this church, except that it is post-Roman and pre-12th century; but the church plan is consistent with a 7th–9th century date. This must be a minster, judged by its great length.

Osric's brother Oshere founded a minster at Withington, between 674 and 704. This was a double minster, and its first grant was to 'Dunne and her daughter Bucge'. In 736–737 the abbess was Hrothwaru, grand-daughter of Dunne, but it seems she had acquired it without legal right, when it should have gone back on her grandmother's death to the church of Worcester. A grant of 774 by Milred, Bishop of Worcester, settled the matter and bequeathed the monastery, for her lifetime, to Abbess Æthelburh. Professor Finberg has argued that the original endowment of the minster, the '20 cassates by the river Coln', was the same as the Roman estate which preceded it, and approximately the same as the parish of Withington today. In 1086, there was a priest at Withington; the present church dates to about 1150.

The minster at Westbury-on-Trym, near Bristol, now swallowed up by Bristol suburbs, was once the dominant ecclesiastical centre of the whole area, long before Bristol grew to a great port. Though probably founded in the reign of Offa, its first mention is in a grant of 804.

In 961, when Oswald was appointed Bishop of Worcester, Westbury-on-Trym was one of the first monasteries to be reformed – perhaps a kind of trial run, to see how reform ideas were accepted before they were tried out in the touchier atmosphere of a cathedral establishment. Oswald introduced Benedictine monks and a number of the canons agreed to undertake the monastic discipline, putting aside wives and worldly possessions. For some ten years Westbury was the only Benedictine monastery in the Worcester diocese. Worcester, the cathedral monastery, was reformed only in 969, followed by Evesham, Pershore, and Deerhurst.

By the 11th century Westbury was in decline. Bishop Wulfstan found that it had only one priest, who seldom said Mass; the church itself was 'half fallen, half without a roof'. Wulfstan repaired and re-endowed Westbury in 1093, and established a community of monks, with his biographer Coleman as Prior; but Wulfstan's successor Samson disbanded the community. A regular Benedictine monastery was founded in 1125 and became Westbury College, whose 15th century remains still stand beside the river Trym at the foot of the hill on which the parish church stands.

Excavations on the site of the College showed fragmentary evidence of timber buildings and a burial ground, both dated 12th century or earlier. Possibly a pre-12th century church stood close by; the excavators suggest that the site of the church was moved to the top of the hill in the late 12th century, and that the 8th century minster church was at the foot of the hill close to or under the College. But since monastic communities could have more than one church, and since Westbury had such an exceptionally chequered history, we should not rule out the parish church as the possible site of an early church, even the minster itself.

Tetbury was founded by 681, when Eethelred, King of Mercia, granted to Abbot Aldhelm at Malmesbury some land in a place described as 'near Tetta's Minster'. Offa granted Tetbury (presumably with its minster) to the church of Worcester; and in 903 during the settlement of a dispute about some land at Sodbury, it was agreed that an annual rent be paid to the bishop 'at Tetbury'. This need not imply that there was still a church there, but it does suggest the presence of an administrative centre, such as a manor house. Tetbury had a priest, and so a church, in 1086.

The site of the church is intriguing; it stands slightly aloof from the town, next to the possible site of the early manor house, both church and manor being surrounded by a substantial earthwork. This is not considered to be an Iron Age fort, and it is probably the banked enclosure of the original minster and manor house (both standing together, as was so often the case). There was once an inner earthwork which was levelled in the 18th century, when traces of buildings and coins of the 10th to 13th century were found.

The monastery of Winchcombe was founded by Offa of Mercia in 787, or possibly by the Hwiccian princes in the late 600s. Most of their minsters, like the original minster at Winchcombe, were dedicated to St Peter, a reflection of the apostolic character of the church at this period. Originally a double monastery, it was a house of monks by 798. Winchcombe was a royal administrative centre, and was also the place where the Hwiccian family records were kept. In the early 800s it was the burial place of two Mercian princes, King Coenwulf (died ?821) and his son Kynhelm (or Kenelm).

In the 10th century the monastery was in decay; it was reformed by Bishop Oswald of Worcester, who introduced monks and made Germanus of Fleury its Abbot. In the 11th century the monastery profited from an increase in popularity of the relics of one of its royal corpses. Anglo Saxons revered relics of saints greatly, and royal child martyrs in particular. Kenelm had died beteen 811 and 821 as a young man; and he did not survive long enough to become King of Mercia. By the 11th century, however, he was considered a royal child martyr. According to his legend, he was treacherously murdered at the instigation of his wicked sister Cwoenthryth. While hunting in the Clent hills, he was killed and his body hidden in a wood. 'But, wonderful to relate, from his severed head, milk-white in the radiance of innocence, a milk-white dove with golden wings soared up to heaven'.

The story is wholly fabrication, except that Kenelm did have a sister Cwoenthryth, who later became abbess of Suthminster in Kent. However, the spurious nature of the story made no difference to the success of the cult, and an impressive array of miracles was reported at Cynhelm's tomb. William of Malmesbury recorded that 'the little saint's body is solemnly

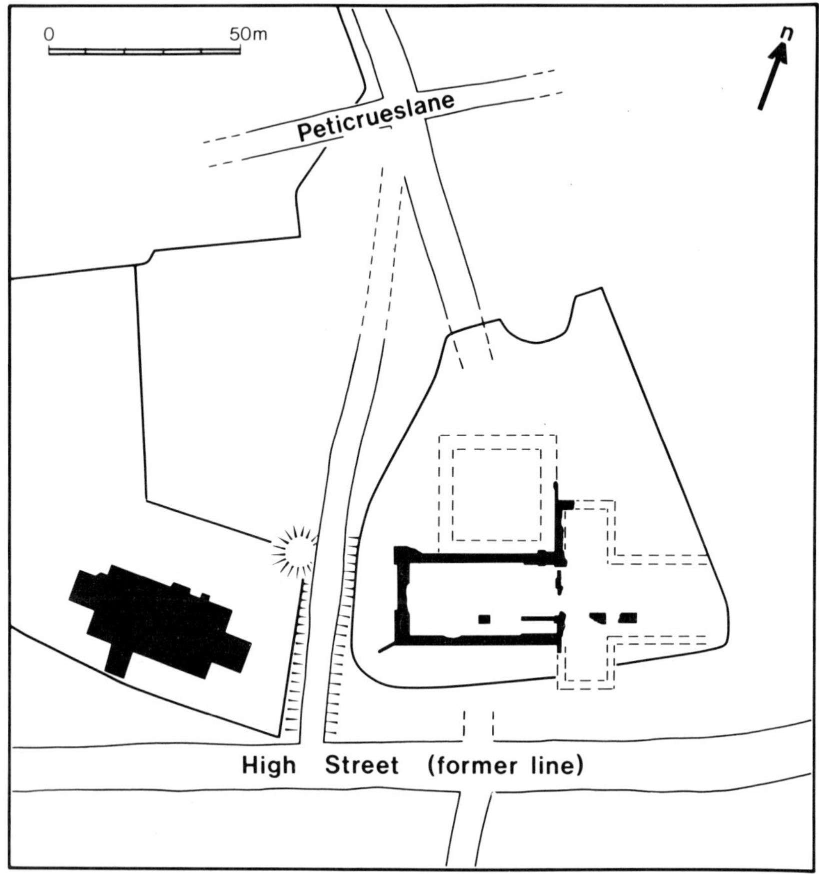

Winchcombe: a plan showing the position of the two Saxon churches; St Peters (now the parish church) on the left and the abbey on the right. The mound between the two is the possible site of the mausoleum of St Kenelm. From Bassett 1986, with permission.

revered, and hardly anywhere else in England is venerated by a greater throng of people attending a festival'.

By the 11th century there were two Anglo–Saxon churches at Winchcombe, one approximately on the site of the present, 15th century parish church, the other to the east of that, where remains of the medieval abbey have been excavated. It is possible that the Abbey was placed on this site when it was reformed, and that the original Saxon minster was close to the present parish church (whose dedication, significantly enough, is to St Peter). Close to the minster was a mausoleum in which the two Mercian princes were buried; a low mound in St Peter's churchyard may mark the position of this tomb.

Deerhurst, the Anglo Saxon tower. The lowest stage was once a porch, and is bonded with the first, 8th century building. As the building grew, the porch was heightened to a tower. The high-level door is common in late Saxon churches; it was probably for the displaying of relics to people outside. Photo: Mick Sharp.

Deerhurst is the most dramatic and complete of Gloucestershire's Saxon churches. It is a church which gave its name to the hundred and to an estate. It was first mentioned in 804 when Ealdorman Æthelric gave it land; but it was not a new church, for Æthelric's father Æthelmund, who had led an invasion into Wessex and been killed at Kempsford in 800, had been buried there. In the 10th century St Ælfheah (Alphege) was a monk at Deerhurst; by 970 he had been appointed Abbot, probably ruling over a newly-reformed monastery. In 975, however, Ælfhere of Mercia began his persecution of the reformed monasteries, and St Ælfheah was driven out. He was appointed to the Abbacy of Bath in 978, and went on to become Archbishop of Canterbury and to die a martyr's death, becoming one of the most famous saints of the Anglo-Saxon church. Captured by the Danes at the siege of Canterbury in 1011, he was kept prisoner by them until a year later, when they were collecting tribute in London. At a feast, the Danes got very drunk

> . . .for wine from the south had been brought there. They seized the bishop, and brought him to their assembly on the eve of. . . . 19th April, and shamefully put him to death there: they pelted him with bones and with ox-heads, and one of them struck him on the head with the back of an axe, that he sank down with the blow, and his holy blood fell on the ground, and so he sent his holy soul to God's kingdom. And in the morning his body was carried to London. . .and buried in St Paul's Minster. And God now reveals there the powers of the holy martyr.

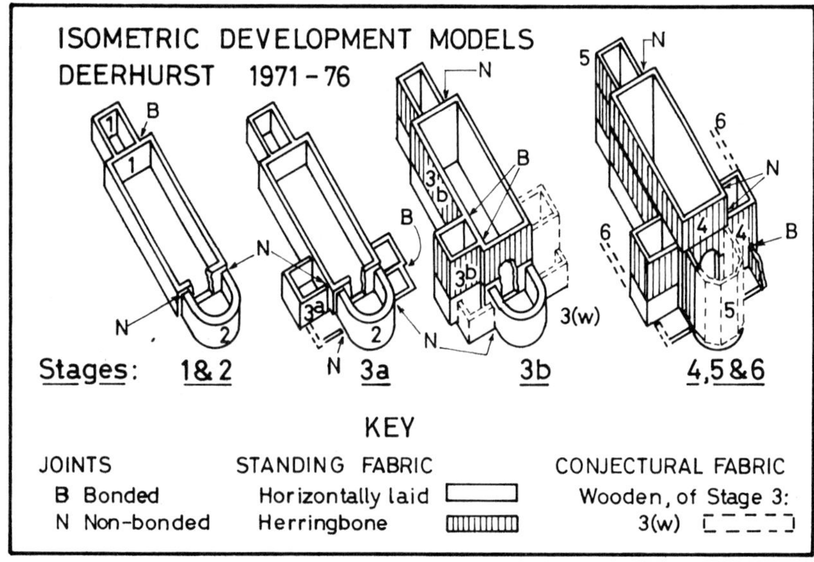

Deerhurst, the development of the plan. Taken from Dr. H. Taylor, Deerhurst Studies, *1977, by permission.*

A few years later, in 1023, St Ælfheah's bones were taken back to Canterbury.

The estates of Deerhurst were dispersed in the reign of Edward the Confessor, but it was still an important place, for Odda, a thegn and favourite of Edward, had a hall and chapel just beside the old church.

The development of the church at Deerhurst has been worked out by Dr Harold Taylor and the members of the Deerhurst Research Project. The original church, perhaps built in the 700s, was a simple rectangle with a porch at the west end. A semi-circular apse was later added at the east end. Subsequently the walls were raised, the porch became a tower, and many chapels, some two storeys high, were added to the side of the nave. By the 10th century, in the reform period, the church had numerous storeys in side chapels and porch, all looking onto a central altar; in the nave there were two galleries, connecting with the chapels in the tower, and also looking onto the central altar.

Some splendid architectural and sculptural detail still remains; the 9th century double triangular-headed window which lights the second floor chapel in the western tower, the 9th century font (rescued in the 19th

Deerhurst, the triangular headed windows in the tower. These formed part of a high level chapel looking down into the nave. At one stage one of these windows was converted into a door, to give access to a gallery in the west end of the nave. These windows might be 9th century in date. Photo: Mick Sharp.

Beast-head from the west door, Deerhurst Church. 9th-10th century. Photo: Mick Sharp.

century from an ignominious life as a horse-trough), the 10th century beast-heads on the chancel arch and on the entrance doorway, and the carved angel high up on the external (now ruined) wall of the apse.

Berkeley was one of the wealthiest and most influential of the Saxon minsters of Gloucestershire. Its earliest mention is in 778, when the records of Worcester say that Tilhere, Abbot of Berkeley, became Bishop of Worcester; his signature appears as witness to several charters. The next mention of the minster is in connection with land disputes. In 802, when Ealdorman Æthelmund was slain at Kempsford, and was buried at Deerhurst, his widow, Ciolburga, was provided for by being created Abbess of Berkeley. This might not imply that there was then a nunnery at Berkeley, for women of rank were sometimes given (no doubt nominal) control of monasteries in order to provide them with employment and income. Her short tenure – only five years – sowed the seeds of endless land disputes concerning the minster at Berkeley.

Æthlemund's son, Æthelric, went on pilgrimage to Rome, and on his return appeared before a church synod to confirm the will he had made concerning his property. Amongst other things, he left land at Westbury on Trym and Stoke Bishop to his mother, 'in order that during her life she might have protection against the claims of the people at Berkeley'. The litigious nature of those in control of the minster were obviously well known to him; probably, too, his mother's title being a nominal one, the priests of the community might be more inclined to dispute her right to revenues, and even to appropriate her personal property. His forebodings of trouble were fulfilled; and after the deaths of himself and his mother, the Westbury and Stoke property were disputed for many years. In 915 Æthelhun, Abbot of Berkeley, became Bishop of Worcester – a sign, probably, of the power and influence of the minster. Its considerable possessions are probably represented by the Hundred of Berkeley.

The end of Berkeley Minster is something of a mystery. The story that Earl Godwin seduced the nuns to get the monastery closed is fiction; and there were probably no nuns at Berkeley anyway. An entry in Domesday book indicates the monastery's destruction,

> Gytha, Earl Harold's mother, held Woodchester. Earl Godwin gave it
> to his wife, so that she could live off it while she lived at Berkeley. For
> she did not wish to consume anything from that manor because of the
> abbey's destruction.

Many people have assumed that the minster was plundered by Earl Godwin, and that his wife strongly disapproved. But the entry does not have to carry this interpretation. If Godwin had obtained the manor for himself it would surely be entered as his son's property in Domesday Book, yet it was then in royal hands. One suggestion is that the minster was destroyed by the Danish raid in 910, and that Gytha was making a protest to her husband in the hope that the abbey would be restored. As to the presence of nuns at Berkeley, the only evidence were two nuns prebends mentioned in 1130.

The site of Berkeley Minster is sometimes said to have been at Old Minster, in Sharpness, but a much more likely site is that of the present parish church in the town of Berkeley, next to the great castle and therefore

Impost and hoodmoulding from Berkeley Church and Castle. These establish that this was the site of the 8th century minster, which must have been richly decorated. Drawings: Richard Bryant.

to the administrative centre of the hundred. The Sharpness 'Old minster' may simply have belonged to Berkeley. The present church is 13th century, but in the churchyard is a post-medieval bell-tower which one source claims to be on the site of an ancient church dedicated to Our Saviour and His Saints. (A Saxon minster church might often have a second, parish church beside it; the two churches were commonly, but not always, in alignment.) There is other evidence of an early church at Berkeley. In the church is a fragment of a 10th century cross-shaft with interlace decoration, and a hood-moulding decorated with key-pattern from an arch. This last is probably of 8th century date, as is a second fragment, similarly decorated, at present in the castle.

Hawkesbury is a very large church in a tiny hamlet consisting only of a manor-house and a few cottages (the main settlement of Hawkesbury Upton is half a mile away on the hill). The church serves a large rural parish; it is also at the centre of the hundred of Upper Grumbald's Ash. The hundred meeting place was in Hawkesbury parish about 2½ miles south-

The church at Hawkesbury. Set in a remote valley, the village at Hawkesbury is only a hamlet. The large church is probably one of Gloucestershire's original minster churches, placed beside an important rural manor which by chance never grew to a village or town. Photo: Mick Sharp.

east of the church. The magnificent Perpendicular church has 12th century elements, but there is also a fragment of interlace sculpture from a cross-shaft, reused underneath the pulpit. Hawkesbury was the parish church which Wulfstan, later Bishop of Worcester, served as priest between 1033 and 1038, and there was still a priest there at the time of Domesday Book. Apart from its large parish and position in the hundred, it is also noticeable that Hawkesbury was by the 13th century the name of the even larger area of the rural deanery.

Bibury, too, has the remnant of a large parish. Its medieval appearance is misleading, for the nave of the church is actually Saxon, and has external pilaster strips, double-splayed circular windows, and a stone crucifixion or Rood over the chancel. The chancel arch imposts are richly decorated and there are also four carved Saxon grave slabs or markers, one of which is built into the north pilaster. An 8th century charter, without mentioning a minster, describes land at Bibury; the payment of soul-scot to Bibury in 899 establishes it as a minster by that date.

Bisley church also once stood at the centre of a large manor, parish, and hundred; the hundred is also named Bisley and the hundred meeting place was close to the village on the old Painswick-Cirencester road. The earlier

Anglo Saxon grave-cover from Bibury. Photo: Mick Sharp

parish included Stroud and Chalford, and no doubt the original minster parish was the same as the hundred. Bisley has a number of carved Saxon stones, a grave slab, and a fragment of frieze, of late Saxon date, and two pieces of interlace-decorated frieze built into the church, although the church itself is mostly 19th century. Bisley had two priests at Domesday.

Many other early minsters – Beckford, Cheltenham, Bishops Cleeve, Twyning, Daylesford, Blockley, are mentioned only once in the 8th or 9th

Anglo Saxon grave-stone from Bibury. The same craftsman probably made the piece from Somerford Keynes.

centuries, and then disappear from history for 300 years, emerging in Domesday Book as parish churches. Only Twyning does not appear as a church in the 11th century. Probably these churches went on being influential ecclesiastical centres, though it is often assumed that they went into decline in and after the Viking period. It is not likely that they moved their sites, even if there was a break in their use. The Anglo-Saxons, in contrast to the Normans, always preferred to add to or restore an existing church rather than to build a new one. Bishop Wulfstan, rebuilding Worcester Cathedral in the new Norman fashion, demolished the two-centuries old Saxon Cathedral, but suffered great remorse at his action, and stood weeping in the churchyard at his own destruction of the past.

THE LAST MINSTER

The last minster was founded in Gloucestershire towards the end of the 9th century. This was the New Minster of St Oswald at Gloucester, founded by Alfred's daughter Æthelflæd of Mercia at the same time that she was restoring the town as a defended centre. The site of the minster appears already to have contained a number of standing crosses, finely carved; these may represent a royal cemetery.

Part of a 9th century cross-shaft from St. Oswald's, Gloucester, showing a pair of opposed 'Mercian beasts' with interlaced tails. Drawn by Richard Bryant.

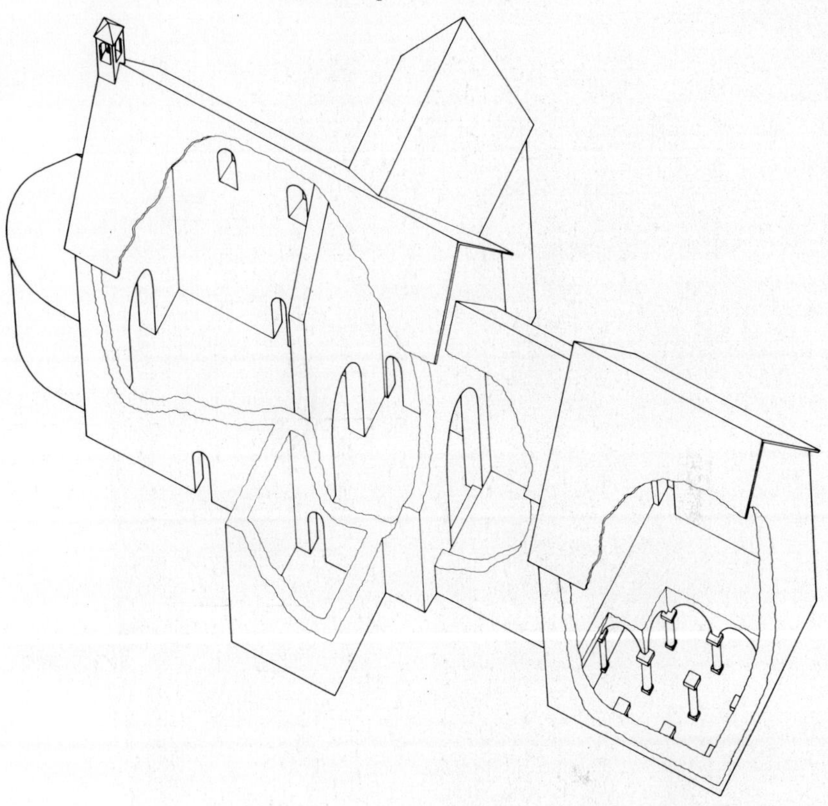

St Oswald, Gloucester, a reconstruction drawing by Jean Williamson of the church as it would have appeared in the mid tenth century. The western apse was a Continental feature, so too was the great pillared crypt at the east end, perhaps the burial place of Æthelflæda of Mercia.

The minster was built at least partly out of Roman stone quarried from the ruined buildings of Roman *Glevum*, but it was decorated too with new sculpture, carved with intricate foliage patterns in the new Continental art styles. Its architectural design can be worked out from the excavation of its plan. Few new churches were built in the 9th century, during the Danish troubles; none have survived to tell what architectural inspiration created at the time. So the archaeological excavations at St Oswald's, which have now uncovered the plan of a church built in the time of Alfred, are a vital 'missing link' in the history of architecture. On the site today is one ruined wall with 12th century arches in it; but the arches are inserted into the wall, which is part of the structure of the original church built by Æthelflæd in the late 800s.

The new church was at once conventional and innovative. Its plan was

A grave slab from St Oswald, Gloucester, drawn by Richard Bryant. The large collection of sculpture from St Oswald's shows how much money was lavished on churches. The sculpture would probably be painted.

standard, even old-fashioned; the simple rectangular box with north and south chapels and a square east end, forming a simple cruciform plan. Unusual was the western apse, a fashion of much larger Continental buildings. Another unusual feature was soon added: a great crypt with four central piers. This might have been the place where Æthelflæd and Ethelred's bodies were placed. It is very like the crypt at Repton, where the bodies of some of Æthelflæd's Mercian ancestors were buried; it may have been modelled on it.

To this new church were soon brought important relics. In 909 Æthelflæd and Edward raided East Anglia, then Danish territory, and brought back in triumph the bones of St Oswald, King of Northumbria, and famous saint. Royal saints were rare in the hierarchy of Anglo-Saxon sainthood; the recovery of these bones was a considerable coup. The presence of St Oswald's relics at Gloucester ensured a stream of enthusiastic and generous visitors; the church acquired treasure and had much wealth in land.

This new minster was unreformed, and indeed retained its community of secular canons until the 12th century. It was very much a private church for the use of Mercian royalty; it had close connections with the palace site at Kingsholm, north of Gloucester, and was to remain a Free Royal Chapel for centuries. It had its own parish, apparently taken out of the parish of the Gloucester Old Minster of St Peter – perhaps those parts which were directly part of the king's estate. The sculpture found in it shows that much money was lavished on its decoration.

By the Norman Conquest, less than 200 years later, its greatness was forgotten, and its possessions had been appropriated by the Archbishop of York. The reason for this was probably political – it was a royal Mercian foundation, and the Mercian kingdom lost all claim to independence with the death of Æthelflæd. Various Archbishops of York repaired and enlarged the church, but it was overshadowed in Norman times by St Peter's Abbey.

WELSH CHURCHES

The Welsh 'clas' churches were similar establishments to the English minsters. They were founded as communities of celibate priests, but soon became merely ecclesiastical corporations, holding the church land by hereditary right, having wives and families, and passing the land on to their heirs. Two Welsh churches in what is now Gloucestershire are Lancaut and Tidenham. Tidenham was probably a 'clas' church and was in existence before about 700, when it was bequeathed by Morgan ab Athrwys, King of Glywyssing to Bishop Bethguin of the church of Llandaff. The peninsula of Lancaut is west of Offa's dyke, part of the lands which were left in Welsh hands when the line of the dyke was drawn. This little tract of land could

The chapel at Lancaut, on the site of a 7th century Welsh chapel.

already have included a church, which is named after the 6th century St Cewydd. It has been claimed that the nave of the chapel is Celtic, but there seems no evidence that the structure is any earlier than the 12th century.

THE FOUNDATION OF PARISH CHURCHES

In the 10th and 11th centuries there was an increasing number of church foundations. The minster churches had been the prerogative of the greater princes: now more of nobles lower down the social scale, the 'local squires' in later terminology, 'thegns' in Anglo-Saxon, began a fashion for building churches. They also attempted to acquire for them burial and baptismal rights, reserved until then to the old minsters. Such rights of course were lucrative, but it was also a matter of local pride to acquire status for the local church. Dozens of parish churches were built, and endowed with land. As with the minster churches, there is every sign that the lord regarded the church as his; he expected to appoint the priest and to gain some revenue from it.

The whole attitude of thegns to their churches is demonstrated by an incident in the Life of St Wulfstan of Worcester. Just after the Conquest, a thegn called Ailsi asked Wulfstan to consecrate a church which he had built

The church at Longney. This church was the scene of a famous dispute in the 11th century, when Wulfstan of Worcester refused to consecrate it on the grounds that the builder, a thegn called Ailsi, held riotous picnics in the churchyard. The present church is 13th century. Photo: Mick Sharp.

on his manor at Longney, on the River Severn. Wulfstan

> came without delay; but the place was full of people gathering to see him as usual. In the cemetery was a nut tree, extending its leafy shade, whose extravagant fullness of braches deprived the church of light. They invited the bishop to begin the ceremony, but he refused to do so until the tree was cut down. He said..that he would not dedicate the church while Ailsi was occupied with frivolity. For he had been told that on summer days Ailsi used to sit beneath the tree, casting dice and eating sumptuous food, or indulging in various boisterous games. Ailsi obstinately refused, and, as he afterwards confessed, declared with impudent madness that rather than have the tree cut down, he would leave the church undedicated. Whereupon the saint, angered by such perversity, placed a curse on the tree. Not long afterwards, the tree died and withered from the root, and Ailsi had to have it cut down. Later, he held . . . that there was nothing more bitter than Wulfstan's curse; nothing sweeter than Wulfstan's blessing.

The important factor in the siting of any church was the dwelling of the lord who had founded it. Parish churches were simply placed beside the thegn's

The Saxon church and medieval manor house at Somerford Keynes. The church, like hundreds of others, stands next to its manor house. A late-Saxon lord lived on the same site and founded the church next to his hall. Photo: Mick Sharp.

hall; hence at Somerford Keynes the manor house and Saxon church are side by side; the village is a tiny hamlet a little distance away, for church and manor predate the village by several centuries. Most parish churches are next to the manor house, and often there is not a village nearby.

The Siting of Churches

Many church sites, not all of them obviously early ones, seem to have a connection with the Roman past. The siting of early minsters in the ruined Roman towns is an obvious example of this, but there are hints that Roman influence may have affected churches all over the county. There are a number of sites, for instance, where the churches are over Roman villas, and even a few where the church is on or very close to the alignment of the villa. Of course, a churchyard producing a few stray Roman finds cannot be claimed as significant, for nearly every inch of land was in use in Roman times. But a church close to or on a villa may be there because the villa represents the Roman estate-centre, the Roman equivalent of the manor-house, the site of which (as at Frocester) moved only a short distance away in the post-Roman period. The continuity is not of Christianity (though this is possible) but of the lord's house, or, even more likely, of the lord's burial ground.

The siting of a church on a Roman or sub-Roman cemetery may also be significant. A burial-place, especially the family cemetery of a powerful

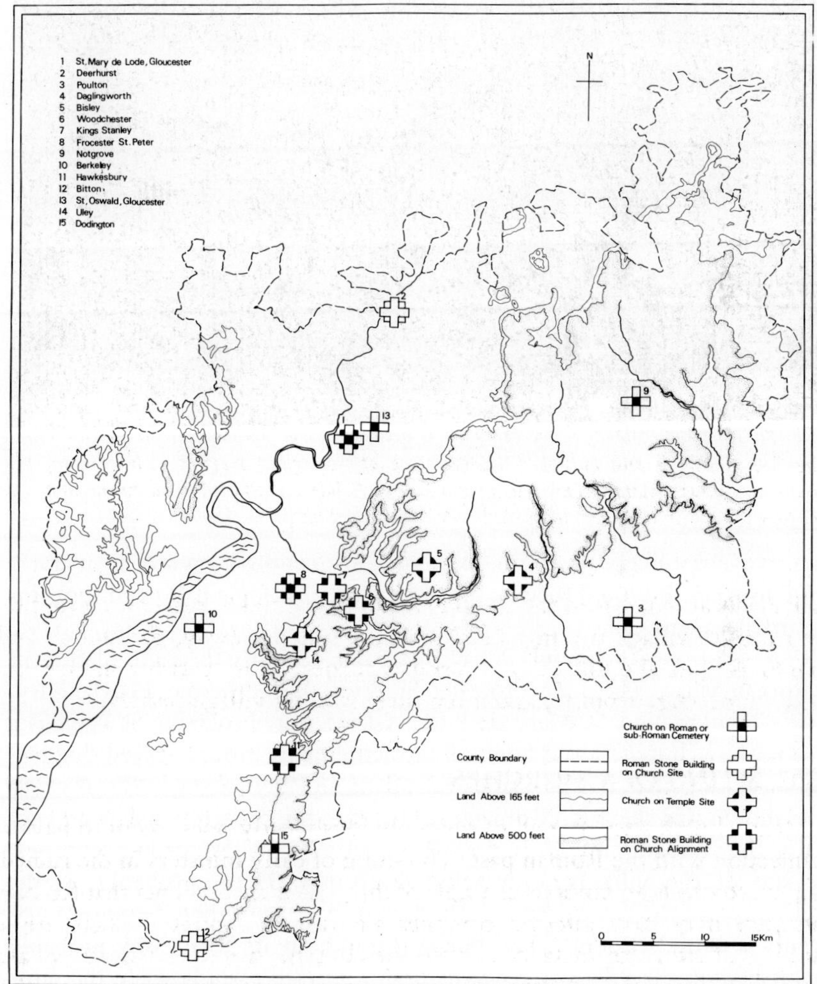

Churches on Roman sites. Map drawn by Brian Cummings. The many churches on Roman villas, some on the villa alignment, suggests there was a correlation between the villa site and the later manor houses, next to which the church was usually built.

Frocester St Peter church. Now demolished, this church has always been in an inaccessible place, far from the villages it serves. This is because it was founded on the private burial ground of a 5th-6th century lord of the manor.

man, was very likely to go on being used for centuries, whether or not it was Christian. It would then be the obvious site, being a hallowed spot, for a Christian church.

There are five churches which have the same, or nearly the same, alignment as Roman villas. These are Frocester St Peter, Woodchester, Hawkesbury, King's Stanley, and St Mary de Lode, Gloucester. Frocester St Peter is a very remote church, so far from all the settlements it once served that it is not surprising that it was made redundant and demolished. Excavations have shown that there is a Roman villa beneath the church which is on very nearly the same alignment. In post–Roman times, the 5th or 6th centuries, the site of the villa became a burial ground. Here, probably, is the explanation of the remote site of the church; it was put there because it was already a burial ground. The burial ground, in its turn, was probably established on the villa site when its owner moved elsewhere. In the same way, 5th and 6th century burials at the other Frocester site were placed in the ruins of the villa, a new house having been built nearby. The closeness of villa and church orientation may be accidental, but is just as likely to have occurred because some remnant of the ruined villa came in handly as a chapel or oratory, and so preserved the original alignment over many rebuildings and generations.

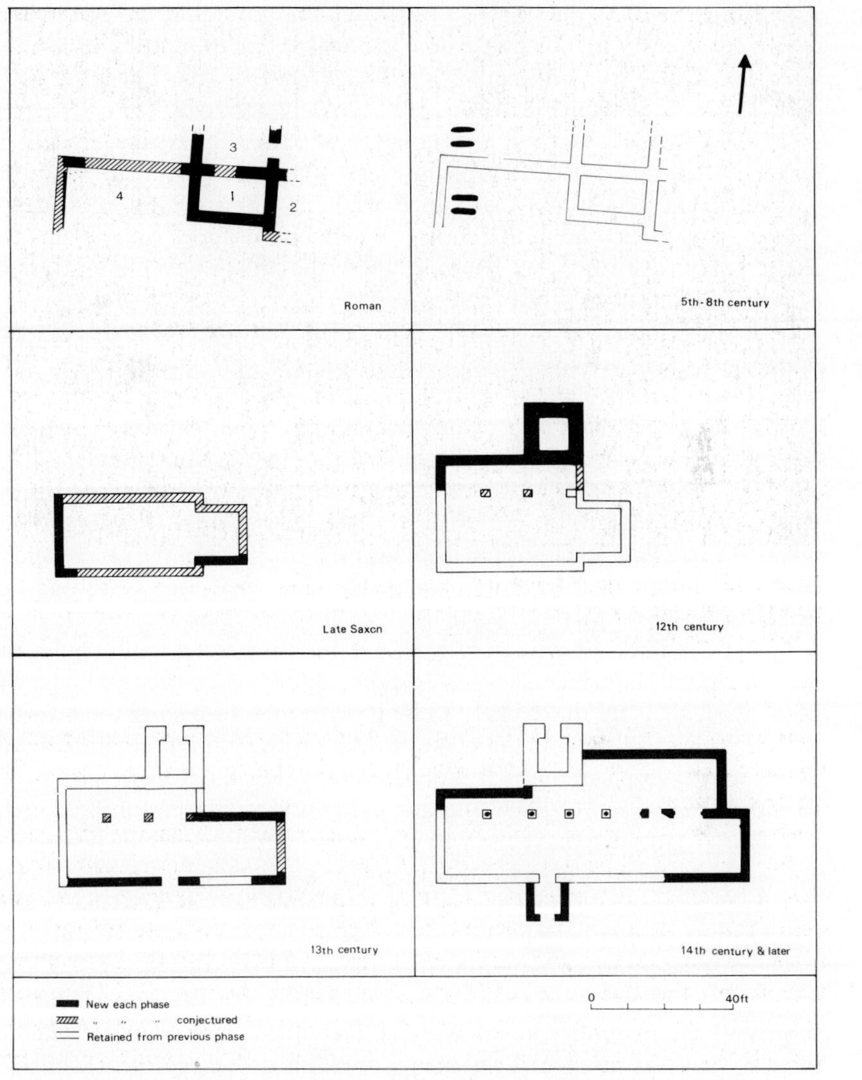

Frocester St Peter church: the development of the site. A Roman villa was first on the site: it covered a much bigger area than the walls shown. Rooms 1 and 2 were heated; Room 4 was probably a courtyard. The walls were still standing, but ruinous, when the villa site was used as a cemetery in the Dark Ages. The cemetery was later chosen as the site of a church.

At King's Stanley, the story is similar, with the church being placed next to an 11th century manor house on a site which had been more or less the same for 700 years. The church is aligned, not on the villa, but on a post-Roman wall which in turn approximately followed the villa alignment. The post-Roman wall is assumed to be 11th century, but it could be earlier. Whatever its date, it probably represents another part of the lord's buildings, and the church was aligned on these. The small town of King's Stanley, created in the 13th century, was some distance away from the church; even today there are grumbles about the church being in the 'wrong place', although it was there first!

At King's Stanley it is possible that the villa is actually a late Roman temple, for there are five Roman altars from the village which may have been found near the church. This might make the site a rare example of a temple being converted into a Christian church. A temple at Uley was also converted into a church in the 5th century, though the church there did not survive. There are other possible examples of temple-conversions at Bisley, where there are signs of a Roman temple, and perhaps Daglingworth, where Roman votive slabs came from near the church. On the other hand, a large villa might well have its own shrines and altars, so we should not make too much of this.

At Hawkesbury all we know is that there are ancient walls under the present church, but since they run at right angles to the nave and under the north wall, they are more likely to be Roman than to belong to an earlier church, and to represent, therefore, a villa on the church alignment. An even better example of this is at Woodchester, where the Roman villa, justly famous because of its Orpheus mosaic, passes under the ruins of the church. The church appears to have the villa alignment. Because the villa is so grand – it could be called a palace – this might be a case where a Roman house church was retained when the villa was demolished, as was the case at Lullingstone (Kent).

The three Roman-villa-alignment churches of Frocester St Peter, King's Stanley, and Woodchester, are remarkably close together (nos 6,7,8, on map) and the magnificence of Woodchester makes one wonder whether these are truly an accidental clustering; does this group represent Christian influence from the Roman villa at Woodchester? But it is also true that these three sites are among the few in the county which have been excavated, so their clustering may imply that many more churches have this relationship to Roman stone buildings.

In once-Roman towns, churches on Roman buildings are, of course, commonplace. Only excavation can show if there is a true connection with the Roman past. The church of St Mary de Lode, Gloucester is in the riverside suburb of Roman Gloucester, and excavations showed that it stands on the site of a well-appointed Roman building. This was delib-

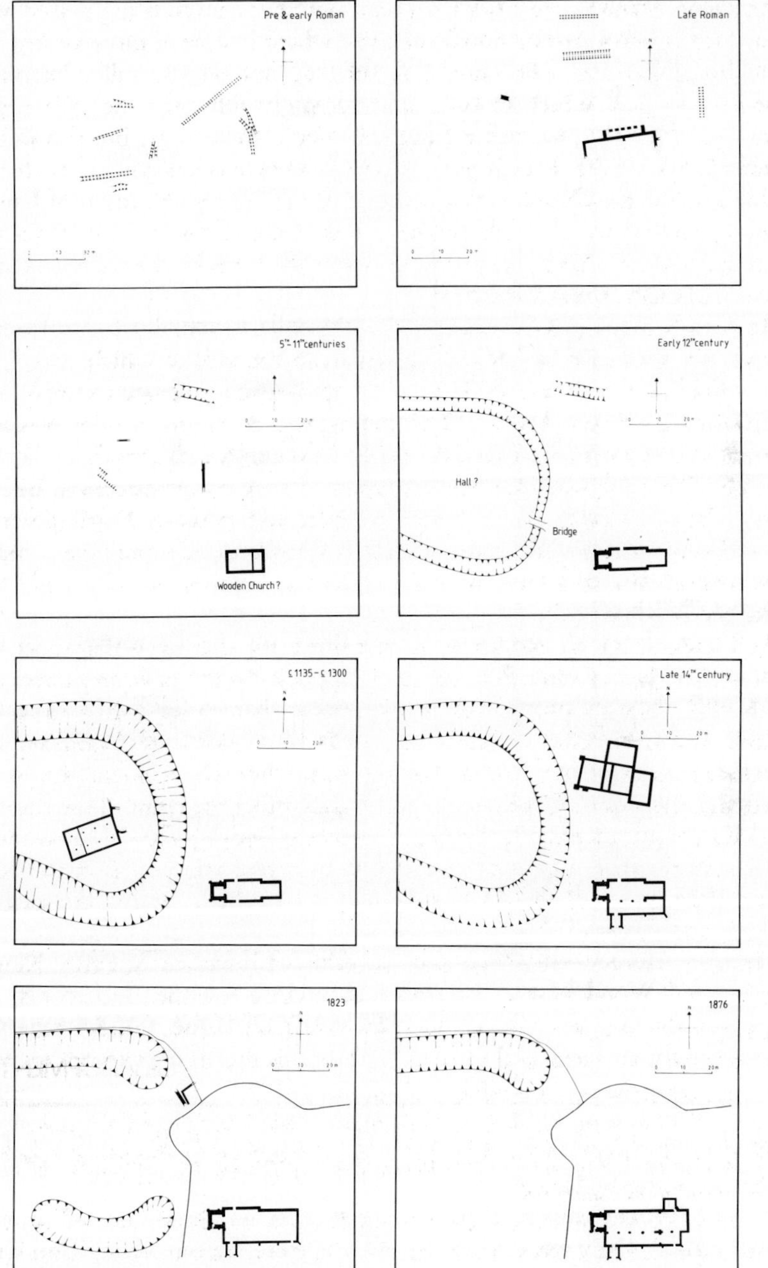

Kings Stanley, the development of a proprietory church. Drawn by Sean Nolan.

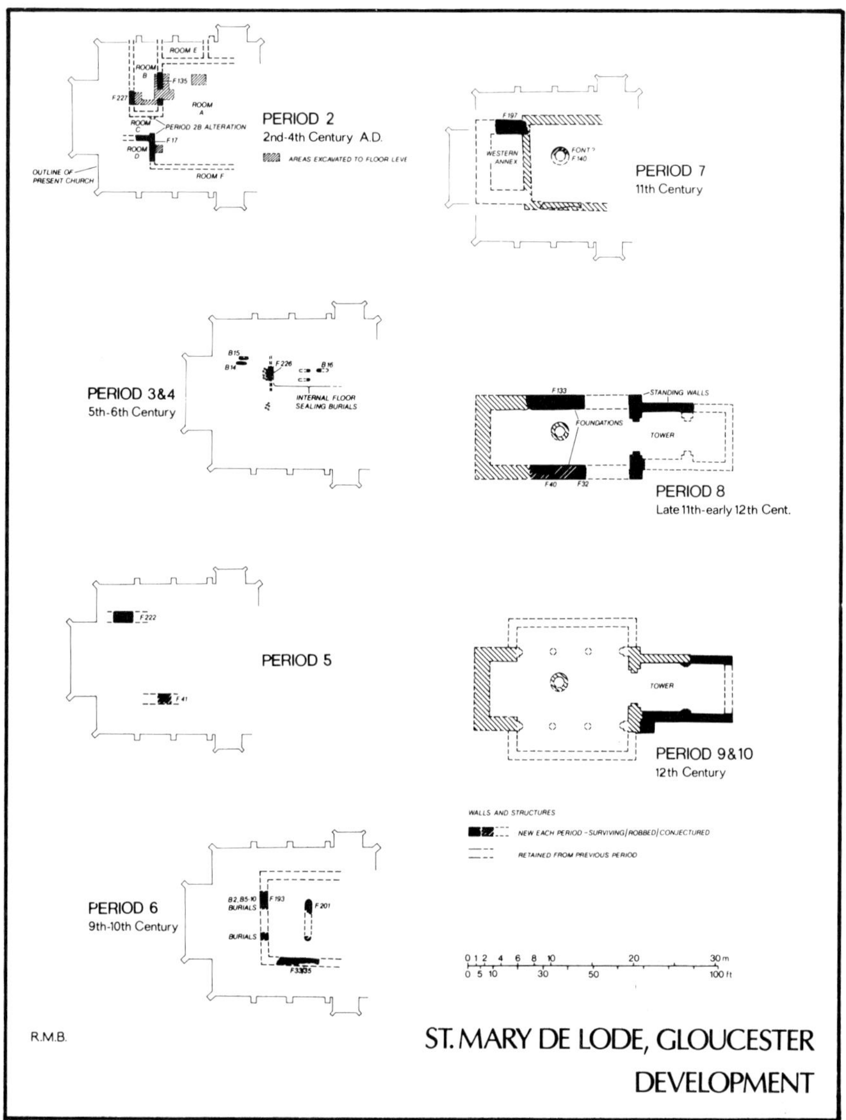

The development of St Mary de Lode Church, Gloucester, drawn by Richard Bryant. The church arose on the site of an early post-Roman cemetery (Period 3), and may be the most ancient church in the county.

erately demolished in the late Roman period and its site occupied by a timber-framed building, in which were east-west burials. This building was on the same alignment as its Roman predecessor. Later, perhaps in the 10th century, a church was built on the site, and was rebuilt a number of times afterwards. In medieval times St Mary's seems to have become the parish church of St Peter's Abbey, and so acquired St Peter's parish. Rumours of its great antiquity are therefore founded on fact, for it is almost certainly a pre-Saxon British church.

With the creation of parish churches went the creation of parishes. In the 10th century the payment of tithes became obligatory, and it was then necessary to know to which church the tax had to be paid. Thus most parish boundaries were drawn in the 10th and 11th centuries – the last subdivision of the ecclesiastical map. The bishoprics had been equivalent, in many cases, to kingdoms, and the old minster churches had each served a hundred or group of hundreds. Now the parish churches served the manors. In many cases, parish boundaries and manor boundaries coincided. Estate boundaries changed often after that, but parish boundaries preserved the outline of the original estate. Some modern parishes (Hampnett, Salperton, Winsor, Hazleton, and Yanworth are those suggested by C. S. Taylor) still represent today a Domesday manor, and there are probably many more, though proof is lacking.

There were also parish churches being created in the towns. Gloucester, for instance had eleven by 1100; many of these must have been Saxon creations. Urban churches were tiny, and often crammed into a single tenement plot, or if the street-front were very crowded, tucked in behind the shop-fronts in back alleyways. At Gloucester, the tiny church of All Saints fitted into one plot and its chancel jutted out into the street. These churches were dominated by their local minster church and were slow to acquire burial and other parochial rights. When they did, their parishes were very small. The earliest urban churches can be recognised because they, being first on the scene, have the largest parishes, extending out into the town fields. At Gloucester the largest parish is that of St Mary de Lode – almost certainly originally the parish of the ancient Abbey of St Peter.

EVIDENCE OF LATE SAXON CHURCHES

It is likely that most of Gloucestershire's 350 or so medieval parish churches had been founded by the time of Domesday Book, though we cannot often prove it. Since so many churches were manorial creations, the compilers of Domesday Book took the view that the church was part of the manor, and seldom mentioned the building, more often mentioning a priest. But Saxon architectural features, or fragments of Saxon sculpture, survive in many churches.

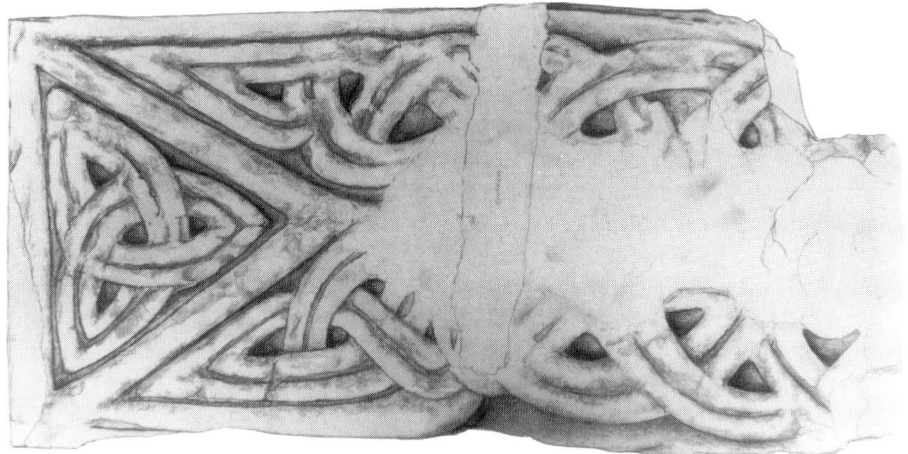

Late-Saxon child's coped gravestone, Avening church. Drawn by Richard Bryant.

At Avening, for instance, are two fragments of 10th century interlace sculpture, one a child's grave-cover. At Daglingworth is a fine collection of reused figural sculpture. Somerford Keynes church has a piece of 10th–11th century sculpture, representing two facing beasts. The sculpture is double-sided and must have been free-standing, perhaps a piece of church furniture.

Somerford Keynes, late Saxon sculpture. Photo: Michael Webber.

At Beverstone there is a full-size figure of Christ built into the south wall of the Norman tower. Bristol Cathedral has a large figure-sculpture relief representing Christ's harrowing of Hell, which pre-dates the foundation of Bristol Cathedral by about a century.

Bristol, the 'Harrowing of Hell' sculpture from the Cathedral. The presence of this suggests an 11th century church on the site of the 12th century monastery.

The cross shaft in the porch at Newent church. This shaft depicts Adam and Eve. This and the 11th century 'pillow stone' show Newent is a Saxon foundation. Photo: Mick Sharp.

At Newent there is a cross-shaft fragment in the porch which is thought to be 9th century; and also a small 11th century funerary tablet. The shaft may not imply a church, as it could have been a preaching cross standing alone, but the tablet probably tells us that there was a cemetery, and therefore a church, at Newent by the 11th century.

Two churches, Daglingworth and Saintbury, have Anglo-Saxon sundials. The Anglo-Saxons did not divide the day into units of twelve, but into 8 tides of 3 hours each. The dial at Daglingworth has lines marking the middle of the tides; it also contain an extra line marking the start of the morning tide at 7.30 a.m., no doubt the time at which Mass was held.

In addition to sculpture fragments there are churches which still contain Anglo-Saxon architecture. The earliest may be at Somerford Keynes, where the north door is usually described as 8th century, though it may not be earlier than the 10th. At Coln Rogers is a delightful church which gives a good impression of what a Saxon church of the 10th to 11th century would have looked like: a small simple nave with a rectangular chancel. On the

Daglingworth church. This simple structure has changed little since it was built in the late Saxon period. The 'Long and short' quoins of the nave can be seen. Photo: Mick Sharp.

Head of Anglo-Saxon south doorway at Daglingworth with original sundial above. The doorway and dial were originally external but are now enclosed by a later porch. Note the extra line on the left-hand side of the dial, marking 7.30 a.m. Photo: Mick Sharp.

The church north door at Somerford Keynes. Photo: Mick Sharp.

Coln Rogers, detail of Saxon chancel arch. Photo: Mick Sharp.

exterior can be seen the long-and-short quoining and pilaster strips so typical of Anglo-Saxon architecture. At Miserden the north and south doorways still retain their Anglo-Saxon hood-moulding; at Duntisbourne Rouse is a little church, apparently 12th century, whose side doors, one triangular-headed, one with a simple flat lintel, betray the fact that the Normans refurbished an Anglo-Saxon church. At Leonard Stanley is a much-mutilated example of a Saxon church just to the south of the Norman one, for when the Priory of Leonard Stanley was founded in the 12th century, the church was rebuilt on a new site. The old church became a chapel, and is now a barn. In its north wall can be seen part of an Anglo-Saxon arch, which once opened into a side chapel, and excavations have shown that the church had a semi-circular east end.

At Bitton, in the extreme south of the county, are the remains of a large Saxon church; an archway in the north wall once opened into a Saxon north chapel. High up on the east end of the chancel are the feet of a great Anglo-Saxon Rood (crucifixion sculpture), cut off by a later lowering of the roof. Bitton is so much larger than the normal, small parish church that it may have been a minster. It had, in the time of King Edward, an endowment of 1 hide of land, another hint of minster status.

Leonard Stanley, detail of an archway of the Saxon chapel.

One church is a rare example of a Saxon building with a precise date attached to it. This is the chapel next to Deerhurst church known as Odda's Chapel. An inscribed stone found in 1675 reads,

> Earl Odda ordered this royal hall to be built and dedicated in honour of the Holy Trinity for the soul of his brother Ælfric which left his body in this place. Aldred, Bishop of Worcester, dedicated it on the 2nd of the Ides of April in the 14th year of King Edward, King of the English [i.e. 12th April 1056].

The royal hall referred to was a complex of buildings of which the chapel was one part. Odda and Ælfric were well-known in 11th century England; they were relatives of King Edward and Odda had been Earl of all the western provinces since 1051. In 1052 he was captain of the royal fleet at Sandwich. Odda and his brother both died at Deerhurst, Ælfric in 1053 and Odda in 1056, so the Deerhurst hall was obviously their main residence.

Bitton: the north wall of the church, showing the entrance to a Saxon side chapel. Inside the church, above the chancel arch, can be seen the feet of a stone crucifix. The rest of the crucifix was lost when the roof was lowered.

The brothers may have been descendants, grandsons?, of that plunderer of the church, Ælfhere of Mercia; their father Ælfric had also appropriated church land, and been banished. Dr Taylor thought that Odda's saintly reputation ('a good man, and pure, and right noble') derived from the fact that having inherited the church lands of Pershore and Deerhurst which Ælfhere had annexed, he then dedicated himself to chastity (so as to have no heir) and also returned some of the church land. Shortly before he died, Odda became a monk. Ironically, not all the land was returned to Deerhurst and Pershore, some was acquired by King Edward and given to his wife, and they passed on her death to Westminster Abbey.

Oddas chapel, Deerhurst, dated to 1056. Until the 19th century it was hidden within a medieval building, the rest of which is still attached to the chapel. Photo: Mick Sharp.

Odda's chapel was one of the dramatic architectural discoveries of the 19th century. In 1885 during repairs to a farmhouse, traces of a semi-circular arch were seen and further investigation revealed the chapel, whose chancel had been divided with floors, the nave put to use as a kitchen. The chapel has a simple rectangular nave with a narrower chancel; there are double-splayed windows on either side of the nave, in one of which can be seen the original wooden frame which held glass or horn panes. The simple chancel arch has through-stones – a Saxon technique in which large stones passed right through the wall – and is outlined by a hood-mould. The door is also constructed of through-stones. Outside, the corners of the building are reinforced by 'long-and-short' quoins. The chapel roof was rebuilt in 1965; the tie beams of the old roof, destroyed by the restorers, may have been the original Anglo-Saxon ones.

Using all the evidence, every scrap of sculpture and of architecture (not all of which is mentioned in this chapter) it is possible to map all known late Saxon churches. The map can be amplified by including all churches and priests mentioned in Domesday Book. This gives a much fuller ecclesiastical map than the record of simple building remains, and corrects the impression that all the county's Saxon churches were on the Cotswolds.

There is in fact a scattering throughout the county. The Cotswolds have many surviving Saxon stone churches, simply because good building stone was readily available; and it is important to remember that most early churches were probably of wood, and so have vanished altogether. The numbers of parish churches probably grew steadily from the 8th century

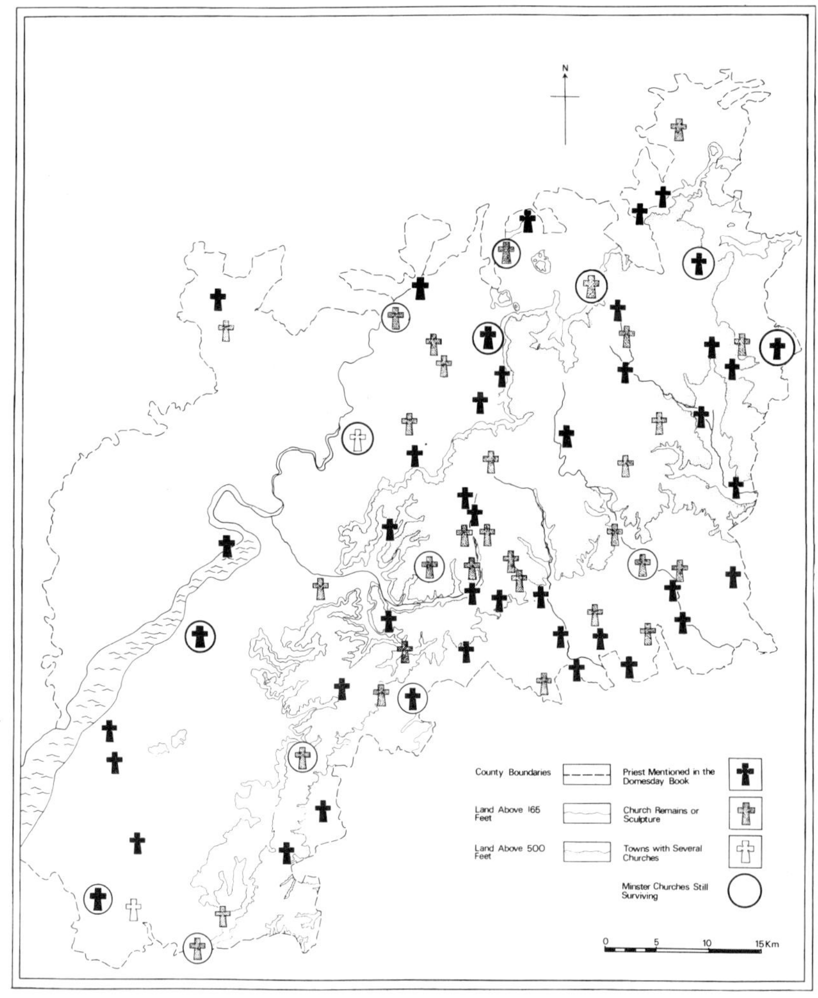

A map of Gloucestershire parish churches known to have existed in the 11th century. The many stone churches on the Cotswolds reflect the convenient Cotswold quarries; most churches would have been of wood and have not survived. This map gives a minimum number of churches; there were probably many more. Drawn by Brian Cummings.

Building a church. A drawing by Heather Brown, based on the Harley Psalter.

onwards, but the non-survival of wood has meant that there appears to be a sudden spate of church building in the 11th century. In fact the process was probably much more gradual. Although many of these churches are not mentioned until 1086, we can assume that few of them were then new; indeed Domesday is careful to say that the little church of Frampton Cotterell 'was not there' in King Edward's time. One church, not in Domesday Book, is mentioned in the life of Wulfstan, and so can be added to our list – the church at Blockley, once an old minster. Wulfstan visited it in the late 11th century and did not approve; he found the altar ornaments unworthy, 'guttered candles in common candlesticks and the linen long unwashed'. Incidentally, this shows that even Wulfstan, who personally did not go in for ostentation, expected a parish church to display some splendour in its ornaments and plate.

PEOPLE AND CHURCHES

The church as an organisation was, by the end of the Saxon period, built deep into the administrative and social fabric. Its bishops were lords and its clerics administrators; the state legislated for it and it helped to maintain the state's authority. It led the field as a patron of the arts. Some great men of the church were venerated holy men; some were competent men of the world. The secular and religious life were not then necessarily seen as separate, and bishops were great lords, who maintained a large household and had to pay their taxes and provide their quota of fighting men. Even the saintly Wulfstan had to keep a company of soldiers. The Marcher bishops in particular were often faced with warfare; Harold Godwin's own priest, Leofgar, became Bishop of Hereford, and wore military moustaches until his appointment. Even then, he 'gave up his chrism and his cross, his spiritual weapons, and took his spear and his sword. . .and went campaigning against Griffith the Welsh king'. He was killed in battle in 1056.

To most people, the church was several things. It was an aspect of authority, to whom had to be paid rents, soul-scot, tithes, or dues paid at baptisms or burials. It was also the local church, part of the community, where the various festivals were held, marking saints' days and also the progress of the agricultural year, when the priest with his cross and people processed about the land. The priest himself was one of the people: Domesday Book shows he was usually ranked with the unfree men. He still had a special status, of course; he was held in law to have the rank of a thegn, and as well as his duties of hearing confession and holding services might represent the people at court hearings, or preside over solemn rituals such as the ordeal.

We do not know how often ordinary people attended church services – it may not have been every week. The laws of Ethelred (1008) urge all people to observe the festivals, both the Sunday festivals and those of the principal saints' days. People were also urged to go frequently to confession, and communion was to be taken at least three times a year. The services were awe-inspiring and mysterious, for they were of course all in Latin. The Mass was the most important, said on Sunday morning and on feast days. Daglingworth church still has a Saxon sundial, with the hour of Mass specially marked, so that the service bell would be rung at the right time.

The priest baptised children, buried the dead, and was supposed to preach sermons, to teach the people about the gospel. This he would do in English. Bishop Wulfstan saw it as his duty to preach to the people, who turned out in enormous crowds to listen, and surely not only because he was a famous bishop and healer. But Wulfstan could not be everywhere, and much would depend on the literacy of the parish priest. There were a number of handbooks with ready-made sermons and instructions for parish priests,

Late Saxon wall-panel in Daglingworth Church. Christ crucified, with Longinus and Stephanus on either side. Photo: Mick Sharp.

although few priests could have access to these, and many of the priests would have found such works beyond their abilities. We do not know how often the average parish priest managed a sermon. For most people, their encounters with Christianity were based not on any intellectual understanding but on their experience of the church rituals and on glimpsed visions of Bible stories, depicted for them in embroidered, painted or sculptured form on the walls of their churches.

Late Saxon wall-panel in Daglingworth church. St. Peter with his book and the keys of heaven. Photo: Mick Sharp.

7
Towns

It is almost amusing to realise that fifty years ago academics were still debating the question of whether Anglo-Saxon towns existed at all. Though the debate came down in favour of such towns it was to be several more decades before the archaeologists confirmed the conclusion by discovering physical evidence of streets, houses, and trades, so that the Anglo-Saxon town was established without doubt.

A surprising number of the urban settlements of Anglo-Saxon England were re-established on the ruins of Roman towns. It is true that no Roman towns survived the troubles of the 5th and 6th centuries, that by the 550s they lay, as Gildas put it, 'in ruins and unkempt'. In this they were in contrast to the towns of south Gaul and Italy, which continued as towns, their walls and streets unchanged, so that many have retained their Roman plan to this day. In Britain, Romano-British towns may have been too superficial an imposition on a clan society to which the idea of a formal town was alien; to them, it was the person, the chief, who was important, not the place. It was not the Saxons who destroyed the towns: by the time the Saxons were in power, the towns were already spent forces. Their ruins were, however, known and revered as representing past greatness.

The two great Roman cities of Gloucestershire were Gloucester (*Glevum*) and Cirencester (*Corinium*), and in the post-Roman period, the region also included Bath (*Aquae Sulis*). None of these towns survived as towns beyond the mid to late 400s, but their walls and gates and, in the case of Bath, the temples, baths, and springs, remained. The reverence which the Saxons had for them was not just an antiquarian interest. There are hints that the towns remained places which had administrative powers. One indication of this is the annal of 577. According to this, when Saxons conquered the Severn valley they captured three cities (Gloucester, Cirencester, and Bath) and three kings – the implication is that the towns were then the controlling centres of regions. Secondly, when monasteries were founded by Saxon princes in the late 600s, each Roman town had a minster placed in it. And finally, when towns were restored in the 10th century, the Roman cities were among them.

The placing of monasteries in the decayed towns is particularly significant. Many monasteries, founded by kings or princes, were placed on royal estates, near a royal vill or palace. Those put in towns, even if among ruins, were presumably also being established on royal property. If there survived any princes' palace within the towns of Gloucester and Cirencester, we do not know of them. The royal halls, like that at Kingsholm, Gloucester, were outside the walls. But minsters were special, and it was probably felt to be eminently suitable that the ecclesiastical corporation should be sheltered by the (albeit mouldering) visible greatness of Ancient Rome. The town did not necessarily include much else; archaeological evidence at Gloucester, limited though it is, suggests just a few people and a lot of agricultural land. These towns were no longer market centres; markets had presumably migrated to the countryside. Some may have continued to be administrative centres for a wide region, the administrative functions being carried out from the royal 'vill'.

In some parts of the country, at Saxon Southampton, London, Ipswich, there were from the 8th century trading centres – 'wics' - which dealt in goods from all over the North Sea area. But Gloucestershire had, as far as we know, no access to these markets, and no early towns of this sort.

In the reign of Alfred, a network of defended centres was established across Southern England. Some were rehabilitated Roman towns; others were newly founded. All had defences of earth, stone, or timber, and an internal grid of streets (modelled on Carolingian examples and perhaps indirectly on Roman forts). After Alfred's death the system was extended to the West Midlands, and more town-fortresses, including Gloucester and Worcester, were established. A charter, dating between 885 and 900, describes how Æthelflæd and Ethelred defended the burh at Worcester, and gave to the Bishop half the profits of the market and of the local court. The idea of a defended market centre continued to be fostered by future kings.

With the creation and promotion of these towns went the creation of districts or shires, dependent on the town and supporting it. Winchcombe and Gloucester became the pricipal centres of Gloucestershire, and in Domesday Book the remnants of a system survived whereby these two towns contained properties which were owned by rural manors – an indication of the usefulness of a stake in the urban market, and also indicating the area which contributed to the towns' defence.

There were other towns beginning to grow in the 10th century, and of them, Cirencester and Bristol had administrative responsibilities for a group of hundreds. These, like many other towns, grew out of royal estate centres, the 'royal vills' to which rents had always been paid, and which often had an old minster which also helped the place to attract settlement.

The kings continued to foster the towns: legislation of Edward the Elder and Athelstan attempted to restrict trade to towns. Towns were also places where the mints were situated: the possession of a mint is one criteria of an

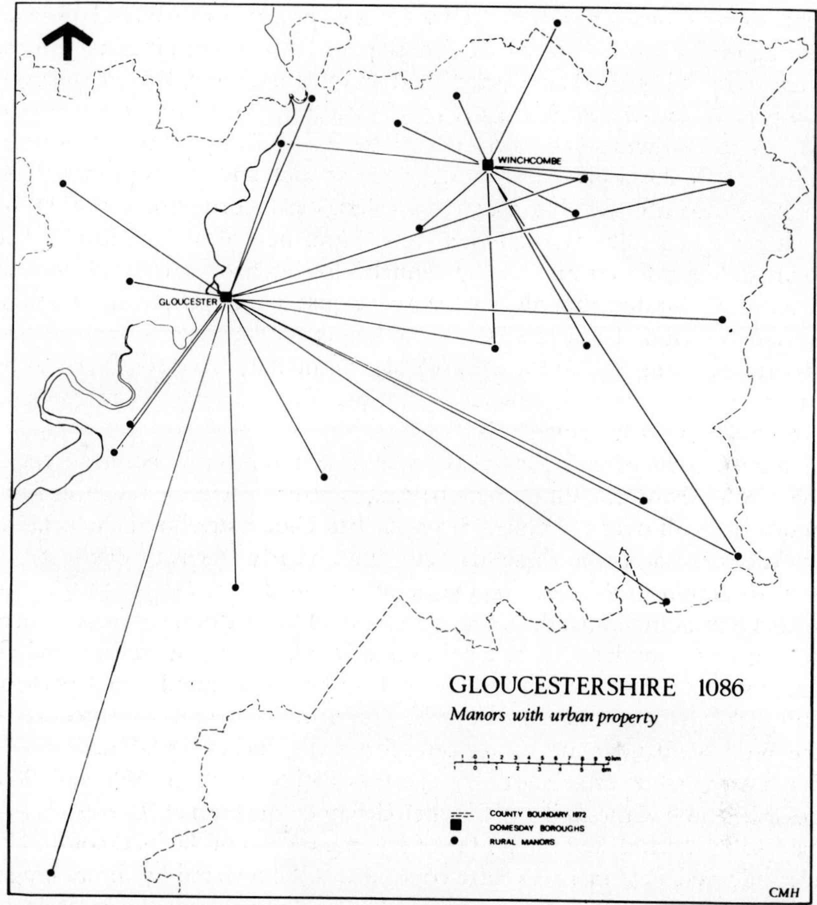

Rural manors with property in the towns in 1086. This shows the importance of Gloucester and Winchcombe in the last century of Saxon rule.

urban place. Control of the coinage was one way in which the kings regulated trade and the economy. Coinage had been in circulation from the reign of Offa (though there was never enough in circulation to permeate the whole of society as it does today). Coinage was a royal monopoly, though the right to make coins was 'farmed out' to moneyers. The penalties for debasing coinage were heavy, and coinage from Edgar's reign onwards was called in and re-issued at frequent intervals. In Gloucestershire, mints existed at Gloucester, Berkeley, Bristol, and Winchcombe.

The 10th and 11th centuries saw the steady establishment of the towns as centres of trade, finance, administration, and ecclesiastical affairs. To begin with the towns were little more than extensions of the countryside, the

Saxon coins of Aethelred, Cnut, Edward the Confessor, and Harold II.

town-dwellers tilling their fields beyond the town. Gradually their trade increased and diversified. By Domesday Book they had acquired the special tenure – 'burgess tenure', by which land held in the town could be passed to an heir. This made a market in property possible. The earliest grants of land in towns suggests that in the late 9th century the town land was subdivided into large blocks, in effect small estates. As towns became more successful these plots were subdivided, each division retaining a bit of valuable street-front. Soon the main streets of the towns acquired the familiar long strips of land reaching many yards back from the principal frontage. This familiar plot-shape has survived in many Gloucestershire towns.

Cirencester was the largest in area of the three Roman towns, though not all the walled area was filled with houses. Towards the end of the 2nd century it had become the capital of Britain's western province, and would have housed the governor's palace and administrative offices. By the late 400s it was not a functioning town, and the amphitheatre had become a defended fort, with the entrance being narrowed and a large timber building erected at the centre.

Cirencester was in contact with Anglo-Saxon immigrants c. 500–550: there was a cemetery just north of the town at Barton Farm. 'Barton' implies a home-farm, probably a royal one, so these Saxons were buried close to the royal manor, Cirencester's administrative centre, and they were probably there in an official capacity, either as rulers or as part of an embassy. The walled and ruined town soon acquired, in the 8th century, a minster church, like Gloucester and Bath. In the winter of 879, the Danes occupied Cirencester. In the 10th and 11th centuries Cirencester had the lordship of seven hundreds. A Welsh poem of the 10th century says that the Welsh had to pay their tribute at Cirencester – a curious fact, since Gloucester was much nearer to Wales. Does this reflect long tradition going back to Romano-British times, when Cirencester was the regional capital?

Cirencester in 1086 was an ancient royal manor; in the 10th and 11th centuries it was also a meeting place of councils; a 'great assembly' was held there in 1020 . Its Roman walls still stood, no doubt encircling much farmland, as it had done even in Roman times. In 1086 it had a 'new market', not necessarily the first. Domesday Book does not credit Cirencester with contributory burgesses, nor indeed with burgesses at all; its importance was still that of a royal manor, though it developed rapidly after the Conquest.

Bristol too had its origins as a royal manor, that of Kings Barton by the town. We would expect Bristol to have been an important trading place at least as early as the 10th century. It had an important mint which operated from the early 11th century onwards; at least six moneyers were working in Bristol before the Conquest. By the time of Domesday Book Bristol was a proper town; it had a number of burgesses and two contributory burgesses.

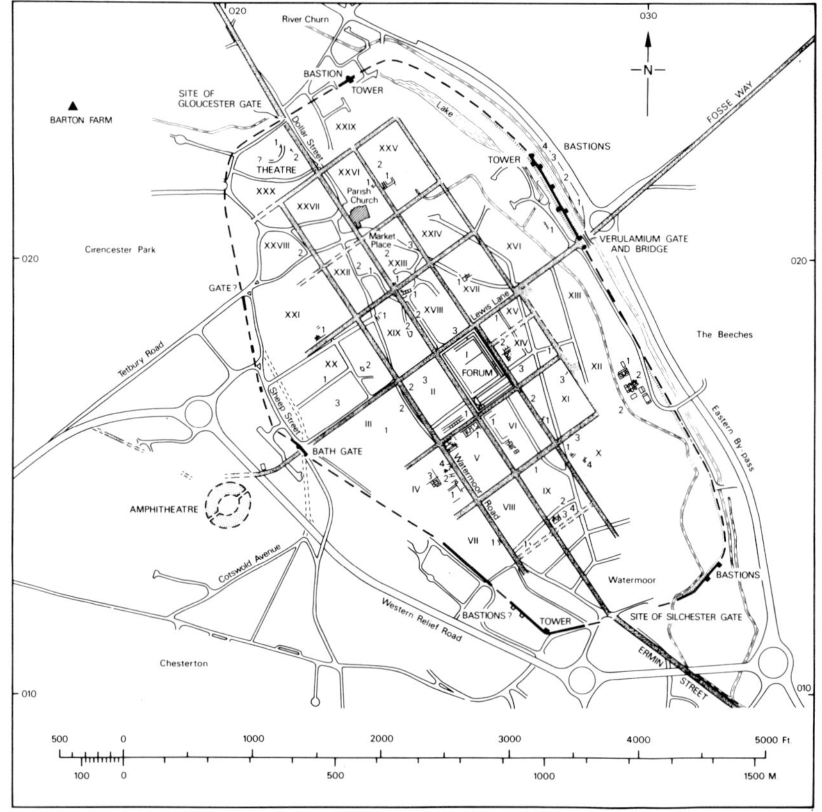

Plan of Roman and medieval Cirencester. The Roman walls survived the Dark Ages, but the loss of the Roman street pattern shows that the place did not continue to be a town. Copyright Cirencester Excavation Committee.

It also had several churches. There is plenty of 11th century pottery from Bristol, and we know from the Life of Wulfstan of Worcester that at the end of the 11th century, Bristol was a flourishing commercial port which exported, among other things, slaves to Ireland. Bristol, like Gloucester, was a military muster-point; Harold Godwineson used it as a base against the Welsh, and it seems to have been defensible in 1067, when the citizens resisted a raid by Irish pirates led by Harold's sons.

The layout of Saxon Bristol is unknown. The name (*brycg stowe*) means 'assembly place by the bridge', and this may refer to the present Bristol Bridge. In Saxon times, before the River Frome was diverted in about 1240, the Avon and its tributary, the Frome, enclosed a promontory with, at its centre, Broad Street, High Street, Wine Street and Corn Street. The line formed by Broad and High Streets aligns on Bristol Bridge, and the layout

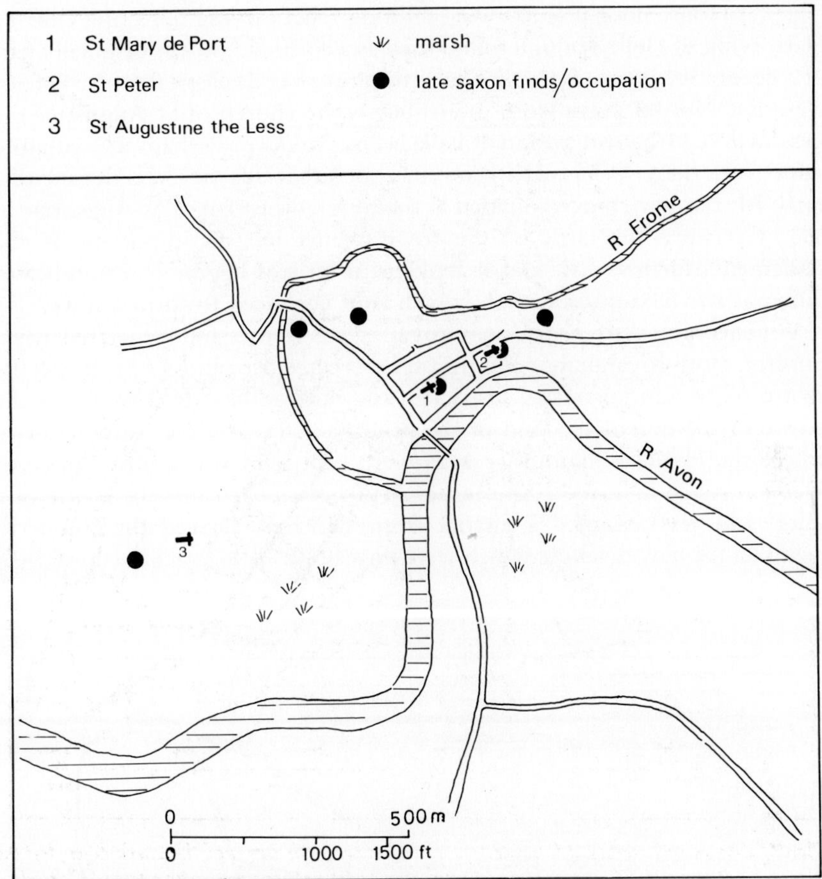

Plan of Anglo Saxon Bristol, c. 1050.

appears planned. It may, however, be a Norman pattern. This was the area which in medieval times was surrounded by a wall.

Evidence of late Saxon occupation comes from this area, but also from under the castle, further east. There are timber buildings and fences, pits, pottery, and metal working debris. Spinning, leather working and iron processing were carried out. St Peter's church, the oldest church in Bristol and originally the parish church of the royal manor of Barton, probably marks the centre of an important area of Saxon settlement. Late Saxon pits found at Tower Lane show that settlement had also spread to the north of the River Frome. There were also pre-conquest settlements at Bedminster and Redcliffe.

Another early centre may have been near the present Cathedral, originally the Abbey of St Augustine founded c. 1140. In 1832 under the

Chapter House floor was found an 8ft long relief carving depicting Christ's Harrowing of Hell. Though found used as a coffin lid, it was originally part of a decorative frieze. It implies an 11th century ecclesiastical centre here or close by. Not far away from the Abbey is the church of St Augustine the Less, where 11th century burials have been excavated. Perhaps the sculpture came from there. It has even been suggested that this area was the site of a early 7th century church founded at the time of the visit of St Augustine in 603. Certainly this area of the town seems just as important as the settlements further east, and it looks as if Bristol begun as a number of different late Saxon settlements which later coalesced to form a town.

Winchcombe also began as a royal estate centre and venerated royal minster. Both royal manor and minster were in existence by 821. It was the centre of an administrative district in the 8th century. It was also at the centre of the hereditary land of the princes of the Hwicce, was the place where the Hwiccian family records were kept, and was a burial place of Mercian royalty. In the 10th century Winchcombe became the centre of a shire, and was assigned a district from which it derived the labour to maintain the new defences which were now built. In 942 a Council was held

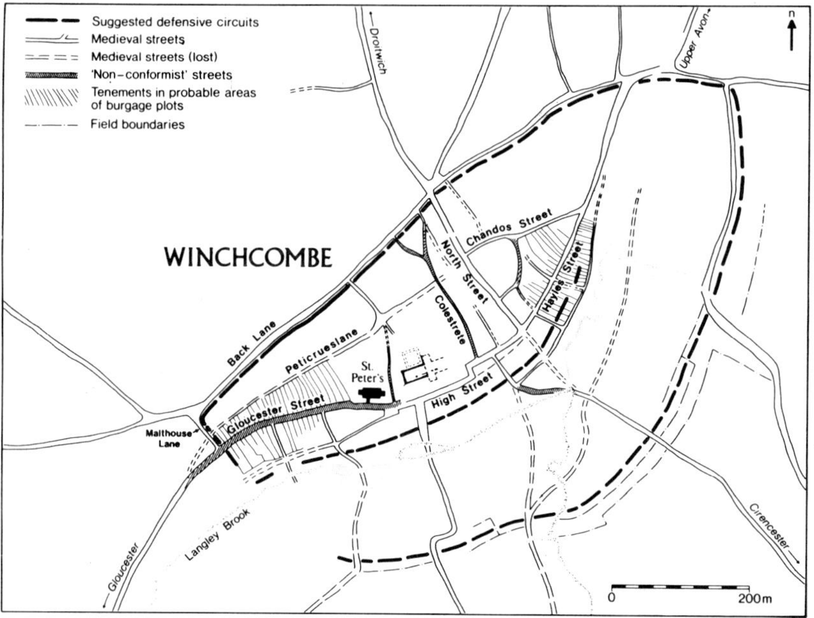

Winchcombe: the town and its defences. The town was probably first defended, by a bank and timber wall, in the early 10th century, when it became a shire town. Drawn by Steve Bassett, and reproduced by permission.

Winchcombe, the Saxon bank on the north side.

'in the very famous place known as Winchcombe'. There was a mint by 973. At about this time the cult of Kenelm had begun, and growing numbers of pilgrims helped to boost Winchcombe's trade. By the 11th century Winchcombe was flourishing: Domesday book records 29 'contributory' burgesses, scattered about the north part of the county. Their positioning indicates roughly the area of the old shire of Winchcombe. The 29 burgesses are probably a Domesday Book underestimate, for there were 141 burgesses by 1100. Winchcombe lost its shire status to Gloucester in the early 1000s, and after the Conquest, it slid into decline.

The town still has a great earth bank which surrounds it on the north. Excavations showed that the bank was preceded by a ditch which marked the settlement boundary in the mid Saxon period. In the late Saxon period this was replaced by an earth rampart with a timber front. Later still the rampart was raised and fronted with a stone wall.

This earth-and-timber type of defence is typically Saxon, and examples have been excavated elsewhere, at Hereford, Tamworth and other places. The rampart at Winchcombe was probably built by Æthelflæd in the early 10th century; the stone-fronted rampart was an addition of the late 10th or early 11th centuries. Both defences are connected with Winchcombe's shire status, for which a defensible circuit was essential. For the rest of the defences, natural features were probably used, the river and marshland.

Gloucester had been a Roman fortress and later became a colonia, one of those Roman implantations which attempted to demonstrate to the provinces the example of urban life. It, too, did not survive as an urban centre, but it did have a minster founded within its walls in 679, and half a mile north of the city was a royal manor which by the 11th century was defined as a 'palace'. The palace site is significant; it occupied a late Roman prestige burial ground, and was probably always an aristocratic centre of some sort; the site represents the sort of continuity which has been described for some churches on Roman sites.

In the 9th century, when the new minster of St Oswald was founded outside its walls, the old Roman town was still an agricultural estate with no apparent urban characteristics, not even any sign of industry. By the early 10th century the decision had been made to fortify Gloucester as part of the burh network. Its walls were repaired and a new street plan laid out, which formed a rough grid and provided a street inside the walls for easy access to the defences. It also had a mint. It probably had, like Worcester, its own market, and its strategic position – it controlled the crossing into Wales – was to be a stimulus to its development. It became the centre of a shire, which contributed to its defence and had a part in its market. Its shire status was even more enhanced in the early 11th century when the shires of Gloucester and Winchcombe were amalgamated.

Archaeologists find an increasing amount of evidence that Gloucester in the 11th century was manufacturing more – iron, glass, pottery – and a greater variety of goods, than before. Cnut and Edmund Ironside chose Gloucester as a meeting-place in 1016; Edward the Confessor visited Gloucester nine times; many councils were held there (probably in the 'palace' at Kingsholm), and campaigns against Wales were planned and troops mustered at Gloucester. In 1051 Gloucester saw the mustering of troops by Edward against Godwin – and no doubt viewed with thankfulness their subsequent disbanding. The Welsh wars were vicious, and the royal hall at Gloucester witnessed some gory moments, as when the head of the Welsh king's brother, Rhys, was brought to Gloucester on Edward's order; or in 1063 when Harold Godwineson mustered troops at Gloucester and led an expedition to Rhuddlan; the Welsh king Griffith was killed and his head brought to Edward at Gloucester.

Gloucester was still a small place, contained mainly within the walls of the Roman town, but with a quayside area to the west, and perhaps a small suburb to the north. Its buildings were of timber, a number with cellars, and set along the two main streets. Roman gates still guarded the north and east approaches; the river was spanned by a wooden bridge. There was still a lot of space inside the walls, occupied by gardens and even by fields. Sections of 11th century streets are often seen when trenches are dug for pipes and cables: the streets were covered with a thick layer of rotting

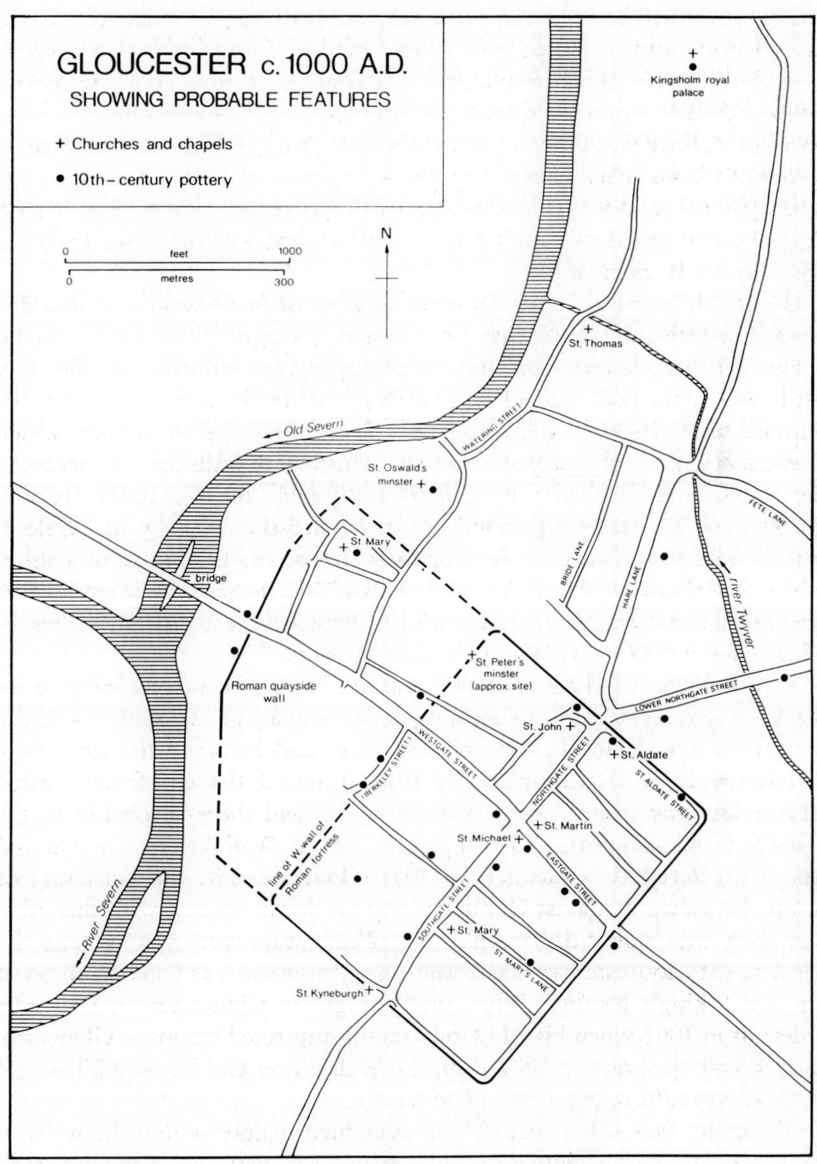

Gloucester in the 10th century. Drawn by Phil Moss. The grid of streets is thought to have been created in the early 10th century by Æthelflæd of Mercia, as part of the policy of fortified towns. It was also at this time that the minster of St Oswald was built on land outside the town to the north-west. The royal palace of Kingsholm, where the Saxon kings had stayed, and which was on the site of a late Roman burial ground, is well out of the town to the north.

refuse, animal dung, and straw, swept out from stables or tumbled from the back of passing carts; it is probable that Gloucester looked much more like an agricultural settlement than a town, with as many pigs and chickens as people. Sanitation left something to be desired; 11th century latrines have been found in back gardens, often not far from the wells, which were the main sources of drinking water.

By 1086 the population of Gloucester comprised a few thousand people; a small fraction of the agricultural population of the countryside, but still a growing town. A number of these people held land by 'burgess tenure'.

The changes made by the Normans in Gloucester were noticeable. First an earth and timber castle was constructed on the south defences of the town, symbolising the new mastery and ensuring military control. The north and east gates were rebuilt, the old Roman gates being mostly demolished. Finally, at the instigation of the new Abbot, Serlo, a new Abbey church was begun. It was at Gloucester that William gave, at Christmas 1085, the order to compile Domesday Book. He was seated, probably, in the Saxon royal palace at Kingsholm, then reaching the end of its useful life.

The growth of many of the smaller towns of medieval England was a product of the post-Norman era, but still many of them had their roots in Anglo-Saxon times. Domesday Book has a habit of not always mentioning such important matters as markets – it gives no market for Gloucester, though it must have had one, and there were probably small towns which

Gloucester: William rides into the town in 1086. Drawn by Phil Moss.

Gloucester: William I gives the order for Domesday Book.
Drawn by Phil Moss.

had markets by 1086, besides the named markets at Cirencester, Thornbury, Berkeley and Tewkesbury. Berkeley had further claim to urban status because it had had a mint in the 10th century: there were a number of places in Anglo-Saxon Gloucestershire which hovered on the edge of being towns, but cannot yet be said to have reached that status.

Tewkesbury was a town by 1086; its market was new and it had 13 burgesses 'living about the hall' – no doubt the great timber hall found under the present District offices in 1975. This hall was the centre of a large and important manor; the town was also a crucial crossing point of the two rivers, Severn and Avon, which join here. But it was a small place: like Thornbury, Berkeley, and so many others, its most important building was its manor house. Norman influence created a market, perhaps a new market, and helped it to full town status.

The Domesday towns were tiny places; we would think them villages. But already their status in feudal society was special. The greatest towns had to have a separate section in Domesday Book: they did not come under the normal category of agricultural land. Then an anomaly, the towns were, as we can see looking back, the beginnings of the urban industrialised world we live in today.

Epilogue

The Norman conquerors made no fundamental changes in the underlying fabric of society. The local government system of shire and hundred remained, as well as the system of justice, the rights and obligations of men, the houses, settlements, and land. The change occurred at the top: the imposition of a new aristocracy. All the English earls and many thegns were killed or dispossessed and William rewarded his followers with their estates. Military domination was maintained and symbolised by the network of castles – the earth and timber motte-and-baileys which were established in every major town and at key points in the countryside. Later they were often replaced in stone.

The castles involved a certain amount of disruption in the urban areas – evictions and demolition – but there was also urban renewal. In the church, the ecclesiastical lords, the bishops, changed more gradually as the old English bishops died off. The new Norman ecclesiastics were powerful, hard-headed men of affairs, patrons of the arts, and great builders. In the new Abbeys at Gloucester and Tewkesbury, we see a great contrast with the small churches always favoured by the Anglo-Saxons, for they, says William of Malmesbury, 'liked to live richly in small buildings, the Normans lived frugally in large ones.'

By the time of William's Christmas court at Gloucester in 1085, the new Gloucestershire was in being. At the court there was one English bishop, the last survivor, the elderly and revered Wulfstan of Worcester. The new Abbey at Gloucester was on the drawing board, and many smaller parish churches all over the country were also about to be transformed. Today there is scarcely a medieval parish church in the county that has not some Norman work in it. The county contained three castles, Berkeley, Bristol, and Gloucester. There were more castles across Offa's Dyke, where the Welsh counties were only recently subdued by the English Earl Harold, and inherited by William. Meanwhile the peasants ploughed and sowed, and the fishermen of Tidenham continued setting their fish-weirs. For them little had changed, except that their exotic fish, their rents, and their services were taken by a new lord.

The nave of Gloucester Abbey, begun by the Norman Abbot Serlo in 1089. The Normans transformed many churches, creating impressive new spaces instead of the small, intimate churches the Anglo-Saxons had built. Photo: The Courtauld Institute.

Notes on Sources

Sources are cited in the order in which they appear in the text.

Preface
Creation of shire. Stenton 1971, p 337; Taylor 1957.
Changes in Gloucestershire boundary, Derby and Terrett 1954.
Regions of Gloucestershire. Derby and Terrett 1954.
Neolithic agriculture. Darvill 1983: see also T. Darvill, *Prehistoric Gloucestershire*,
    forthcoming.
Forest clearance, by Roman times. Fowler 1979, p 17; McWhirr 1981, p 81.
Forest clearance, in 4th millenium bc. Brown 1982; Darvill 1983.
Hwicce and Dobunni. Hooke 1985, p 17.

Chapter 1   A sub Roman Kingdom
Population, at end of Roman period. Taylor 1983, p 106; Campbell 1982, p 9.
Roman sites, on M5. Fowler 1979, pp 17–18; Fowler 1977.
Population, survival of Celtic. Campbell 1982, pp 38–9; Jackson 1953; Gelling 1976.
Villas, late Roman. Branigan 1972.
Towns, declining in 4th century. Reece 1980.
Fleet, Roman in the Severn. McWhirr 1981, p 166.
Roman Britain, end of. Salway 1984.
Gildas. Winterbottom 1978.
Frocester villa, burials. Gracie 1970; Gracie and Price 1979.
Frocester St Peter, burials. Gracie 1963. Though the report does not make it clear,
    the burials are associated with grass-tempered pottery.
Frampton-on-Severn, burials. Baddeley 1928.
Cannington, Somerset. Rahtz 1977.
Frocester villa, decline of. Gracie 1970, p 31.
Frocester villa courtyard, 5th cent. Gracie and Price 1979; one burial reported in
    Gracie 1970.
Barnsley Park. Webster 1981, esp Fig 3.
Gildas on towns; Winterbottom 1978, ch. 26.2
Gloucester in 4th and early 5th century. Heighway and Garrod 1980; Hurst 1976.
Wroxeter. Barker 1980.
Gloucester, 6th century pottery. Darvill, Gloucester Castle, report forthcoming.
Cirencester, in 5th century. Wacher 1976, p 15.
Cirencester amphitheatre. See *Antiquaries Journal* 44 (1964), pp 17–18.
Bath. Cunliffe 1976.
Lydney Roman temple. Wheeler and Wheeler 1932; Rahtz and Watts 1979.
    Wheeler's date for the Roman buildings has been reconsidered; see Casey 1981.
Uley. Ellison 1980.
Blaise Castle. Rahtz and Brown 1959.
S E Wales in 5th-8th centuries. Davies 1978.

Llandaff charters on Kingship. Quote from Davies 1978, pp 106–7.
Gildas. Winterbottom 1978; Sims-Williams 1983b.
Kingsholm burial. Hurst 1985.
Genealogy of Vortigern. Morris 1980, p 33.
Crickley Hill: information from P Dixon and R. Savage; text in forthcoming book.
Pottery, red slipped from Mediterranean. Thomas 1981a.
Grass-tempered pottery. Vince 1984a; Hodges 1981, pp 55–6.
Saltways, see Chapter 4.
Finberg and continuity of estates. Finberg 1955.
Eric John on servitude; John 1966, p 126.
Wansdyke. Taylor 1904; Myres 1964; Fox and Fox 1960; Aston and Burrow 1982, p 95.
Clothes and jewellery. Pretty 1975, pp 48–53; Ashe 1968, section on clothing by Jill Racey, pp 205–13. Types of pennanular brooches from Fowler, E. 1963. Type G pennanulars; Dickinson 1982.
Change in population and climate. Hill 1981, p 9.
Irish pirates. Branigan 1976.
Thames Valley, environmental changes. Miles 1984, p 210.
Saxon Chronicle, annal for 577, its reliability. Sims-Williams 1983a. For all references to the Anglo-Saxon Chronicle (ASC), Whitelock (ed) 1961.

Chapter 2   The Anglo Saxons take over
Pagan Saxons, evidence. Hills 1978.
Pagan Saxons, cemeteries. Meaney 1964; Bishop's Cleeve, unpublished; inf. David Brown.
Pagan Saxon burial mounds.Hooke 1985, pp 40–48; EPNS iv, p 139; O'Neil and Grinsell 1960.
Bledisloe Tump, excavation. Dornier 1966.
Fairford, Chavenage: see references in Meaney 1964.
Lechlade. Miles and Palmer 1986.
Place-names, dialects. Mills 1960.
Place names. British. EPNS iv, pp 28–9; Gelling 1976.
Place names in 'wicham'. Gelling 1967.
Place names, *wealh* names. Cameron 1980; EPNS iv, pp 28–9.
Penda of Mercia. Stenton 1971.
Hwicce, origins and area. Wilson 1969; Hooke 1985, p 13, 16; EPNS iv; Mills 1960.
Hwicce, archaeology. Pretty 1975; Hooke 1985.
Avon valley, importance to Hwicce. Bassett 1977, pp 35–6.
Original area of Hwicce. Mills 1960.
Northumbrian princes; Finberg 1972; Stubbs 1862; Hooke 1985, p 11.
Hwicce, derivation of name. EPNS iv, p 33, note 1; also Hooke 1985, p 11.
Worcester, derivation of name. Hooke 1985, p 19.
Oshere and Osryth. Finberg 1972.
Lypiatt Cross and Berkeley sculpture. See Chapter 6.
Minsters, foundation of. Taylor 1892; 1894a.
Tidenham. Finberg 1972, no.7, p.32.
Magonsaetan. Mills 1960; Stenton 1971.
Mercia, kings in 8th century. Hart 1977; Stenton 1971.
Offa of Mercia. Levison 1946.
Offa's dyke. Hill 1981, p 75; Lewis 1963.

Chapter 3 Vikings
Danish raids: quotations and main events from ASC.
Tidenham. Finberg 1972, p 49, no 81; p 54, no 101.,
Early fortresses in Mercia. Biddle 1976 and references there cited.
Alfred. Keynes and Lapidge 1983.
Æthelflæd of Mercia. Wainwright 1975.
Gloucester, restoration of. Heighway 1984 a and b.
Athelstan. Wood 1982.
Athelstan's election. William of Malmesbury, account in EHD, p 303.
Cirencester, payment of tribute at. quoted in Davies 1982, 113-114.
Athelstan, quote from William of Malmesbury, EHD p. 304
Eadred. Taylor 1900.
Reform of monasteries. Taylor 1900.
Ethelred. Keynes 1978, pp 227–270.
Alney Island, treaty of. Taylor 1902, p 235; Chronicle of 'Florence of Worcester' in
    EHD, p 310. Site of Alney: EPNS ii, p 79; also M. Aston in unpublished survey
    for Deerhurst Research Committee.
Stirrup, 11th century. Seaby and Woodfield 1980.
Cnut, reign of. 'Florence' of Worcester's Chronicle; see EHD.
Gloucestershire, creation of shire. Stenton 1971, p 337; Taylor 1957.
Edward Confessor, reign of. Barlow 1970.

Chapter 4 The land
Hides, size of. Taylor 1889; Dyer 1982.
Charters, in general. Finberg 1972; Grundy 1936.
Stoke Bishop. Lindley 1959; Everitt 1961
Blockley. Finberg 1957, p.7
Pucklechurch. Grundy 1936, pp 199–220.
Deerhurst. Finberg 1972, p 80; also information from Mick Aston, unpublished
    survey for Deerhurst Research Committee. Map in Wool 1982.
Donnington. Hooke 1986, p 69; Grundy 1936, p 108.
Woodchester. Translation of charter in TBGAS v, p 149; Harmer 1914, p 56;
    interpretation of bounds in Grundy 1936, pp 274–5.
Hundreds. EHD p 429; Darby 1954.
Hundred names. EPNS, iv, p 52.
Hundred meeting places. Cam 1944.
Hundred courts. EHD p 429.
Bookland. EHD pp 376–77.
Westbury Charter. EHD p 507.
Blockley charter. EHD p 528.
Uhtred's grant of 770. EHD p 502, no 74.
Early fortresses. Biddle 1976.
Peasant armies. Dyer 1982, p 42.
Woodland, general. Rackham 1976; Darby 1954
Early estates. Jones 1976; Ford 1976.,
Woodland, Kingswood Forest. Aston and Isles 1987, p 91..
Woodland, negotiation of rights. Hooke 1985, p 85; Aston 1985, pp 109–11.
'The Haw'. EPNS, iii, p 150. 'Haywardsfield House', Stonehouse. EPNS, ii, p
    202–3.
Woodland, in Domesday Book. Darby 1954.
Blackfriars, Gloucester, timber for. Rackham, Blair and Munby 1978.

Arable farming systems. Rowley (ed) 1981; Aston 1985.
Frocester ridge and furrow, dating etc. Information from Eddy Price.
Welsh system of partible inheritance. Jones 1981.
Strip fields at Upton St Leonard's. Scobell 1901.
Blockley, Upton DMV. Rahtz 1969.
Wharram Percy. Hurst 1984.
Crops. Rowley (ed) 1974.
Animals. Clutton Brock 1976.
Sheep. Clutton Brock 1976, p 380; Finberg 1957, 12–14.
Charlemagne's letter to Offa. EHD, i, p 847.
Cats. Clutton Brock, 1976, p 384; for cat-skin, see Darlington 1928, p 46.
Dogs. Quote from William of Malmesbury, in EHD, p 307.
Fishing. Derby 1954; Hooke 1985, p 130–131; rent of Tidenham, Finberg 1972, p 77.
Lead digging. Hooke 1985, p 126.
Forest of Dean industry. Hart 1971.
Building stone and sand. Hooke 1985, p 126–8.
Mills. Derby 1954.
Roads, names. EPNS, i, p 15–120. 'Ricknield Street' is a post-conquest name: see
  EPNS Worcs, p 2–3.
Salt roads and industry. Hooke 1985, pp 145–9, 120, 126–7.
Roman roads in Saxon period (Wilts). Pelteret 1984.
Roads. Aston and Burrow 1982.

Chapter 5 People
Tidenham survey. EHD ii, pp 879–880.
Domesday fisheries. Darby 1954.
Rectitudines. EHD ii, pp 875–879.
Slaves, in laws of Alfred. EHD p 416.
Mills. Darby 1954.
Kings Barton, render. Moore 1982, I.2.
Cnuts laws on hunting. EHD, p 467.
Diet. O'Connor 1986.
9th century pit in Gloucester. Heighway et al 1983, p 246–7.
Weaving, evidence in 9th century. Heighway, Garrod and Vince 1979.
Wulfstan's cat skin. Darlington 1928, p 46.
Clerical dress edict; EHD p 881.
Short Viking hair. EHD p 843 and p 896.
Wulfstan and his pocket knife. Darlington 1928, p 23.
Baths. Colgrave p 166.
Lice. O'Connor 1986.
York in 10th century. Kenward et al 1978.
Skeletons at St Oswalds. Information from Dr. Juliet Rogers.
Skeletons, Roman at Cirencester. McWhirr, Viner and Wells 1982.
Family size, etc. Laslett 1984; Herlihy 1982.
Wulfstan's young men. Darlington 1928, pp 50–51.
Cnut's laws on children. EHD p 457.
Athelstan's laws on children. EHD p 423.
Houses. Rahtz 1976.
Huts at Bourton on the Water. Dunning 1932.
Tewkesbury hall. Information Alan Hannan.
Gloucester, 9th century finds. Heighway, Garrod and Vince 1979.

Pilgrimages. Biddle 1986.
Wulfstan and the 5 brothers. Darlington 1928, pp 38–9.
Justice. EHD p 366–8.
Wulfstan, his biography. Darlington 1928; translation: Peile 1934.
Wulfstan at Gloucester. Darlington 1928, pp 36–7.

Chapter 6   Christianity
Roman Christianity. Thomas 1981b.
Barnsley Park, ring. TBGAS c (1982) pp 139–40.
St Augustine's visit. Bede, II.2.
St Augustine's Oak, location. EPNS iii, p 127; EPNS iv, p 33.
Aust. Taylor 1901a and b.
Lancaut. Wood, Dobson and Hicks, 1936.
St Tecychius. J. Knight, *Monmouthshire Antiquary* III. 1, pp 29–36.
St Pancras. Atkins 1712, p 550; see also Wool 1982.
St Arilda. Lindley 1951.
St Briavels stone, now in Dean Heritage Museum, Sudeley. Unpublished.
Welsh Christian memorials. Thomas 1981b.
Christianity, survival of British. Pretty 1975, pp 90–91; Taylor 1891.
Pagan burials, cessation of. Hawkes 1986, p 92.
Hwicce, conversion of. Bede IV.13.
Monasteries, foundation, status etc. Stenton 1971; Taylor 1891; Wormald 1978. For
    some references not cited here, see Appendix 1.
Lypiatt Cross. Cox 1985.
Bede on minsters, his letter to Archbishop Egbert. EHD p 805–6.
Life in minsters. Wormald 1978.
Ælfhere of Mercia. Taylor 1900.
Bath. Sims Williams 1975, Taylor 1900; Cunliffe 1986.
Gloucester. Finberg 1972; Heighway 1984a and b. Kyneberg may have been the
    widow of St Oswald of Northumbria, though this seems very unlikely. Finberg
    1972, p 165.
Cirencester. Evans 1976; Brown 1976; Fernie 1983, p 69; Evans forthcoming; she
    argues for a 9th-10th century date for the minster at Cirencester.
Withington. Finberg 1972, p 32, 35, 38.
Westbury. Finberg 1972 p 43; EHD pp 512–13, 516–17; Anon 1901; a grave slab in
    Westbury parish church (Lindley 1960) is claimed as Saxon, on very uncertain
    grounds.
Westbury, reform. Taylor 1894.
Westbury, restoration by Wulfstan. Darlington 1928.
Westbury, evidence of minster site. Ponsford 1981; Wilson and Hurst 1969.
Tetbury. Finberg 1972, p 31. Leech 1981.
Winchcombe. Levison 1946, pp 249–59; Bassett 1977 and 1985.
Kenelm, legend of. Hartland 1916.
Kenelm, mausoleum. Bassett 1985.
Deerhurst. Taylor 1902, p 336; Taylor and Taylor 1975.
Alphege or Aelfheah. Taylor 1902, p 236; death of Ælfheah, quote from ASC.
Berkeley. Taylor 1895; Finberg 1972, p 43, no 53; Williams 1956; Sabin 1970. The
    Domesday book entry is in Moore 1982, I.63. Site of church: Leech 1981. Name
    'Oldminster': EPNS ii, pp 234–5.
Women in charge of monasteries: Stubbs 1862, p 248.
Hawkesbury. Hundred meeting place, name 'Hundred Path', EPNS iii, p 23, 24.

Roman walls under church: Bethell 1889. Bibury. parish, VCH, vii, p 21. Charters: Finberg 1972, p 34 and p 51. Fabric of church in Taylor and Taylor 1975.

Bisley. Parish, VCH xi, pp 3–4. Roman altars: RCHM 1976, p 14.

Wulfstan, rebuilding Worcester Cathedral. Darlington 1928, p.52.

St Oswald's, Gloucester. Heighway and Bryant, 1986; Heighway 1978 and 1980.

Welsh churches. Davies 1982. Lancaut. Wood, Dobson and Hicks 1936; inf. Charles Parry.

Parish churches. General: Barlow 1979, pp 183 ff.

Longney. Darlington 1928, pp 40–41. Translation mine.

Churches on villa sites. Morris and Roxan 1977.

Frocester St Peter, minster church. Gray 1963. The 13th century reference to Frocester as 'Old Minster' does not decide its minster status; for instance nearly all the churches in Gloucester were called 'Old Minster' in the 13th century (VCH, xi). The status of Frocester St Peter does not in any way detract from its interest as a site.

Kings Stanley. Unpublished excavation by P. Griffin and D. Evans; interim report forthcoming.

Parishes, estates and Domesday manors. Taylor 1889, p 43.

Urban churches. Biddle 1976, p 133.

Sculpture. Dobson 1933, and additional information from M. Hare and R. Bryant.

Bristol. Sculpture from Cathedral, note by G. Zarnecki in *English Romanesque Art 1066–1100*, Arts Council 1984, p 150. Early church on site of Cathedral, Dickinson 1976.

Newent. Zarnecki 1953.

Sundials. Green 1927.

Somerford Keynes. Taylor and Taylor 1975, pp 556–8; Taylor 1969; Finberg 1972, p 31, no 3; ibid., p 32, no 4A; ibid., p 78, no 180; see also TBGAS, 88, 1969, p 208.

Coln Rogers, Duntisbourne Rous, Leonard Stanley. Taylor and Taylor 1975.

Duntisbourne Rous. Study by M. Hare forthcoming.

Bitton. Taylor and Taylor 1975.

Odda's chapel, inscription. Okasha 1971; Taylor 1902, p 230.

Odda's chapel, building. Taylor and Taylor 1975, p 209–10; Taylor 1977.

Odda's chapel, roof. Currie 1983.

Odda and Ælfric. Taylor 1902.

Leofgar, bishop of Hereford. Entry in ASC for 1056.

Churchgoing in early medieval Wales. Davies 1982.

Church services in Saxon England. C. J. Godfrey, *The Church in Anglo Saxon England*, 1962, pp 376–8.

Ethelred's code of 1008. EHD pp 444–5.

Chapter 7 Towns.

General. Biddle 1976; Darby 1954, pp 43–8; Tait 1936; Leech 1981.

Gildas, quote. Winterbottom 1978, p 28.

Dyrham, battle in 577. See reference for Ch.1.

Administrative regions, pre-shire. Slater 1976; Cam 1944.

Saxon towns in 10th century. Biddle 1976; Biddle and Hill 1971.

Worcester charter: EHD p 540.

Shires, creation of etc. Stenton 1971, p 337; Darby and Terrett 1954; Taylor 1957; Taylor 1909.

Coinage. Loyn 1962; Stenton 1971.

Cirencester. McWhirr (ed) 1976; Evans 1987; market, Moore 1982, I.8. Cirencester as administrative centre. Slater 1976.

Bristol. Watts and Rahtz, 1985; Taylor 1909b; Walker 1971; Lobel and Carus-Wilson 1975.

Bristol: St Augustine the Less. Boore 1986.

Winchcombe. Bassett 1977; Ellis 1986.

Winchcombshire in early 10th century. Stenton 1971.

Gloucester. VCH xi, forthcoming; Heighway 1984a and b.

Gloucester, condition of streets. Straker and Heighway 1985.

Bath. Cunliffe 1986; Taylor 1900.

Epilogue
Douglas 1957; Price 1983.

Appendix 1: Places shown on map of Minster Churches

(giving references where not given in notes to text)

Doubtful minster churches – not on map

Tewkesbury.   The evidence for a minster at Tewkesbury is wholly unreliable.
  Only in a 16th century manuscript is there mention of a 7th century foundation at
  Tewkesbury, and it is a garbled account which puts some known 11th century
  personages in the 8th century. Tewkesbury cannot be counted as an early
  minster, but it is still a possibility. (Blunt 1898). A forthcoming article in *Southern
  History* by Anthea Jones suggests that Twyning minster is actually Tewkesbury.
Yate.   It has been said that a monastery at Yate was founded at the same time as that
  of Westbury. 10 'mansiones' of land at Yate were granted to Eanulf by Ethelbald
  of Mercia in 716 × 757 and were again granted by Offa to the church at Worcester
  between 777 and 779. In the second grant the earlier one is referred to as 'the same
  church' but since Yate was in Domesday Book a member of Westbury, it is not
  certain that the chuirch referred to is not Westbury itself. If Yate was a minster
  church, nothing more is known of it. (Taylor 1892, p 222; Finberg 1972, p 34, p 39).

Minster churches : documentary evidence

Bath 675 Osric (not on map)
Gloucester 679 Osric
Withington 674x704 Oshere
Westbury on Trym by 793x796?
Deerhurst by 803
Frocester St Peter (Gray 1963)
Tetbury by 681
Beckford by 803 (Finberg 1972, p 43; VCH viii, p 259)
Cheltenham by 803 (as for Beckford)
Bishops Cleeve by 768x779, dedicated to St Michael. (Finberg 1972, p 38, no 30;
  Grundy 1936, p 71)
Twyning by 740. A minster at Twyning existed by about 740; it had three cassates
  of land east of the Severn, and 10 'manentes' west of the same river. It still existed
  in 814 (Finberg 1972, p 35, no 22).
Daylesford ?727. Land was given by Ethelbald, King of Mercia, for founding a
  monastery in about 727; a description of the land boundary survives. Finberg
  1972, p 44, no 57; Grundy 1936, p 102-4.
Berkeley by 759

Blockley by 855. (Finberg 1972 p 48, no 76; Finberg 1957, pp 5-11.) A church in late
   11th century, when visited by Wulfstan (Darlington 1928, p 41).
Winchcombe by 787

Minster churches: fabric, sculpture, or excavation

Bitton
Cirencester
Deerhurst by 803

Welsh churches – documentary evidence

Tidenham (Finberg 1972, p 32, no 7)
Lancaut (EPNS iii, p 263; Wood, Dobson and Hicks 1936; VCH x, p 77)

Minster churches – deduced from large parish, and also from other evidence

Bibury
Bisley
Hawkesbury
Westbury on Severn

Appendix 2: Places shown on map of Late Saxon Churches

Evidence of Architecture, Sculpture, and Archaeology

Abson — Sculpture fragments
Avening — 2 Sculpture fragments
Ampney Crucis — North doorway. Taylor and Taylor pp 25–6.
Aston Blank — Cross-shaft fragment.
Berkeley — Sculpture fragments.
Beverstone |— Figure of Christ in S wall of tower.
Bibury — 5 pieces of sculpture; remains of Rood over chancel arch; also architectural
   remains. Taylor and Taylor pp 63–6.
Bisley — Collection of sculpture.
Bitton — Rood above chancel-arch. Taylor and Taylor pp 73–6.
Bristol Cathedral — Harrowing of Hell relief.
Broadwell — Sculpture fragment
South Cerney — Cross-shaft in south porch.
North Cerney — Earlier building found underneath Norman Chancel. U.
Daubeny, *Cotswold Churches*, 1921, p 185. Fragment of crucifixion.
Coberley — Late Saxon sculpture fragment, now missing. Inf. parish and British
   Museum.
Coln St Aldwyns — Sculpture fragment.

Coln Rogers — Architectural detail; also late Saxon sundial.
Deerhurst; St Marys. — Architectural evidence; Taylor and Taylor pp 193–209.
Deerhurst; Odda's Chapel. — Architectural evidence, dated by inscription. Taylor and Taylor pp 209–11.
Daglingworth — Architecture; Taylor and Taylor pp 187–190; also sculpture.
Duntisbourne Rouse — Side doorways of nave. Taylor and Taylor, p 221.
Duntisbourne Abbotts — long and short quoins on nave (inf M. Hare)
Elmstone Hardwicke — Sculptured stone with trumpet spiral ornament.
Hawkesbury — Fragment of sculpture.
Dymock — Probably on Anglo Saxon foundations. Taylor and Taylor p 221-2.
Edgeworth — Sculpture fragment. Architecture: Taylor and Taylor p 227–8.
Elkstone — Grave cover.
Gloucester, St Oswald. — A late minster foundation. Heighway 1978 and 1980.
Leonard Stanley — Remains of Saxon chapel. Taylor and Taylor p 567–8.
Miserden — Remains of doorways in side walls of nave. Taylor and Taylor p 430–1.
Newent — Cross shaft and pillow-stone. Zarnecki 1953.
Saintbury — Sundial.
Somerford Keynes — Sculpture fragment; north door usually said to be 8th century. Taylor and Taylor 1965, p 556; Taylor 1969.
Temple Guiting — Sculpture fragment in N wall of porch.
Winstone — Taylor and Taylor, p 672–3.
Wormington — Crucifixion built into east wall of south aisle.

Priest or church in Domesday Book (or other 11th century document)

Awre,	Eastleach Martin (the manor of Southrop)
Ashton under Hill and Beckford,	
Down Ampney	Fairford,
Ampney Crucis	Hasleton
Berkeley	Hampnett
Blockley – visited by Bishop Wulfstan	Lasborough
Bristol	Guiting Power
Bibury	Littleton on Severn
Bourton on the Water	Maugersbury
Broadwell,	Meysey Hampton
Bisley (2 priests)	Miserden
Badminton,	Marshfield
(Gt) Barrington,	Minchinhampton
Brimpsfield	Olveston
Brockworth,	Oakley
(Bishops) Cleeve,	Prestbury
Bitton (2 hides, one of them paid tax, the other belonged to the Church.)	Painswick
	Quenington
Cheltenham	Rodmarton
Coln Rogers?	Stoke Giffard
Cutsdean	South Cerney
Cirencester	Salperton
Daylsford	Siddington
Driffield	Stow on the Wold (St Edward)
Dymock	Stanway (a minster)

Stratton
Shipton Oliffe,
Side
Tidenham
Temple Guiting
Tetbury
Tewkesbury
Tormarton

Upper Swell
Withington (priests)
Willersey
Weston sub Edge
Wheatenhurst
Westbury-on-Trym (restored by
   Wulfstan)
Winchcombe

Appendix 3:
Map of Churches on Roman Sites

Churches on Roman or sub-Roman cemeteries

Dodington. Cremation in glass vessel near church. RCHM 1976, p 43.
Frocester St Peter. Gracie 1963.
Notgrove. Cinerary urn and other Romano British pot found 19th century beneath St Bartholomews church. RCHM 1976, p 88.
Poulton. RB sherds, late RB burials. Main Roman settlement 100 yds west of church. RCHM 1976, pp 94–5.
St Mary de Lode, Gloucester. Bryant 1980.
St Oswald's, Gloucester. Heighway 1978, 1980a and b.

Roman stone building on church site

Bitton. Coins, tesserae and pottery from churchyard and vicarage garden. RCHM 1976, pp 16–17.
Deerhurst. Roman stone building close to church. Rahtz 1976, p 6 and subsequent excavation.

Roman stone building on church alignment

Frocester St Peter. Gracie 1963.
Hawkesbury. Bethell 1889.
Kings Stanley. Unpublished.
Woodchester. Lysons 1797; RCHM 1976, pp 132–134..

Temple site

Bisley. Roman altars and votive plaques in sufficient numbers to suggest a religious centre. RCHM 1976, p 14–15.
Daglingworth. Roman votive slabs in churchyard and nearby. RCHM 1976, p 41.
Uley. Roman temple converted into Christian church? Ellison 1980.

Bibliography

Note: *TBGAS* = *Transactions of the Bristol and Gloucestershire Archaeological Society*

Abbot, R D 1962. An Anglo-Saxon Cauldron from Kempsford, Glos. *TBGAS* 81, pp 196–7.

Anon 1901. [Visit to Westbury on Trym]. *TBGAS 24*, pp 22–31.

ASC. Whitelock, D (ed) 1961. *The Anglo Saxon Chronicle*.

Ashe, G 1968. *The Quest for Arthur's Britain*.

Aston, M and Burrow, I 1982. *The Archaeology of Somerset*.

Aston, M 1985. *Interpreting the Landscape*.

Aston, M. and Isles, R. 1987. *The Archaeology of Avon*.

Atkins, R 1712. *A New History of Gloucestershire*.

Baddeley, St Clair 1928. A Post-Roman settlement near Frampton on Severn. *TBGAS* 50, pp 123–133.

Barker, P 1980. *Wroxeter Roman City: Excavations 1966–80*.

Barlow, F 1979. *The English Church 1000–1066*.

Barlow, F 1970. *Edward the Confessor*.

Bassett, S 1977. *The Origins and Early Development of Winchcombe and its District*. Birmingham University MA Thesis.

Bassett, S 1985. A probable Mercian Royal Musoleum at Winchcombe, Gloucestershire. *Antiquaries Journal* 65, pp 82–111.

Bazeley, W 1884. Notes on Buckland Manor and Advowson AD 709–1546. *TBGAS* 9 (1883–4), pp 103–124.

Bede. *A History of the English Church and People*. Translated L Shirley-Price (Penguin 1977).

Bethell, W W 1889. Hawkesbury Church. *TBGAS* 13, 1888–89, pp 10–15.

Biddle, M and Hill, D 1971. Late Saxon Planned Towns. *Antiquaries Journal* 51, pp 70–85.

Biddle, M 1976. Towns, in *The Archaeology of Anglo Saxon England* (ed D Wilson).

Biddle, M 1986. Archaeology, Architecture, and the Cult of Saints, in *The Anglo Saxon Church* (ed R Morris).

Blunt, J H 1898. *Tewkesbury Abbey*.

Bonney, D 1972. Early boundaries in Wessex, in *Archaeology and the Landscape* (ed P Fowler), pp 168–186.

Boore, E 1986. The Church of St Augustine the Less, Bristol: An Interim Statement. *TBGAS* 104, pp 211–14.

Branigan, K 1972. The end of the Roman West. *TBGAS* 91, pp 117–28.

Branigan, K 1976. Villa settlement in The West Country, in *The Roman West Country* (ed K. Branigan and P. Fowler).

Brown, D 1976. Archaeological evidence for the Anglo-Saxon period, in McWhirr 1976, pp 19–45.

Brown, A G 1982. Human impact on the former floodplain woodlands of the Severn, in British Archaeological Reports, S 146 (eds M Bell and S Limbrey), pp 93–104.

Bryant, R 1980. The church of St Mary de Lode, Gloucester. *Glevensis* (Journal of Gloucester and District Archaeological Research Group), 14, pp 4–12.

Cam, H 1944. *Liberties and Communities in Medieval England*.

Campbell, J 1982. *The Anglo Saxons*.

Cameron, K 1980. The meaning and significance of Old English 'walh' in English Place Names. *Journal English Place Name Society* 12 (1979–80), pp 1–46.

Casey, J 1981. Excavations at Lydney Park, Gloucestershire, University of Durham and Newcastle on Tyne, *Archaeological Report for 1980*, 4, pp 30–32.

Charles-Edwards, T M 1976. Boundaries in Irish Law, in Sawyer 1976, pp 83–87.

Clutton-Brock, J 1976. The Animal Resources, in *The Archaeology of Anglo- Saxon England* (ed D Wilson).

Colgrave, B (ed) 1985. *Life of Bishop Wilfrid* by Eddius Stephanus.

Cox, C 1985. The Lypiatt Cross – A Discussion. *Glevensis* 19, pp 16–23.

Cunliffe, B 1986. *The City of Bath*.

Currie, C R J 1983. A Romanesque Roof at Odda's Chapel, Deerhurst, Gloucestershire? *Antiquaries Journal* 63, pp 58–63.

Darby, H C 1954. Gloucestershire, in *The Domesday Geography of Midland England* (eds H C Darby and I B Terrett).

Darlington, R 1928. *The 'Vita Wulfstani' of William of Malmesbury*.

Darvill, T 1983. *Excavations at the Buckles, Frocester 1983, lst Interim Report*.

Darvill, T forthcoming. Excavations on the site of the early Norman Castle at Gloucester. *Medieval Archaeology*.

Davies, W 1978. *An Early Welsh Microcosm: Studies in the Llandaff Charters*.

Davies, W 1982. *Wales in the Early Middle Ages*.

Dickinson, J C 1976. The origins of St Augustine's, Bristol, in *Essays in Bristol and Gloucestershire History* (eds P McGrath and J Cannon).

Dickinson, T M 1982. Fowler's Type G Pennanular Brooches Reconsidered. *Medieval Archaeology* 26, pp 41–68.

Dobson, D P 1933. Anglo Saxon buildings and sculpture in Gloucestershire. *TBGAS* 55, pp 261–276.

Dornier, A 1976. Bledisloe Excavations 1964. *TBGAS* 85, pp 57–69.

Douglas, D. Gloucestershire and the Norman Conquest. *TBGAS* 76, pp 5–20.

Dunning, C G 1932. Bronze Age Settlements and a Saxon Hut near Bourton on the Water, Gloucestershire. *Antiquaries Journal* 12, pp 279–93.

Dyer, C 1982. *Lords and peasants in a changing society*.

EHD. *English Historical Documents* 1, c.500–1042 (ed. D Whitelock), 2nd edition 1979.

EHD ii. *English Historical Documents* 2, 1042–1189 (ed D Douglas and G W Greenaway), 2nd Edition 1981.

Ellis,P 1986. Excavations in Winchcombe, Gloucestershire, 1962–1972. *TBGAS* 104, pp 95–138.

Ellison, A 1980. Natives, Romans and Christians on West Hill, Uley; An Interim Report on the excavation. . .in Rodwell 1980, pp 305–328.

EPNS. *The Place Names of Gloucestershire*, parts i-iv (ed A H Smith), Cambridge 1964 and 1965.

Evans, B 1976. The Collegiate Church at Cirencester: A critical examination of the historical evidence, in McWhirr 1976), pp 46–60.

Evans, B forthcoming. The Church at Cirencester; Historical Evidence, in Cirencester Excavations, 4, forthcoming

Everitt, S 1961. A reinterpretation of the Anglo Saxon survey of Stoke Bishop. *TBGAS* 80, pp 175–8.

Fernie, E 1983. *The Architecture of the Anglo-Saxons*.

Finberg, H P R 1955. *Roman and Saxon Withington, a Study in Continuity*.

Finberg, H P R 1957. *Gloucestershire Studies*.

Finberg, H P R 1972. *The Early Charters of the West Midlands*.

Ford, W J 1976. Some Settlement Patterns in the Central Region of the Warwickshire Avon, in Sawyer 1976, pp 274–294.

Fowler, E 1963. Celtic Metalwork of the 5th and 6th centuries. *Archaeological Journal* 120, pp 98–160.

Fowler, P J 1977. Archaeology and the M5 Motorway, Gloucestershire 1969–75; a summary and assessment. *TBGAS* 95, pp 40–46.

Fowler, P J 1979. Archaeology and the M4 and M5 motorways, 1965–78. *Archaeological Journal*, 136, pp 12–26.

Fox, A and Fox C 1960. Wansdyke Reconsidered. *Archaeological Journal* 115, pp 1–48.

Gelling, M 1967. English Place Names derived from the Compound 'Wicham'. *Medieval Archaeology* 11, pp 87–104.

Gelling, M 1976. The Evidence of Place Names, in Sawyer 1976, pp 200–211.

Gilbert, E 1968. The First Stone Church at Deerhurst. *TBGAS* 87, pp 71–95.

Gracie, H S 1958. St Peter's Church, Frocester, and an underlying Roman building; Interim Report. *TBGAS* 77, pp 23–30.

Gracie, H S 1963. St Peter's Church, Frocester. *TBGAS* 82, pp 148–167.

Gracie, H S 1970. Frocester Court Roman Villa, First Report 1961–67. *TBGAS* 89, pp 15–89.

Gracie H S and Price E G 1979. Frocester Court Roman Villa: Second Report. *TBGAS* 97, pp 9–64.

Gray, I E 1963. Some Early Records of Frocester. *TBGAS* 82, pp 143–7.

Green, A R 1927. Anglo Saxon Sundials. *Antiquaries Journal*.

Grundy, G B 1936. *Saxon Charters and Field Names of Gloucestershire*.

Harmer F E 1914. *Selected English Historical Documents*.

Hart, C 1977. The Kingdom of Mercia, in *Mercian Studies* (ed A Dornier).

Hartland, E S 1916. The Legend of St Kenelm. *TBGAS* 39, pp 13–65.

Hart, C E 1971. *The Industrial History of Dean*.

Hawkes, S C 1986. The Early Saxon Period, in *The Archaeology of the Oxford Region* (ed G Briggs, J Cook, and T Rowley), pp 64–108.

Heighway, C M 1978. Excavations at Gloucester: fourth interim report: St Oswald's Priory, Gloucester 1975–76. *Antiquaries Journal* 58, pp 103–132.

Heighway, C M 1980. Excavations at Gloucester 1977–78; 5th Interim Report: St Oswalds Priory. *Antiquaries Journal* 60, pp 207–226.

Heighway, C M 1980b. The cemeteries of Roman Gloucestershire. *TBGAS* 98, pp 57–72.

Heighway, C M et al 1983. *The East and North Gates of Gloucester*.

Heighway, C M 1984a. Anglo Saxon Gloucester, in *Anglo Saxon Towns in Southern England* (ed J Haslem), pp 359–83.

Heighway, C M 1984b. Anglo Saxon Gloucester to AD 1000, in *Studies in Late Anglo-Saxon Settlements* (ed M Faull), pp 35–53.

Heighway C M 1984c. Anglo Saxon Gloucestershire, in *Archaeology in Gloucestershire* (ed A Saville), pp 225–247.

Heighway, C M , Garrod, A P and Vince, A G 1979. Excavations at 1 Westgate St, Gloucester, 1975. *Medieval Archaeology*, 23, pp 159–213.

Heighway, C M and Garrod A P 1980. Excavations at nos 1 and 30 Westgate Street, Gloucester. *Britannia 11*, pp 73–114.

Heighway, C M and Bryant, R M 1986. A Reconstruction of the 10th century church of St Oswald, Gloucester. in *The Anglo Saxon Church* (ed R Morris), CBA Research Report 60, pp 188–195.

Herlihy, D 1985. *Medieval Households*.

Hill, D 1981. *An Atlas of Anglo Saxon England*.

Hills, C 1978. The Archaeology of Anglo Saxon England in the Pagan Period, in *Anglo Saxon England*, 8 (ed P Clemoes), pp 297 ff.

Hodges, R 1981. *The Hamwih Pottery*. CBA Research Report 37.

Hooke, D 1985. *The Anglo Saxon Landscape, The Kingdom of the Hwicce*.

Hurst, H 1976. Gloucester: A Colonia in the West Country, in *The Roman West Country: Classical Culture and Celtic Society* (ed K Branigan and P J Fowler), pp 63–80.

Hurst, H. 1985. *Kingsholm*.

Hurst, J 1984. The Wharram Research Project: Results to 1983. *Medieval Archaeology* 28, pp 77–111.

Jackson, K 1953. *Language and History in Early Britain*.

John, E 1966. *Orbis Britanniae*.

Jones, G R J 1976. Multiple Estates and Early Settlement, in Sawyer 1976, pp 15–40.

Jones, G R J 1981. Early Customary Tenures in Wales and Open-Field Agriculture. In Rowley (ed) 1981, pp 202–225.

Kenward et al 1978. The Environment of Anglo Scandinavian York. in *Viking Age York and the North* (ed R Hall), CBA Research Report 27, pp 58–73.

Keynes, S D 1978. The Declining Reputation of King Aethelred the Unready. in *Ethelred the Unready* (ed D Hill), British Archaeological Reports 59, pp 227–254.

Keynes S and Lapidge, M 1983. *Alfred the Great*.

Knight, J K. St Tatheus of Caerwent: An Analysis of the Vespasian Life. *The Monmouthshire Antiquary* III.1, pp 29–36.

Laslett, P 1984. *The World We Have Lost, Further Explored.*

Leech, R 1981. *Gloucestershire Towns.*

Levison W 1946. *England and the Continent in the Eighth Century.*

Lewis, J M 1963. A Section of Offa's Dyke at Buttington Tump, Tidenham. *TBGAS* 82, pp 202–4.

Lindley, E S 1951. St Arild of Thornbury. *TBGAS* 70, pp 152–3.

Lindley, E S 1959. The Anglo Saxon charters of Stoke Bishop. *TBGAS* 78, pp 96–109.

Lobel, R and Carus-Wilson, 1975. *Atlas of Historic Towns, 2: Bristol.*

Loyn, H. 1962. *Anglo Saxon England and the Norman Conquest.*

McWhirr, A. 1976 (ed). *The Archaeology and History of Cirencester.* British Archaeological Reports, 30.

McWhirr, A 1981. *Roman Gloucestershire.*

McWhirr, A, Viner, L and Wells, C 1982. *Romano British Cemeteries at Cirencester.*

Meaney, A 1964. *Gazeteer of Early Anglo Saxon Burial Sites.*

Miles, D and Palmer, S 1986. *Invested in Mother Earth: the Anglo Saxon Cemetery at Lechlade.*

Miles D 1984. Romano British Settlement in the Gloucestershire Thames Valley, in Saville (ed) 1984, pp 191–211.

Mills, A D 1960. *A Linguistic Study of Gloucestershire Place Names.* PhD Thesis, University of London .

Moore, J S (ed) 1982. *Domesday Book; 15, Gloucestershire.*

Morris, J (ed) 1980. *Nennius: British History and the Welsh Annals.*

Morris R and Roxan, J 1980. Churches on Roman Buildings, in Rodwell 1980, pp 175–209.

Myres, J N L 1964. Wansdyke and the Origins of Wessex, in *Essays in British History Presented to Sir Frank Feiling* (ed H Trevor-Roper), pp 1–27.

O'Connor, T 1986. What The Vikings Left Behind. *New Scientist*, 6 Nov 1986, pp 42–7.

Okasha, E 1971. *Handlist of Anglo Saxon non-runic inscriptions.*

O'Neil, H and Grinsell, L V 1960. Gloucestershire Barrows. *TBGAS* 79, pp 5–144.

Peile, J H F 1934. *William of Malmesbury's Life of St Wulstan, Bishop of Worcester.* Oxford.

Pelteret, D A E 1984. The Roads of Anglo Saxon England. *Wilts Archaeological and Natural History Magazine* 79, pp 155–163.

Ponsford, M W 1981. Excavations at Westbury College, Bristol. *BARG Review* 2, pp 24–6.

Pretty K 1975. *The Welsh Border and the Severn and Avon Valleys in the 5th and 6th centuries AD: An Archaeological Survey.* PHD Thesis, University of Cambridge.

Price, D 1983. *The Normans in Gloucestershire and Bristol.*

Rackham, O 1976. *Trees and Woodland in the British Landscape.*

Rackham, O, Blair, W J and Munby, J T 1978. The 13th century roofs and floor of the Blackfriars Priory at Gloucester. *Medieval Archaeology* 22, pp 105–122.

Rahtz, P 1969. Upton, Gloucestershire, 1964–68. *TBGAS* 88, pp 74–126.

Rahtz, P 1976. Buildings and Rural Settlement, in Wilson (ed) 1976, pp 49–98.

Rahtz, P 1976b. *Excavations at St Marys Church, Deerhurst 1971–3.* CBA Research Report 15.

Rahtz, P 1977. Late Roman cemeteries and beyond, in Reece (ed) *Burial in the Roman World.*

Rahtz, P. 1979. *The Saxon and Medieval Palaces at Cheddar.* British Archaeological Reports 65.

Rahtz, P and Brown, J C 1959. Blaise Castle Hill, Bristol, 1957. *Proceedings of the University of Bristol Speleological Society* 8, pp 147–171.

Rahtz P and Watts L 1979. The End of Roman Temples in the West of Britain, in *End of Roman Britain* (ed J Casey), British Archaeological Reports 71, pp 183–210.

RCHM 1976. *Iron Age and Romano British Monuments in the Gloucestershire Cotswolds.*

Reece, R 1980. Town and Country: The End of Roman Britain. *World Archaeology* 12, pp 77–92.

Rodwell, W (ed) 1980. *Temples Churches and Religion in Roman Britain.* British Archaeological Reports, 77.

Rowley, T (ed) 1974. *Anglo Saxon Settlements and Landscape.* British Archaeological Reports, 6.

Rowley, T (ed) 1981. *The Origins of Open Field Agriculture.*

Royce, D (ed) 1892–1903. *Landboc sive Registrum Monasterii de Winchelcumbe* (2 volumes).

Sabin, A 1970. St Augustine's Abbey and the Berkeley Churches. *TBGAS* 89, pp 90–98.

Salway, P 1984. *Roman Britain.*

Sawyer, P (ed) 1976. *Medieval Settlement: Continuity and Change.*

Scobell, E C 1899. The Common Fields at Upton St Leonards and the recent enclosure 1897. *PCNFC* 13, pp 215–30.

Seaby, W A and Woodfield, P 1980. Viking Stirrups from England and Their Background. *Medieval Archaeology* 24, pp 87–122.

Sims-Williams, P 1983a. The Settlement of England in Bede and the Chronicle, in *Anglo Saxon England* 12, pp 1–41.

Sims-Williams, P 1983b. Gildas and the Anglo-Saxons, *Cambridge Medieval Celtic Studies* 6, pp 1–30.

Salter, T 1976. The Town and its Region in the Anglo Saxon and Medieval Periods, in McWhirr (ed) 1976, pp 81–108.

Stenton, F M 1971. *Anglo Saxon England*, 3rd Edition.

Stubbs, W 1962. The Cathedral, Diocese and Monasteries of Worcester in the 8th century. *Archaeological Journal* 19, pp 236–252.

Straker, V and Heighway C 1985. Organic matter from medieval deposits outside St Nicholas Church, Gloucester. *TBGAS* 103, pp 223–5.

Taylor, C S 1889. *An Analysis of the Domesday Survey of Gloucestershire.*

Taylor, C S 1891. Early Christianity in Gloucestershire. *TBGAS* 15, pp 120–138.

Taylor, C S 1892. Gloucestershire in the eighth century. *TBGAS* 16, 1891–2, pp 208–230.

Taylor, C S 1894. The Benedictine Revival in the Hwiccian Monasteries. *TBGAS* 18, 1893–4, 107–133.

Taylor, C S 1895. Berkeley Minster. *TBGAS* 19, 1894–5, pp 70–84.

Taylor, C S 1900. Bath: Mercian and West Saxon. *TBGAS* 23, pp 129–161.

Taylor C S 1901a. Did St Augustine Meet the British Bishops at Aust? *TBGAS* 24, pp 14–22.

Taylor, C S 1901b. Aust, The Place of Meeting. *TBGAS* 24, p 159–171.

Taylor, C S 1902. Deerhurst, Pershore, and Westminster. *TBGAS* 25, pp 230–50.

Taylor, C S 1904. The Date of Wansdyke. *TBGAS* 27, pp 131–155.

Taylor, C S 1909. The Northern Boundary of Gloucestershire. *TBGAS* 32, pp 109–139.

Taylor, C S 1909b. The Chronological Sequence of the Bristol Parish Churches. *TBGAS* 32, pp 202–218.

Taylor, C S 1957. The Origin of the Mercian Shires. Reprinted in Finberg 1957, pp 17–51.

Taylor, H M 1969. The Eighth Century Doorway at Somerford Keynes. *TBGAS* 88, pp 68–73.

Taylor, H M and Taylor, J 1975. *Anglo Saxon Architecture.*

Thomas, C 1981a. *A Provisional List of Imported Pottery in Post-Roman W Britain and Ireland.* Institute of Cornish Studies Special Report 7.

Thomas, C 1981b. *Christianity in Roman Britain.*

VCH. *Victoria History of the Counties of England: Gloucestershire.*

Vince, A G V 1984. An Appendix on Grass-tempered Pottery, in Heighway 1984c, pp 240–41.

Wacher, J 1976. Late Roman Developments. in McWhirr 1976, pp 15–17.

Wainwright, F T 1975. Æthelflæd, Lady of the Mercians, In *Scandinavian England* (ed H P R Finberg), pp 305–324.

Walker, D 1971. *Bristol in the Early Middle Ages.*

Watts, L and Rahtz, P 1985. *Mary-le-Port, Bristol: Excavations 1962–3.*

Webster, G 1981. Barnsley Park, Report 1. *TBGAS* 99, pp 21–71.

Wheeler, R E M W and Wheeler, T V 1932. *Report on the Excavation of the Prehistoric, Roman and Post-Roman Site in Lydney Park, Gloucestershire.*

Williams, E W 1956. Godwin and Berkeley: A Legend. *TBGAS* 75, pp 205–209.

Wilson, M 1969. The Hwicce, in The Origins of Worcester, *Transactions of the Worcestershire Archaeological Society*, 3rd Series 2, 1968–9, pp 20–25.

Wilson, D M and Hurst, D G . Note on Excavations at Westbury College. *Medieval Archaeology* 13, p 244.

Winterbottom M (ed) 1978. *Gildas: The Ruin of Britain.*

Wood, M 1982. *In Search of the Dark Ages.*

Wood, J G, Dobson, D P and Hicks, F W P. The Church and Parish of Lancaut. *TBGAS* 58, pp 207–218.

Wool, ST 1982. *Fundus and Manerium: a Study of Continuity and Survival in Gloucestershire from Roman to Medieval Times*. Phd Thesis, University of Bristol.
Wormald, P 1978. Bede, Beowulf, and the Conversion of the Anglo-Saxon Aristocracy. In *Bede and Anglo Saxon England* (ed R T Farrel), British Archaeological Reports 46, pp 32–95.
Zarnecki, G 1953. The Newent Funerary Tablet. *TBGAS* 72, pp 49–55.

Index

Page references to illustrations are in italics

Abson 168
Ælfhere, ealdorman of Mercia 49, 101
Ælfric, bro. of Odda 137
Ælfwyn, dr. of Æthelflaeda of Mercia 45
Æthelflaed of Mercia 43, 45, 119, 146, 153
Æthelmund, Ealdorman 111
agriculture 13, 18, 63–70, *59, 66,* 77–8.
Alfred, K. of Wessex 43, 117, 146
Alfred, son of Ethelred II 50
Alvington 70
Ampney Crucis 168, 169
Anglo-Saxons, origins 20
animals 69
Ashton under Hill 169
Aston Blank 168
Athelstan, K. of England 45–6, *46,* 146
Augustine's Oak 94
Aurelius Caninus 10
Avening 23, *130,* 168
Awre 70, 169

Badminton 169
Barnsley Park (Roman) 4, (Christian ring) 93
Barrington 169
Bath 8, 37, 47, 50, 101–3, 145, 167
Beachley 94
Beckford 114, 167
bees 78
Beowulf 38
Berkeley 39, 101, 110–12, *112,* 157, 167, 168, 169
Beverstone 53, 131, 168
Bibury 55, 101, 113, *114, 115,* 168, 169
Bishop's Cleeve (cemetery) 19, 23, *24* (church) 114, 167, 169
Bishton 76
Bisley 98, 113, 126, 168, 169, 170
Bitton 136, *138,* 168, 169, 170
Blaise Castle 9, 94
Bledisloe Tump 25
Blockley 57, 62, 114, 168, 169
Bookland 61
Botloe 25
Bourton on the Water (burials) 23 (hut) 85 (lead tanks) 93 (church) 169
bridge work, fortress, work, military service 62

Brimpsfield 169
Bristol Cathedral (sculpture) 131, *131,* 152, 168
Bristol 146, 149–52, *151,* 169
Bristol, King's Barton 149
Broadwell 168, 169
Brockworth 170
Buckland 61
Burgred, K. of Mercia 41
burials 3, 20–31, *21, 22,* 24–5, 123–4
Buttington, Salop 42–3

Cadbury-Congresbury 10
Cambridge, Glos 44
Cannington, Somerset 3
cats 69
cattle 69
cauldrons 14–15
Ceolwulf, K. of Mercia 41
Chalford 114
Charters 55–9, *56,* 62
Chavenage (cemetery) 18, 23, 25, *29*
Chedworth 93
Cheltenham 98, 114, 167, 169
children 84–5
Chirbury 44
Christianity 9, 38, 93–144
churches, late Saxon *140, 141,* 139–141, 167–8
church attendance 88–9, 142
Churchdown 32
Cirencester *2,* 7, 8, *8,* 18, 35, 42, 47, 50, 103–4, *103,* 145, 149, *150,* 157, 168, 169
climate 15
clothes *9,* 15, 79–80, 101
Cnut, K. of England 50, 52
Coberley 168
Coenwulf, K. 105
coins *148;* see also mints
Coln Rogers 133, *136,* 169
Coln St. Aldwyn's 168
combs 23
Conan 10
cooking 14–15, 87
Cricklade 50
Crickley Hill 12, *12,* 13
crops 68